70000032883

The Ballet Companion

A Dancer's Guide to the Technique, Traditions, and Joys of Ballet

Eliza Gaynor Minden

A Lark Production
A Fireside Book
Published by Simon & Schuster
New York London Toronto Sydney

FIRESIDE
Rockefeller Center
1230 Avenue of the Americas
New York, NY 10020

FIRESIDE and colophon are registered trademarks of Simon & Schuster, Inc.
For information regarding special discounts for bulk purchases,
please contact Simon & Schuster Special Sales at 1-800-456-6798
or business@simonandschuster.com.

Designed by Susan Evans, Design per se, New York
Cover photograph of Gillian Murphy, American Ballet Theatre,
by Eduardo Patino.

Manufactured in the United States of America
10 9 8 7 6 5 4 3 2 1
Library of Congress Cataloging-in-Publication Data
Minden, Eliza Gaynor.
  The ballet companion: a dancer's guide to the technique,
traditions, and joys of ballet / Eliza Gaynor Minden.
    p.   cm.
  "A Lark production."
  "A Fireside book."
  Includes bibliographical references and index.
  1. Ballet dancing—Handbooks, manuals, etc. I. Title.
  GV1788 .M56 2005
  792.8—dc22   2005044102

ISBN-13: 978-0-7432-6407-5
ISBN-10:   0-7432-6407-X

To my own ballet companion, John Minden, with gratitude and love.

Contents

Acknowledgments

I am really lucky to have had the help of so many talented, knowledgeable, and extremely generous people. Thank you all.

The idea for *The Ballet Companion* came from Lisa DiMona, of Lark Productions, a ballet mom who wanted a better book for her dancing daughter. It was a pleasure to create one with her.

I am very grateful to Eduardo Patino, whose unfailing eye and amazing timing resulted in the beautiful photographs that illustrate the cover and the chapters on technique. My thanks also to Rick McCullough for the knowledge and help he provided throughout the shoot and to our dancer-models, Maria Riccetto, of American Ballet Theatre, and Benjamin Millepied, of New York City Ballet, for their patient, cheerful, and impeccable demonstrations of ballet's steps and positions.

Sarah Burns assisted in writing and researching, as did Karen Lacy, who made the glossaries a reality, advised on the manuscript, and contributed to the project in so many ways. My special thanks to Leigh Witchel for wordsmithing, researching, interviewing, and good humor. Leigh is a talented choreographer, and I bet he's a divine partner as well—he cheerfully does the heavy lifting while making the girl look good.

I cannot say thank you enough to all the dancers and dance teachers who so generously shared their stories and their expertise: Alexandra Ansanelli, Peter Boal, and Nikolaj Hübbe of the New York City Ballet; Kristi Boone, Gillian Murphy (who also jumped tirelessly for our cover shot), and Ethan Stiefel of American Ballet Theatre; Michael Bjerknes of the American Dance Institute; Mignon Furman of the American Academy of Ballet; Diana Byer of New York Ballet Theater; Henrik Emmer and Anne Marie Vessel Schlüter of the Royal Danish Ballet School; Elisabeth Platel of the Paris Opera Ballet School; Melissa Hayden of North Carolina School of the Arts; Raymond Lukens of the Boston Ballet; Joan Kunsch of the Nutmeg Conservatory for the Arts; François Perron of Studio Maestro; Kathryn Sullivan of Steps on Broadway; Maria Youskevitch of American Repertory Ballet's Princeton Ballet School; Rebecca Wright of the Washington School of Ballet; Moira

Murphy Wright of Connecticut Dance School; Robin Hoffman and Sandra Aberkalns of the Dance Notation Bureau; Liz Cunliffe and Diana Curry of the Benesh Institute, The Royal Academy of Dance; Gail Choate-Petit of the Cecchetti Council of America. My thanks also to David Howard, Lourdes Lopez, and most especially to A.B.T.'s Kirk Peterson and Connecticut Dance School's Alan Woodard. Mindy Aloff, Lynn Garafola, Marc Haegeman, Lynette Halewood, Abby Kahn, Sandra Kurtz, Miro Magloire, Alexander Meinertz, Jeffrey E. Salzberg, Jane Simpson, and Alexandra Tomalonis kindly provided answers to many dance, theater, and music questions. Gail Beaufays assisted with the French.

"The Healthy Dancer" section of this book benefited immeasurably from the advice of Colleen Dean, National Dance Association; Peter Frame; Dr. Adam Glassman; Margo Maine; Alycea Ungaro, Real Pilates; Dr. Heinz Valtin, Dartmouth Medical School; Mary Virginia Wilmerding, International Association for Dance Medicine and Science; Megan Richardson; and especially—for his invaluable help discussing injury prevention and treatment—Dr. David Weiss of New York University Medical Center and Harkness Center for Dance Injury. Sandra Foschi graciously allowed us to adapt an article she contributed to Gaynor Minden's Web site. There is no way to sufficiently thank Katy Keller, P.T., for the hours she gave in providing information and making sure I got it right.

My gratitude to Francesca DeRenzi for the initial photo research and for so ably helping to manage the photo shoot, and also to Siobhan Burns, Susan Danziger, Peter Diggins, Jean Gaynor, Mireille Gaynor, Matt Lincir, Emily Rothman, and Kelly Ryan for their assistance on the project. To Carabosse, Carlota de Cardenas, Alexandra Kenin, Melissa Mohan, Brenda Neville, Natasha Shick, Johnson Stevens, Kiley Stoker, Amanda Tindal, Evie Tochterman, Julia Welsh and everyone else at Gaynor Minden—thank you all for your help and support.

I greatly appreciate the work of the people at Simon & Schuster: Trish Todd, Cherlynne Li, Mark Gompertz, Linda Evans, Nora Reichard, Martha Schwartz, Sara Schapiro, Jeff Wilson, Marcia Burch, Lisa Considine, and particularly my editor, Doris Cooper, for her belief in this project and her wise, sensitive guidance along the way.

Like the ballerina who makes the arduous appear effortlessly graceful, Susan Evans and her staff at Design Per Se, Lorie Pagnozzi and Sarah Pokora, created a harmonious and beautiful design out of disparate elements that seemed hopelessly incompatible. My grateful thanks to them, and also to the team at Lark Productions: Robin Dellabough, Karen Watts, Ingrid Roberg, and Ariana Barth.

Phil Karg, Dance Division, Research Libraries, New York Public Library, provided indefatigable research help and unflagging effort. Also: Tom Lisanti, New York Public Library; Michel Rosenfeld, Bibliotheque Nationale de France; Matteo Sartorio, Museo Teatrale Alla Scala; Dina Makarova; Costas Cacaroukas; Paul Kolnik; Martha Swope; Victor DeLiso; Rosalie O'Connor; Myra Armstrong; Beth Olsen, Alvin Ailey American Dance Theatre; John Kane; Josh Mora and Mark Antman, the Image Works; Rona Tuccillo, and Rosa DiSalvo, Getty Images; Ann Vachon and Nicole Tronzano-Speletic, José Limón Dance Foundation; Johann Persson; Laura Raucher and Jennifer DePauw, Martha Graham Center of Contemporary Dance; Robby Barnett and Mikey Rottman, Pilobolus; Christina Johnson; Virginia Johnson, *Pointe* magazine; Joanna Harp, Lifestyle Media; Amanda Golucki, Joffrey Ballet; Evan Gunter, Norton Owen and the School at Jacob's Pillow; Maggie Christ, Ballet Tech; Andrew Grossman, Columbia Artists Management, and the Georgian State Dance Company; Nancy Wolff and Helene Godin, Wolff & Godin, LP; Arks Smith; Lois Greenfield; Paul B. Goode; Diane Grumet, Steps on Broadway; Jérôme Maurel, Ballet de l'Opéra National de Paris. My thanks also to Bonnie Hofkin for beautiful anatomical drawings and Monica Rangne for intrepid illustrations.

Parents and families are the sine qua non of ballet. My loving thanks to my husband's family for all their support and encouragement, and especially to my mother-in-law, Marilyn Minden, who gave so many weekends to this project, who tirelessly corrected and improved draft after draft with gentle rigor.

My own parents and siblings have always helped me, and I will always be grateful. My thanks to my father, Edwin Gaynor, for the photograph herein, and for his support and encouragement of all my endeavors. And thank you to my mother, Elizabeth Gaynor, whose influence is on every page of this book. She shared her extensive dance library with its many rare volumes, and she read and advised on most of the manuscript. Most important, by enrolling me in ballet classes and by taking me to so many memorable performances, she introduced me to the joys of ballet.

Finally, my thanks to my daughter Lucy for her patience, and to my husband, John, to whom this book is dedicated.

Introduction

When Anna Pavlova was a young dancer in Russia, she faced stiff competition from a bevy of imported hotshot Italian ballerinas. With their tricked-out shoes and their formidable technique they performed marvels on full pointe: endless balances, dazzling pirouettes, even an unheard-of thirty-two fouettés. Pavlova toiled to make herself into a virtuosa in their mold.

Fortunately her teacher Pavel Gerdt advised her to leave off the tricks and turns and focus on developing her own innate qualities: delicacy, lyricism, expressivity. In the end Pavlova triumphed as a Romantic dancer at a time when hard-boiled classicism was all the rage, and she went on to foment balletomania the world over. Of course, she never stopped working on her technique; she even got the greatest Italian ballet master of all, Enrico Cecchetti, to give private lessons to her and no one else. And she did adopt the newfangled Italian shoes (albeit doctored in her secret way), but not just for flash or bravura. Pavlova did the opposite: she used pointework to convey achingly beautiful vulnerability.

Pavlova became a legend by tapping into her genius for self-expression rather than by technique alone. She cultivated her own eloquent "voice." And you can do the same even if you never set foot on a stage. Certainly executing steps well provides tremendous satisfaction. But ballet's joy lies not just in doing steps; it's in *dancing* them—in the pleasure of expression through movement, of union with music, of singing with your body. I hope this book helps you not only in developing proficiency but also in discovering your voice.

The Ballet Companion offers a discussion of technique that is not just how to, but why. You already know what tendus are because you do them in class. But you may not realize why you do so many, or that the meaning of the word in French ("stretched") defines the quality of the movement, or that a famous choreographic passage, the opening of Balanchine's *Theme and Variations*, is based on them—or how by perfecting your tendu you can improve your technique overall. Throughout the book, I connect the work you do in class to the bigger picture.

That picture, of course, includes performance. Looking as much as doing sparked my own love of ballet. My first impressions were formed watching Fonteyn and Nureyev, Baryshnikov, Fracci, Makarova in *Swan Lake*, Kirkland in *Giselle*, and the opening night (a school night at that) of Balanchine's 1972 Stravinsky Festival with its landmark premieres. Granted, that's a hard act to follow, but every generation has its own superb dancers. Let today's inspire you.

In the back of this book you will find a collection of choreographic "greatest hits" along with some of my favorites that are less well known. Go to the ballet as often as you can. If you can see a work repeatedly, that's even better. A second or third viewing reveals the craftsmanship in the choreography and lets you compare different interpretations. In deciding what you admire and what you don't, what you allow to influence you and what you reject, you will shape your own character as a dancer.

Sometimes the first step toward finding your voice is to realize that it's okay to have one. This book is generously sprinkled with nuggets of ballet history that show how often a distinctive choreographic or performing personality has influenced and enriched ballet. Things we take for granted today—the one-act ballet, the tutu, the overhead lift, the blocked pointe shoe, even women dancing professionally—all were innovations in their time and sometimes bitterly resisted. Dance history is full of skirmishes between rebels and traditionalists, but ultimately dance embraces new voices and rewards those who take risks.

As a student I was captivated by ballet history and contrived to write every school term paper I could on a ballet subject. An assignment on great Americans became an essay on Ted Shawn, an art history project a study of Diaghilev's collaborations. My poor logic professor asked for an example of a well-constructed argument and got a scathing critique of the dance program at Yale. I took great pleasure in using my obsession with dance as a means of enlivening schoolwork; you might, too.

Ballet history is delicious—it's rich and glamorous and fun. It's also important for your dancing in a serious way. You develop an informed artistry when you understand why the Sylph holds her arms differently from the Sugar Plum Fairy, or why a Bournonville allegro must bounce along the way it does. Petipa and Ivanov's *Swan Lake* and Fokine's *Dying Swan* were choreographed only ten years apart and both feature swan-women in white, feathered tutus. But to dance Fokine like Petipa would be to miss the point. Fokine loathed—among other things—classicism's stale verticality and lack of expressivity, so his reforms included a liberation of the arms and upper body. This isn't a stylistic nicety; it's a wholly different approach. We know about it from history: from his own manifesto and from the accounts of the dancers he trained.

I hope the historical tidbits in this book intrigue you enough so that you read more. Dancers' autobiographies are often delightful and engrossing. It's fascinating to read about your own familiar exercises and routines as they were in other times: in Imperial Russia or with the Ballets Russes or under Communism or for Balanchine. Some of the dancers' stories will surely resonate with you and contribute to the creation of your own dancing personality.

Ballet training rightly focuses on technique and artistry, but dancers are not indestructible, and they ignore their health at their peril. Ballet has become more overtly athletic. Although dancers still pretend not to sweat on stage, and still conceal their exertions under serene smiles, their bodies are being pushed and pulled as never before. Fortunately, there is now far more awareness and knowledge of dancers' health.

A whole new field of medicine has sprung up, and its practitioners have much to offer on the subject of injury prevention and safe training. Eating disorders, once a shameful secret, are now brought into the sunlight for compassionate confrontation and cure. Cross training is widely recognized as a complement to class that can speed the process of building strength and flexibility. I have devoted an extensive section of this book to the healthy dancer.

Like a strong and flexible dancer, ballet itself is hardy. It phoenixed out of the aristocratic pomp of the Baroque age. Powdered wigs and snuff boxes are long gone, but ballet has endured and maintained its traditions—vestiges of its royal origins—while resiliently absorbing new ideas. From a boys-only club to the cult of the ballerina, from six-foot hoop skirts to nudity, from courtiers elaborately curtsying to the king to performances that incite antigovernment protest, throughout its rich history ballet has repeatedly remodeled itself and survived.

So go ahead: cultivate your technique, your voice, and your ideas. No great choreographer ever picked a boring dancer for a muse. Ballet needs distinctive personalities to inspire new choreographic genius, to make the classics fresh, and to keep the audience interested. Your self-expression may lead you beyond ballet to other forms of dance, or to the theater. You may become a choreographer, dance teacher, dance historian, dance doctor, dance critic, dance notator, dance photographer, dance administrator or, as I did, a pointe shoe designer. You may decide to be the next Martha Graham and invent a whole new dance language. In all these endeavors your ballet technique, along with your knowledge of ballet's traditions, is the foundation on which you build. And even in nondance pursuits, qualities you develop in the studio—physical intelligence and confidence in your own voice—will serve you very well outside it. I hope this book helps you in joyfully creating your foundation. I hope it encourages you to soar.

Part One

To Be a Dancer

Getting Started

Selecting a Ballet School

Your mother says you danced in the crib. You love moving to music. Perhaps you want to perform. Perhaps performing is not for you, but the exhilaration of a well-executed tour jeté in class is. Perhaps you've been advised to try it for medical reasons, to make you strong or improve your posture. Or maybe, like Alexandra Ansanelli, principal dancer at the New York City Ballet, you were knocked out cold on the soccer field and your parents wanted you in something safer. Whatever draws you to ballet, finding the right school will make all the difference to your experience.

In the United States anyone can hang out a shingle and call him- or herself a ballet teacher. There is no organization or governing body to license teachers and maintain standards. But there are many indicators of a school's merits. Here are some things to look for when considering where to study, many of which are described in more detail later in this book:

1. Teacher's Credentials

The instructor with the most glamorous and prestigious performing credentials may not be the best teacher. The ability to dance brilliantly is different from the skills that make a great teacher: the ability to analyze, to break down steps, to explain, to inspire. Some people possess both performing and teaching abilities; some don't.

In France no one is allowed to teach without a state diploma. In the United States, the Cecchetti Society, the Cecchetti Council of America, and the London-based Royal Academy of Dance (R.A.D.) are highly respected institutions whose founders cared deeply about how ballet is taught. Teachers who have been trained through these organizations have learned a well-established syllabus—a known commodity with a proven track record of providing safe, solid, classical training. These are by no means the only good choices. There are other major training

Sauté in a modified retiré.

systems (see Major Schools of Ballet, page 63) that certainly produce excellent teachers, too. Don't be shy about asking about your teachers' backgrounds.

2. Pure Classical Ballet Technique

A school that offers nonballet classes such as jazz, modern, or tap is a plus, but if you want to learn ballet, the school's focus should be on classical ballet technique. Your classes should be pure ballet, not a hybrid.

3. Progressive Training and Syllabus

Before attempting the thirty-two fouettés in *Swan Lake* you must master the single pirouette, but before you can do that you must be able to balance in retiré on demi-pointe, and to do that you must have developed control of your turnout. In the best schools, students progress from one level to the next by mastering skills in a logical order. Ideally your school follows a graded syllabus that is informed, at least in part, by the philosophy of one of the major training systems. A syllabus helps ensure that nothing is left out and that there is a solid foundation of strength and technique on which to build in a safe, sensible way.

Some schools divide students into many levels; often each has its own leotard color, and the higher levels usually require more frequent attendance. The R.A.D. and Cecchetti systems offer examinations that students pass before moving up to the next grade. Other schools are more informal, have looser attendance requirements, and simply designate students as beginner, intermediate, or advanced. The important thing is careful, progressive training in a pleasant environment in which *you* are comfortable.

4. Attitude

A ballet school should exude a disciplined and serious but cheerful atmosphere. (See What Class Expects of You, page 11.) Students should be well groomed, neatly dressed, and display good studio etiquette. Sweatpants and other loose, concealing garb should not be allowed. (See Studio Attire, page 11.)

5. Forcing Turnout and Extension

Rotation of the leg in the hip socket so that the knees and feet point out to the side rather than to the front is essential for classical ballet. A turnout of 180 degrees is most desirable but rarely achieved. Forcing it can damage knees, hips, or ankles. A careful teacher will try to help her students achieve the desired flexibility by working within the range of a student's potential turnout and without putting the joints at risk. If students are struggling to achieve a perfect heel-to-toe-toe-to-heel fifth position, and are unable to straighten their knees or hold the knees over the toes correctly, they are forcing turnout. (See Alignment, page 78.)

6. Pointe Shoes

At what age are the girls allowed to go on pointe? Starting too young can cause injury; a lot of very little girls in pointe shoes is a red flag. Ideally pointe class is not an option but, at the appropriate level, part of the training. (See When to Begin Pointework, page 17.)

7. Facilities

The ideal space is large, open, airy, well ventilated, with high ceilings, a good floor, no obstructing pillars or pipes, and plenty of mirrors. The best studio floors are "sprung" (meaning there is air space underneath) wood and covered with a nonslip surface. Things should be clean and neat, especially the dressing rooms. A piano indicates a real accompanist instead of recorded music. This can be a tremendous enhancement, though not a requisite; plenty of schools do just fine with recorded music.

8. Health and Safety

Good ballet training improves your body and your self-esteem. Bad training can have the opposite effect. Beware of a teacher who pooh-poohs health and injury prevention; she may well have a long, sad history of injured pupils. If most of the class has tendinitis at the end of term, think twice about what's going on. Sick or injured dancers can neither create art nor experience the joy of dancing.

9. Weight

When assessing the health and safety-consciousness of a school, ask yourself whether the students look happy and healthy. Are they lean, bright-eyed, and eager, or are they frighteningly thin and joyless? How much emphasis is being placed on being thin? (See Body Esteem, page 214.)

10. Competition

Is the emphasis on progressive training or on competitions? Performing experience is valuable and should be encouraged, but in the long run an overemphasis on rehearsing for a competition can be a distraction from building solid technique.

Choosing Your Level of Commitment

You get out of ballet what you put into it. Ballet rewards both the ballerina who basks in a standing ovation at Lincoln Center and the ardent amateur who is thrilled to have just done her first double piqué turn. If your ambition is to become a professional dancer, your training will follow a certain exceptionally rigorous path—especially if you hope to dance classical ballet roles with a major company. If you are reconciled to not dancing *Swan Lake* at Covent Garden but still entertain the idea of a dance career, then you have a little more flexibility in the number and in the types of classes you choose. If you are lucky enough to study ballet for the sheer joy of it, and because there is nothing like the satisfaction of having had a terrific class, then you have more options still.

Many schools offer performance opportunities in recitals, workshops, or, often, a production of *The Nutcracker*. These can be great fun, and wonderful experiences. But be warned that auditions, rehearsals, and performances add significantly to the amount of time that you devote to ballet. Sometimes there are extra costs, too, such as costume rentals or new pointe shoes. Some schools require that you attend a minimum number of classes each week in order to participate. And if you do, you will be expected to be at every rehearsal and every performance.

Girls with professional aspirations, at about age twelve, usually in the third or fourth year of training, take class five or six days a week, often more than one class a day. Or they may put in the same number of hours

Young dancers at Ballet
Academy East in New
York City.

with longer classes over fewer days. That's a lot of time and still more if there are rehearsals, too, plus the daily trek to and from the studio. Serious preprofessional training is also expensive. In addition to tuition there is the cost of practice clothes, shoes, and perhaps summer programs as well.

To make it to the highest levels in professional ballet, you should be dancing full time during the years when most people finish high school and go to college. Ballet careers are short, and those years are formative and crucial: your youthful vigor, resilience, and strength are at their peak, your body can best absorb advanced ballet technique and you can most easily adapt to an artistic director's vision and a company's style. This presents a difficult choice for dancers' parents (usually the dancer knows that there is nothing in the world she would rather do than dance).

Forgoing or postponing higher education is not always a requisite for a professional career. Many colleges and universities offer excellent dance programs, some with prominent choreographers in residence. Conservatories such as Juilliard produce world-class dancers who also have solid academic backgrounds. Modern dancers can often start later than ballet dancers, as can musical theater dancers. Plenty of companies require that their dancers have a good command of ballet but not that they be virtuosi— either because the repertory is not the most technically demanding or because it is not limited to ballet. Being a charismatic performer who can also handle modern or jazz sometimes counts for more than pure ballet technique.

Top-notch training and all the other benefits of ballet are available even to dancers without professional ambitions. Many schools, including some professional conservatories with "open divisions" (programs that do not require you to commit to the preprofessional track and allow you to enroll in fewer classes), offer excellent classes for students who want to dance for the sake of dancing. Most schools don't turn away the once-a-week dancer; just know that it isn't realistic to expect progress beyond the basics if that's all the time you can allow. To improve your technique, you must take at least two classes a week. Three is better. Most schools require regular attendance at several classes a week in order to begin pointework.

Even if you don't intend to dance professionally, there are reasons to make the commitment to frequent if not daily classes. Ballet class gives your day structure and focus. Patient, daily study pays off not only in what it does for your technique. The applied discipline it takes will help you tackle other tasks in other areas of your life. It makes you stand out on college applications, too. But watch out: ballet class can be addictive. You may find that your problem isn't taking too few classes but wanting to take too many.

Ballet Moms and Dads: Sine Qua Non

Behind almost any successful dancer are devoted, supportive people who sacrifice to make ballet dreams come true. Your parents and family pay for all those classes and for all that special ballet gear. They drive you to lessons and rehearsals whether they're around the block or in another state, and they often wait in the lobby while you get to dance. They give up weekends and family vacations, sew costumes, and sell tickets for school performances. Their holiday celebrations have to accommodate your *Nutcracker* rehearsals, and they never miss the show. Mom's the shoulder you cry on and Dad's your biggest fan. It's a ton of work, and your commitment becomes theirs as well.

What to Expect of Class

Ballet classes last from one to two hours and are divided into two parts, barre and center. Exercises at the barre warm up and strengthen your muscles and help you practice the basic movements of ballet. Center work usually starts with stationary exercises, progresses to combinations that travel, then moves on to leaps and turns "across the floor," often along the diagonal from a back corner to a front one. The exercises vary from lesson to lesson, but always follow the same general order and build logically.

Levels

Ballet students are grouped in classes according to skill level and/or age. In large schools, they are sometimes grouped by sex. When enrolling at a new school, tell the registrar where you've studied, for how long, and how often. "Advanced Beginner" may mean different things at different studios. New students are often obliged to take a placement class to determine the appropriate level.

There is a good reason for this. Technique can only build progressively. If you're in a class over your head, you won't improve and you may be in the way. It's okay to challenge yourself with a harder-than-usual class, and it's tremendously inspiring to work alongside really good dancers, but the class is meant for the students at that level and you should defer to them. If you're an advanced student in a more elementary class, do demonstrate the steps if the teacher asks you to, but keep in mind that it's the beginning students' class.

Learning Combinations

Combinations can be tricky for beginners. Learning them has less to do with intelligence or a good memory than with concentration and focus. You don't learn steps with your mind alone; your muscles must learn them, too. Deliberate and continuous repetition ingrains movement patterns into your body and develops "kinesthetic memory." Be patient: mastering steps takes time and practice. The best way to pick up a combination is to mark it as the teacher gives it (see page 16). Certain steps are frequently combined. For example, sissonne tombée often precedes

9

Teacher, David Howard, and student, Jennifer Gelfand.

pas de bourrée, glissade, and grand jeté. The more you do these steps in familiar sequences, the more you can think of them as phrases that come automatically rather than as individual words.

The Teacher

Your teacher observes and offers corrections, sometimes as you are dancing, sometimes in between combinations. To keep the class moving and students' muscles warm, pauses between exercises are kept to a minimum. Don't interrupt the teacher. If you're lost when everyone else knows the steps, try to learn them by watching the others dance. In your regular class with your regular teacher, it's okay to raise your hand and ask a question if the answer would benefit the whole group; it's not okay if the question pertains only to you. See your teacher privately after class if you need help or advice.

Expect physical contact in ballet class. It's often helpful for a student to feel an instruction as well as to hear it, so don't be surprised if your teacher touches you to correct your placement or your line: it's essential and it's absolutely professional. It is inappropriate, and never necessary, for a teacher to touch breasts or private parts. But your arms, hands, feet, ankles, knees, ribs, shoulders, abdomen, and even your jaw or hip bones may all be adjusted. One of my teachers favored a stick for this purpose, as do many others.

Studio Attire

Check the dress code of your school. All of the following are available at dance supply shops, through dancewear catalogs, and on the Internet.

Basic Studio Attire for Women:

▶ A leotard with or without sleeves. Check if your school has prescribed colors for each level. If not, black is always a safe choice.

▶ Pink dance tights. Regular hosiery is not strong or thick enough.

▶ Soft ballet slippers in pink canvas or leather. Elastics sometimes come with the shoes, and you sew them on yourself.

▶ A short wrap skirt (optional, and only if allowed).

▶ Warm-ups (optional, and only if allowed).

You need not wear underpants with tights and a leotard. Many leotards include a built-in shelf bra, but it's fine to wear a regular one, too.

Basic Studio Attire for Men:

▶ T-shirt. Plain white is traditional, but some schools allow more latitude.

▶ Long tights, with or without feet. Some schools allow shorts or three-quarter-length tights. Black is most common, though some teachers request gray so they can see your leg muscles better.

▶ A belt or an elastic waistband to hold up your tights.

▶ Black or white socks.

▶ Soft ballet slippers in black or white canvas or leather. Elastics often come with the shoes, and you sew them on yourself.

▶ A dance belt, which is similar to an athletic supporter.

What's in Your Dance Bag?

▶ Hair kit: coated elastics, barrettes, large hairpins, bobby pins, hairnets

▶ Nail clipper and nail file

▶ Band-Aids

▶ Antibiotic ointment

▶ Deodorant

▶ Joint wrap bandage

▶ Sewing needle and thread

▶ Safety pins

▶ Toiletries

▶ Towel

▶ Water bottle

▶ Granola, fruit, or other energy food

▶ A spare pair of ballet slippers (optional)

And for dancers on pointe:

▶ Pointe shoes

▶ Pointe shoe accessories: toe tape, heel grippers, toe pads, fitting kits, extra ribbon and elastic

11

What Class Expects of You

In today's world of instant informality and less than perfect manners, ballet class provides an oasis of true courtesy and dignity, a remnant of the royal decorum of the Baroque age. Studio etiquette may seem mysterious at first, but its importance soon becomes apparent. You are creating an environment conducive to learning, and you are physically demonstrating the esteem in which you hold your art, your teacher, and your fellow students.

Considerate, respectful behavior is expected. Courtesy is especially important for performing artists; putting a show on stage requires cooperation among directors, managers, performers, technical crew, and front-of-house staff. A performance is a complicated machine with a lot of moving parts, and politeness is the essential lubricant.

Be on time. Arriving late disturbs other students. Your teacher has carefully planned the class so that it builds on the exercises done at the beginning. If you must be late, ask permission to enter (you can do this with eye contact and a hopeful and contrite look). Locate a spot at the barre before walking into the room, and take your place quickly and quietly. Do a few pliés on your own to warm up. It's especially important that you not try to sneak in unobserved after roll call. If the teacher does not note your presence, your attendance record looks bad and that can make all the difference in when you are allowed to go on pointe or how you are cast in a production.

Be neat. Keep your hair off your face and neck. Hair that moves is a distraction. It should be tight against your head so that you can spot freely. If it's long, fasten it securely in a bun or French twist. (See Ballet Bun, page 28.) Ponytails and long braids are hazardous; they could smack you or someone else.

A general rule: Don't wear jewelry in the studio. It could fly off or stick someone, especially in a partnering class. Small stud earrings are allowed in some studios, but never dangling earrings, bracelets, large necklaces, or a wristwatch. Dark or bright red nail polish looks creepy on stage and for that reason it is often prohibited in class as well.

Be clean. Respecting others means wearing clean clothes and sweet–smelling shoes, and attending to your personal hygiene. Air out your shoes between classes. Shower before class and use antiperspirant or deodorant; keep some tucked in your bag as well. Avoid strong perfumes or cologne. What smells fine to you may be overpowering to someone else.

Dress the part. Follow the dress code. The intention is not to quash individuality but to enable the teacher to see clearly. Even if there is no uniform, don't wear wild outfits or hide under layers of clothing. Wear clothes that show you are ready to take class. This not only sends a message to the teacher about your seriousness, it also sends a message to yourself. You will dance better if you are properly dressed for class.

Mind your manners. Dancers are ladies and gentlemen. They are polite. They don't lean against the wall or on the barre, and they don't sit down unless directed to do so. They wouldn't dream of chewing gum in class.

It is a privilege to have live piano or other instrumental accompaniment rather than recorded music. Treat the accompanist with the utmost respect, and never lean on the piano, use it as a barre, or place things on it.

Rudeness to teachers or the accompanist is unthinkable in ballet; you could be dismissed from class or even expelled from the school. Yawning, talking, whispering, or having private giggles with your friends counts as rudeness.

Pay attention. You're there to work, so watch and listen, especially when the combination is given. Some teachers may not show it twice.

Stash your stuff. Your school may well be so honest that you can blithely leave your dance bag unattended in the dressing room. Sadly, that's not the case everywhere. Especially in big cities, your dance bag goes with you into the studio. Look for the pile of dance bags and place yours with it, making sure it is safely out of the path of dancers. In crowded, unfamiliar studios put it where you can keep an eye on it.

Do the combination as given, and do it in its entirety. If everyone is doing one thing and you've decided to "improve" it, it's not only a distraction, it's downright disrespectful to your teacher. There are exceptions: a teacher might ask more advanced students to do a combination on demi-pointe or to add beats. If there are steps you must modify because of a physical condition, speak to the teacher beforehand so it isn't a surprise to her.

Always finish every combination. Even if you flub it completely, the discipline of ballet requires that you finish it, and finish it with as much poise as you can. Sighing, making faces, or otherwise showing your frustration or other emotions is inappropriate.

Know where to stand. If you're new in class, notice whether the other dancers have set places at the barre. Dancers are as territorial as lions, so try not to displace anyone. The teacher may suggest a spot for you. Otherwise, find an empty place, ask your neighbors if there's room, and settle in. You need to be able to extend your leg in grand battement as far as it can go both front and back without whacking the person next to you. If there isn't enough room, angle out when doing extensions.

Tour de Force

CATHERINE DE MEDICI AND *LE BALLET COMIQUE DE LA REINE*

Catherine, born in 1519 to the fabled Medici family, was orphaned as a child and raised in a convent, where she learned Latin and Greek and became one of the best-educated and cleverest women of her time. At fourteen, in an arranged marriage, she wed Henry of Orleans, the future king of France. In addition to becoming one of the most influential queens in its history, she introduced to France the delights of artichokes, ice cream, and ballet de cour.

Catherine's major contribution to the advancement of ballet was an extravaganza known as *Le Ballet Comique de la Reine*. Commissioned on the occasion of her sister's wedding celebration in 1581, it was staged by a popular Italian violinist, Baldassarino de Belgiojoso—known in France as Balthasar de Beaujoyeulx—who brought to the French court the kind of lavish dancing spectacle already popular with Italian nobles. *Le Ballet Comique de la Reine* lasted nearly six hours and combined dramatic narrative, dance, and vocal performance to tell the mythological story of Circe and her enchantment of Apollo.

The ballet, witnessed by ten thousand guests, took place in the Petit Bourbon Palace in the center of a great hall, with elaborate scenery and audience seating arranged around the sides. This magnificent showpiece demonstrated the lengths to which the French court, with the widowed Catherine presiding, would go to dazzle European society. It became the model for court entertainments throughout Europe and is widely recognized as the first ballet.

If there are portable barres in class, help set them up and remove them. If you're new, offer to help, but let someone who knows where the barre goes place it. Men, be cavaliers: Take the barres away for the women.

When class moves on to center floor, the teacher may find a place for you in line. In some schools the lines rotate when the combination repeats so that everyone gets a chance to check placement in the mirror. In many classes no one is allowed to hide in the back and be a habitual follower; all must take a turn at being in front and on their own. If the lines don't rotate, then the honor of standing in front usually goes to the best students: it means the teacher trusts you to be an example to others. Work hard for that honor.

When everyone lines up to dance across the floor, take your place in line and be ready to go. Know the right number of phrases or counts between groups so that you start on cue. If you're not going to go, make it clear by getting out of the way.

Drink politely. Do drink before class starts and carry a water bottle— but the norms of the gym don't apply to ballet class. If the teacher allows it, you may drink from your water bottle between barre and center, but not between barre exercises and never while a teacher is giving a combination.

Ask permission to leave. Even if you are suddenly taken ill, you should ask permission to leave the studio. Wandering in and out of the room is not allowed. If you absolutely must leave early, get the teacher's okay before class starts. Don't leave in the middle of a combination. Acknowledge the teacher by catching her eye and communicating your thanks with a silent wave, then leave unobtrusively.

Getting the Most Out of Class

Make time for ballet. Your brain understands what you ought to be doing before your muscles do. Coordination, line, speed, and strength develop only if you train your muscles through regular repetition. It's great fun to take ballet recreationally, but you can't expect much improvement in your technique if you take class only once a week.

Make time for rest. Professional dancers generally take one day off a week. Allow yourself at least this much rest. Your body needs it.

Be ready for class. Arrive in time to bring your mind into focus, warm up, and stretch. If you need them, have your pointe shoes ready in your dance bag, no fumbling with toe pads in the middle of class. Once class starts there are no bathroom breaks except for real emergencies; plan accordingly. Don't eat a big meal just beforehand, but don't dance on an empty stomach either. (See Eating Right, page 209.)

Take barre in a different spot periodically. Don't fall into the "this is my spot" trap. It's helpful to see yourself from different angles to be certain of your placement and line. Face the mirror straight on at some times; look at yourself in profile at others. Also practice without the mirror—there isn't one on stage.

Mark the combination. To mark means to move through steps without doing them fully. Most people learn combinations much faster if they mark while the teacher demonstrates or explains. Lift your leg just a little rather than to your full extension or walk a step instead of jumping it. Change direction and orientation. Arm movements, however, should be done full out, not marked, to avoid developing bad habits. Be mindful of getting in the way of other students.

Work on corrections immediately. Even for professionals, class is not about being perfect. Don't be frustrated by a correction; be honored that the teacher feels you are worthy of his personal attention. Take corrections very seriously; they not only improve your technique, they protect you from injury.

Teachers expect you to try the combination again, incorporating their corrections right after they give them. Do the best you can: you may be able to correct the error immediately, or it may take more practice.

Stay after class and practice any step that's giving you trouble. Use a quiet corner or an empty studio. Don't practice at home or unsupervised when you are beginning ballet. If you do a step incorrectly repeatedly, it's that much harder to set right. Bad habits can sink into your muscles as easily as good ones.

The world's greatest, and probably shortest, commencement speech is said to have contained only three sentences, "Never give up. Never give up. Never give up." Take this to heart and realize that you are not alone. When the combination seems so fiendishly difficult that you despair of ever getting it, look around; if you're having trouble it's likely others are as well. An amateur dancer told me that he was about to admit defeat on a series of turns when he noticed that a principal dancer from a major company was falling over, too. Try again.

When to Begin Pointework

It takes a long time to develop a body for dancing—especially the feet. The pointes for girls have to be, I always say, like an elephant's trunk; strong and yet flexible and soft. It takes some time.

—George Balanchine

It is hard to tell an eager young dancer that she is not yet ready for pointe shoes. Students—and parents—must realize that teachers have to be firm: there is a risk of serious injury in introducing pointework too soon. Starting pointework is not just a question of age or physical maturity; readiness depends on strength, technique, attitude, and commitment.

Pointe shoe fitting at Gaynor Minden.

The bones of the foot are not fully developed, strengthened, and hardened until sometime in the late teens or early twenties. Of course, there is a great deal of individual variation. If a young dancer attempts pointework without proper strength and technique, the significant

Ribbons and Elastics

Sewing Elastics on Slippers

You need a piece of elastic about five inches long and about half an inch wide for each shoe. Fold the heel of the shoe down to meet the sockliner as shown. Mark the inside of the shoe along the creases with a pencil. Sew one end of elastic in a square pattern over the pencil mark,

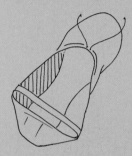

Sew technique shoe elastic at the creases made by folding the heel forward.

using a whip stitch on the sides and a running stitch along the bottom and the top near, but not through, the drawstring. About a half inch of the elastic should be attached on each side, stitches should be about an eighth of an inch long. Pin the other end of elastic in place and try the shoe on for comfort before you finish sewing. It should be taut but not too tight.

Note: The terms "technique shoe" and "ballet slipper" are interchangeable.

Sewing Ribbons on Pointe Shoes

The more you dance, the more particular you will become about how and where to sew the ribbons on your pointe shoes. Their location and their angle determine how effectively they keep the shoe attached to your foot, and how attractively they do it. Because every foot is different, every dancer must determine the positioning that is right for her, and most dancers insist on sewing their ribbons themselves. However you choose to sew them—more angled, less angled, staggered, or with your personal good luck number of stitches per side—you are participating in one of ballet's tedious but cherished rituals.

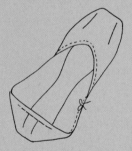

Fold the heel forward then mark the crease with a pencil.

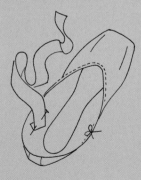

Pin the ribbon in place so its back edge aligns with the crease you made by folding.

Most pointe shoe ribbon is nylon or polyester satin with either a shiny or matte finish. It should be seven-eighths to one inch wide and cut into four pieces, each about twenty-two inches long. Some dancers singe the ribbon ends with a match to keep them from unraveling.

Although you will fine-tune your own method with every pair you sew, the basic procedure is this: Fold the heel of the shoe down to meet the sockliner as you would for technique shoe elastics. Mark the inside of the shoe along the crease with a pencil; this line will correspond to the position of the back edge of the ribbon and ensure that

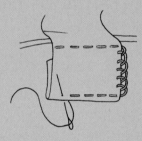

Fold the end of the ribbon under so the raw edge is not visible and sew the ribbon with running stitches along top and bottom and whip stitches at the sides.

Most dancers prefer that the ribbons angle forward.

the ribbon is angled. Ribbon should overlap shoe by at least one inch.

Using strong thread (some dancers use dental floss), sew the ribbon securely onto the shoe, using whip stitches and running stitches in a square pattern as for technique shoe elastic (see above). For a neater and stronger result, fold the bottom end of the ribbon under so the rough edge does not show and so you are sewing through a double thickness of ribbon. If your pointe shoes have a separate, unattached lining, sew your ribbons onto the lining only. If the lining is bonded to the outer satin and you must sew all the way through, use running stitches throughout. Also, use a good strong needle and be sure the thread matches the color of the satin.

Sewing Elastics on Pointe Shoes

Many dancers use elastics as well as ribbons to keep their pointe shoes from slipping off their heels. Pointe shoe elastic tends to be wider and more heavy-duty than technique shoe elastic. Some dancers sew the elastics near the ribbons, which helps conceal them once the ribbons are tied. Others sew them at the back of the heel, on the outside of the shoe, to prevent chafing the Achilles tendon. Still others find that the ideal position is in between, often a thumb's width in front of the back seam. For additional security and support, you can do what men often do with their technique shoes: use two pieces of elastic per shoe, crisscrossing them over your instep.

Tying Ribbons

Ribbons add support but should never be so tight that they hurt your Achilles tendon or restrict movement of your ankle.

For the cleanest line, wrap one ribbon at a time. With your foot flat on the floor, grasp the inside ribbon and wrap it over your foot and around the back of your ankle. Continue wrapping the ribbon around to the front of your ankle and back around again, stopping at the inside of your ankle.

Then wrap the outer ribbon over your foot and around the back of your ankle, bringing it around to the front to meet the first ribbon at the inside of the ankle, just between the bone and the Achilles tendon; the knot will go here, never directly on the tendon. Tie the ribbons securely in a double knot—never in a bow!— and tuck in the knot and loose ends. The knot should be invisible: if it makes a bulge when you tuck it in, trim the ribbons.

Wrap the inside ribbon over the top of your foot and around the back of your ankle.

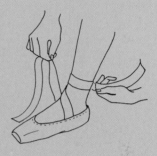

Then grasp the outside ribbon.

19

Wrap the outside ribbon over the top of the foot and around the back of the ankle.

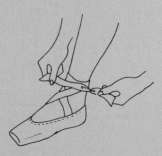

The outside ribbon meets the inside ribbon at the inside of the ankle. Tie the ribbons in a small knot and tuck the knot in so it disappears.

forces created by the combination of body weight and momentum can permanently damage those not-fully-developed bones. Yet if a dancer is truly ready, if the introduction to pointework is gradual and always carefully and knowledgeably supervised, if the pointe shoes are well chosen and properly fitted, there is minimal risk of injury even if the bones are not fully formed.

Most dancers are ready to begin pointework between the ages of ten and twelve. Occasionally a supremely strong nine-year-old can safely go on pointe, but this is unusual. There is rarely any harm in waiting. A dancer who starts pointework a year later than her classmates almost always catches up. Many adult beginners are not ready for pointe either, but there is much less risk in their using pointe shoes because their feet have fully grown. In general, these are the criteria for readiness for pointe shoes:

Commitment

Most dancers need at least two to four years of training in ballet technique, with a good attendance record, before going on pointe. Other forms of dance, or classes that mix ballet with other forms, don't count.

Someone who regularly takes several classes a week can probably start at a younger age than someone who attends less frequently. During the first year of pointe you will probably be expected to take at least three or four ballet classes a week (a minimum of five hours).

Maturity

Your demeanor shows that you have the maturity for pointework. Your attitude is attentive and hardworking, and your studio etiquette is exemplary.

Technique

Pointework requires a continual lifting up and out of the shoe. It's the same strength and skill needed for attaining and sustaining a balance on a high demi-pointe on one leg. That means that you can always hold your turnout when you dance, that your abdomen and lower back— your core—are strong, and that your legs, and especially your knees, are really pulled up.

You must be able to both relevé and piqué up to a balance. Calf and ankle strength are essential. Your relevé must be particularly strong; at least sixteen flawless ones onto a high demi-pointe center floor should be easy. You must demonstrate the correct use of plié in your dancing and know how to work your feet properly in tendu and all other exercises that require pointing the foot—no sickling.

Health and Physique

You should be in good health, not recovering from illness or injury, and of normal weight. You must possess the stamina to make it through a full ballet class several times a week. You don't need insteps arched like bananas, but your feet must not be so flat or your ankles so stiff as to prevent you from properly "getting over" onto full pointe.

It's the rare dancer who is not tremendously excited about going on pointe. It's a good sign: an indifferent dancer may not have the perseverance needed for the repetitive exercises pointe training entails. *But don't let your enthusiasm tempt you to practice at home or to wear your new pointe shoes around the house.* Proper supervision is so important that some schools require that their students keep their pointe shoes at the studio. And when you are ready to go on pointe, congratulations. You have worked hard for this moment. See How to Select and Fit, page 192.

All That Jazz, Modern, and More

Ballet has been called "the Latin of dance," the language the well-educated dancer knows. Still, it never hurts to learn another language. Just as ballet provides technical precision, strength, and fluidity to students of modern, jazz, and tap, you—the ballet dancer—can learn much from other dance forms.

Modern and Contemporary

"Modern" usually refers to the techniques created by Martha Graham, Doris Humphrey, and their many choreographic descendants including Paul Taylor, José Limón, and Merce Cunningham. It may also refer to the lunging, swinging style of dance developed by Lester Horton and carried on by his students, among them Alvin Ailey.

Tour de Force

REBELS, RIVALS, AND THE "SHAKESPEARE OF BALLET"

By the late 1600s ballet had begun to evolve from a princely pastime
enjoyed in the relative privacy of the palace to a popular entertainment in public theaters. The transition altered both ballet and the
ballerina over the ensuing century. Leading the changes were
Noverre, the "Shakespeare of ballet" and a pair of rival ballerinas,
Camargo and Sallé.

A French ballet dancer turned choreographer, Jean-Georges Noverre
(1727–1810), helped codify the pioneering principles of what was
to become modern-day ballet. Noverre believed that ballet was stiff
and artificial and that a new narrative ballet, ballet d'action, offered
a richer experience. He strove to unite ballet's disparate elements—
music, costumes, and scenery, as well as choreography—in the
service of the story. While he didn't shun virtuosity in technique, he
didn't believe in it for its own sake. Like Shakespeare, Noverre gave
prominence to character and plot while invigorating the language

His famous *Lettres sur la Danse*, published in 1760, was a call to arms for the ballet world to shed its artifice—wigs, masks, high heels, and elaborate costumes that disguised the body and hid the face. He encouraged dancers to be as dramatic as possible, to use natural movement, gesture, and facial expression, as well as their ballet vocabulary. To maximize expressivity, traditional masks had to go—a radical notion—and looser, simpler, and more realistic costumes that allowed greater freedom of movement were encouraged.

Noverre worked all over Europe, but he did not reform ballet single-handed. In England, John Weaver (1673–1760) combined pantomime with ballet, producing numerous comic and serious ballets d'action between 1702 and 1733. And soon Marie Sallé (1707–1756), a French ballerina and choreographer, would also, ever so gracefully, rewrite the rules.

Sallé epitomized the dramatic expression and the costume reform that Noverre later expounded upon, interpreting her roles with exquisite realistic acting and a modest style. At a Covent Garden performance in 1734, Sallé choreographed and danced in her own production of *Pygmalion*, in the role of Galatea, the statue who comes to life. She wore an unadorned, flimsy muslin tunic and literally let down her hair, which fell loose without any ornamentation. The audience was shocked. And delighted.

Sallé's rival, the Belgian Marie-Anne de Cupis de Camargo (1710–1770), was known more for her extraordinary technique—the height of virtuosity at the time. Like Sallé, Camargo dressed for success. She dared to remove the heels from her shoes and caused a scandal by shortening her skirts—the better to perform and to be seen performing flashy, elevated steps like entrechat quatre and cabriole, steps that had previously been the exclusive property of the male dancer.

Their tremendous rivalry was terrific for the box office; it appealed to audiences in much the same way the competition between the Yankees and Red Sox attracts fans today. Their styles represented the ongoing argument between the virtuosic and the dramatic—it's the rare dancer who excels at both—and their dancing achieved new heights of each. Both succeeded, in part, because they had the courage to reject conventional notions of what was appropriate for women, mores that got in the way of their artistry and their technique.

Voltaire immortalized them in verse, which went, in part, "Ah! Camargo. How brilliant you are! But, great gods, how ravishing too is Sallé."

Marie Camargo

Modern dance is more weighted than ballet; modern dancers speak of being "into the floor." Working turned-in as well as turned-out with bare feet flexed as well as pointed, using a nonballetic port de bras, breathing at specified times, falling—it's all part of the mix. Graham's technique emanates from the lower torso; her signature movements include the tightening of the body into itself, the contraction, and its opposing movement, the release. Modern class may include floor work—seated, kneeling, lying—as well as or instead of barre work.

"Contemporary" encompasses a wide array of styles that have their roots in both modern and ballet. In the United Kingdom, contemporary dance is usually what Americans refer to as modern.

Jazz class at Steps on Broadway, New York City.

Jazz

An unleashed, makes-me-wanna-sing-and-dance energy fills a good jazz class. Like jazz music, jazz dance has developed into a variety of forms: from the theatrical work of Jack Cole, Michael Bennett, and Bob Fosse to the rhythmic exuberance of Billy Siegenfeld to the sharp, funky styles that sprouted up along with rap and hip-hop music.

Jazz emphasizes isolations—freely moving one part of the body such as the head, shoulder, or pelvis while the rest is absolutely still. Ballet dancers who must carefully hold the pelvis in place especially benefit from isolations and the coordination they develop. Both modern and jazz also practice suspension: moving through a position rather than stopping there to balance. Mastering the suspension adds fluidity and nuance to your dancing.

Ballroom and Social Dance

Discover the glamour of swirling around the dance floor like Fred and Ginger. Social dance develops smooth grace. Best of all, it's useful in real life. So many dancers are shy about dancing socially—what, you mean dance without rehearsal? With ballroom classes, you won't feel awkward at a formal party. If you're interested in choreography, ballroom is the thing to learn. The partnering and steps can flow right into ballet composition.

Balanchine celebrated the waltz in *Vienna Waltzes;* other choreographers have explored the tango: Hans van Manen's *Five Tangos* and Paul Taylor's *Piazzolla Caldera*. And Julio Bocca, the Argentine ballet star, even formed a company dedicated to the fusion of ballet and modern with his country's national dance, the tango.

Tap

Tap focuses on percussive rhythm and precise patterns of sound. Tap is good aerobic exercise: it builds muscle control and rhythm. It can be improvisational, which can be liberating for the ballet dancer. Whether it's virtuosic like that of Fred Astaire, Gene Kelly, Gregory Hines, and Savion Glover or just hoofin' and making your own music with your feet, there's something undeniably energizing—and liberating—about this great American style of dance.

West African

West African dance challenges and rewards the ballet dancer who dares. In sharp contrast to the upright ballet stance, West African dance works low to the ground, constantly using the floor. And what flexibility in the spine! Though the steps are codified and specific, the number of times a particular sequence of steps is performed is dictated solely by live drummers playing complex rhythms. You have to be highly attuned to the music because you can't go on to the next step until they give you the signal.

Folk and Character

Dance has arisen all over the globe, and there's a world to choose from. Whether you are drawn to capoeira, the dance form from Brazil that's also a martial art, or to Irish step dancing, with its compelling rhythmic vigor and precision, you will find something to incorporate into your ballet training. For example, the "flower finger" position of classical Chinese dance differs greatly from ballet's hand and wrist, but the classical Chinese mandate that "eye follows hand" develops a lovely coordination of head and arm in the ballet dancer. The isolation of the head acquired in Indian dancing—moving it directly side to side while the eyes and chin stay level—might not seem applicable to ballet until a renowned contemporary choreographer asks you to rub an imaginary surface with your ear.

It's useful and enlightening to step outside ballet's physical confines, to dance in positions and alignments that are not balletic. In addition, some dancers, the shy types, can benefit from a dance form in which assertiveness is a requisite. Studying Spanish flamenco certainly increases your chance of being cast in the Spanish divertissement in *The Nutcracker,* and, more important, it develops a supremely confident stage presence. A flamenco dancer often improvises, solo, in the middle of a circle formed by others, which forces her to show personality and self-assurance. The chest is lifted and thrust commandingly forward. The hips release so the feet can stamp strongly accented, propulsive rhythms beneath swirling arms, circling wrists, and clicking castanets. Every step must have boldness and brio.

Most of the major ballet training systems require some study of folk or "character" dance. Broadening your experience of music and movement enriches your ballet technique and enlarges your perspective, enabling you to better understand and appreciate ballet. It makes you a more knowledgeable, more versatile, and ultimately more interesting dancer.

Ballet at Any Age

Ballet is not just for the athletic, the artistic, or the young. Homemakers, physicists, philanthropists, lawyers, secretaries, movie stars—ballet is more popular than ever among people of all metiers, all ages, and both sexes. Ballet offers both a break from daily life and a challenge with its own distinct mental and physical rewards. In class you become a part of the grace and beauty you see on stage, and it becomes part of you. Ballet also provides a great workout, with lasting benefits of toning, lengthening, and stretching. The camaraderie in class can be the best part. Your classmates become a second family because no one else understands so well your passion for dance.

Ballet class for adults has the same structure as ballet class for children: barre to warm up and center to move. But adults learn differently, by analysis as well as by repetition. Class may be more aerobic, with fewer stops so that muscles stay warm. Combinations are less gruelingly academic and more "dancey."

There's seldom a dress code in adult classes. If you feel too exposed in standard class attire, wear a T-shirt or wrap sweater and sweatpants or a skirt in which you can move freely. As you progress, you may find yourself gaining definition and shedding pounds—and a layer or two of clothing along with them.

Ballet need not start at age four and end at thirty, but adult beginners and returning students do need to be realistic about physical limitations. An older body with a set bone structure can't be pushed the way a younger, more malleable one can. You won't acquire much turnout as an adult, but you can strengthen the lower abdominal muscles to better use what you do have. To prevent injury and maximize enjoyment, aim for proper form, not that extra half inch of extension or two degrees of turnout.

You can certainly improve flexibility. Stretch frequently but carefully and only when you are warmed up. Cross training such as Pilates builds core strength and may make all the difference in your développés.

Many schools offer beginning pointe for adults. The classes concentrate on barre work and must be taken in conjunction with several weekly technique classes. Strength and alignment are prerequisites just as they are for younger students. Be sure your pointe shoes are fitted by an expert.

The Ballet Bun

Ballet's classic hairstyle has come to define the dancer herself: "bun-head" is dancers' own affectionate term for ballerinas and ballet students. Meticulous grooming is part of ballet; dancers quite literally keep every hair in place. You rarely see a really good dancer with sloppy hair, and good schools never allow it. I once suffered agonies of embarrassment when my hair fell down in class, and I was banished until I got the bun right. Sleek, disciplined, functional, and beautiful, the ballet bun tops off your elegant line and holds your hair away from your face.

You need a brush and comb; large, sturdy two- to three-inch hairpins; bobby pins; a fine hairnet that matches your hair color; and elastic hair bands (the plush fabric ones are best; rubber bands or elastics with metal parts can break your hair). It can be helpful to moisten your hair using a spray water bottle, or tame it with an antifrizz styling gel before you start. For performances you may need hairspray for the finishing touch.

High Ballet Bun

1. Gather hair up from your jawline to the top part of the back of your head. Use an elastic band to make a tight ponytail.

2. Twist the ponytail itself and then coil it around the elastic band, making at least one complete circle; tuck the end of the ponytail under the bun and hold everything in place with your hand.

3. Use large hairpins around the bun to secure it to the rest of your hair. Use only as many as you need; three or four are usually enough. Flying hairpins are dangerous in class or on stage, so be sure your bun is fastened firmly and that pins pose no threat to fellow dancers. Dancers have actually been fined for dropping hairpins in performance.

4. Place the hairnet around the bun, wrapping it as many times as necessary to secure it completely. If the bun sticks up too high, flatten it with your hand and pin it down again so that the bun top is closer to your head and forms a smoother line. Use bobby pins to tidy any wisps.

Chignon

The chignon, or low bun, which is positioned at the nape of your neck, is the hairstyle of many a Giselle; it is also a great option if your hair is shorter than shoulder length. Make a low ponytail, then form the chignon as described for the high bun. Dancers with very short hair may use a hairpiece bun for performance; otherwise, securing hair away from your face with pins or inconspicuous barrettes should do the trick for class.

French Twist

The sophisticated French twist provides an even cleaner line than a bun.

1. Gather hair back into a low ponytail as for chignon, but do not secure the ponytail with an elastic band.

2. Grasp the ponytail underneath with one hand and begin to twist the ponytail, lifting the hair up as you twist. Work quickly and twist tightly. Use your free hand to hold the roll that begins to form against your head as you twist.

3. Tuck the end of your ponytail into the roll as you continue to hold the hair in place with your hand. Use large pins or a sturdy, flat barrette to secure the roll; start pinning at the bottom and follow the direction of your twist.

And Always Secure Your Tiara

Position the headpiece, then secure it all along its length with pairs of bobby pins, each pair crisscrossed into an X shape.

High bun

Chignon

French twist

28

Starting Late but Serious?

Most ballet dancers' professional careers begin in their late teens, after years of training begun in early childhood. But there are exceptions. Carmen Corella, soloist at American Ballet Theatre, was a basketball player until, at age thirteen, she saw what fun her brother Angel was having in ballet. It's a myth that all sports conflict with ballet training; in fact, sports, especially gymnastics, can give you a leg up with a late start. Sylvie Guillem of the Paris Opera Ballet was a gymnast before taking up ballet, as was Igor Youskevitch, the great *danseur noble* of the 1930s, '40s, and '50s. Men can often begin later than women; Youskevitch started at the ripe old age of twenty.

If you're serious about dancing but playing a game of catch up, you will have to work especially hard and find the best training you can. Enroll in a rigorous school that is either attached to a ballet company or regularly sends its students on to ballet careers. You must take class daily, and probably more than just one class a day.

Plenty of dancers who start training late are cast in community productions or even on Broadway. And lots of ballet students with no performing aspirations progress enough to learn pointework and variations. Get into class and dance!

Ballet and Pregnancy

There was a time when ballerinas were discouraged from having babies and pregnant women were discouraged from exercising. Fortunately both the dance and the medical professions are now more enlightened. Many women take class during pregnancy, and some, like American Ballet Theatre's Julie Kent, have even performed beautifully during the first trimester. Check with your doctor or midwife, and unless she has a specific reason for advising against it, by all means dance. This is a time in your life when dancing may be especially joyful.

You may even find that your pirouettes improve because your weight is more forward. Be prudent, as you would be during any form of exercise, to avoid injury or exhaustion. You may wish to do only barre. Toward the end of pregnancy the body produces a hormone, appropriately called relaxin, that relaxes some of the tissues in the pelvis in preparation for childbirth. It can produce a very loose-legged sensation; be cautious with your newfound flexibility.

Getting Serious

Backstage and Onstage

What you learn in class is only part of the picture. Ballet is a performing art, and, for many if not most dancers, performance is both the goal and the reward. Familiarity with the traditions of the theater, the unwritten rules of backstage and onstage etiquette, and the mechanics of putting on a show are expected of dancers. As you become more comfortable with the process that transforms you from ballet student to performing artist, you acquire the confidence that frees you to go beyond technique and to really dance.

Casting

Not everyone has the rock-solid balance to dance Aurora, the dazzling fouettés required of Odile, or the delicacy essential to the Sugar Plum Fairy. But the corps needs dancers with special gifts, too. To lead the way down the ramp in *La Bayadère*, for example, you must do nearly forty consecutive arabesques without a wobble.

Someone needs to decide who will dance these parts, and the decision often involves the choreographer, the artistic director, and the ballet master or mistress. In a school production your teacher may also have a say in who dances what. Casting is not just a matter of rewarding effort, or seniority, or even the best technique. Sometimes a dancer must be a particular height, or fit into the one existing costume. A director may pick a dancer who has the right stage presence or comic flair for a particular role. At other times directors may see potential in a less advanced dancer and want to offer her a challenge, knowing that a certain role may help her grow. And when dancers perform more than one part in the same ballet, casting becomes even more complicated. Conscientious directors agonize over casting and strive for fairness.

Supported arabesque
penché.

When the cast list goes up, elation and disappointment are inevitable. You may get the part of your dreams or it may just as easily go to your best friend. Casting decisions are not always easily understood, even by professional dancers. Know that some frustration comes with the territory, and don't take casting personally. Share disappointments with your parents, but don't ask them to intercede on your behalf. Go to auditions with a positive, open mind and without actively campaigning for a specific part.

Rehearsing

When you learn and rehearse a new ballet, the choreographer creates the dance "on" you. She makes up new steps for you to dance. If a ballet has already been choreographed, a ballet master or mistress who knows all the parts usually teaches them. The two kinds of rehearsal are much the same: you are warmed up and ready to dance before rehearsal begins; you learn your part and practice it repeatedly.

But there are differences between rehearsing with a choreographer and rehearsing with a ballet master. Creating something new takes more time than teaching existing choreography. There is more stopping and starting and waiting while the choreographer makes up steps or works with other dancers. And while a choreographer may welcome your creativity, a ballet master needs your accuracy. Asking a ballet master a question— such as "Is this on count two or three?"—is helpful. But asking a choreographer the same question when she's trying to create may interrupt her train of thought.

Your practice in picking up combinations in class comes in handy here. Learn your part the same way you'd learn an exercise and know it completely. Note taking helps: write down your steps after each rehearsal and go over your part at least once a day. No need to dance it full out, just walking the steps helps you recall their sequence. Work after class on sections you have trouble with. Once you can do your part without following anyone else, you know it well enough. Then focus on polishing.

As performance day approaches, the ballet master calls cleaning or touch-up rehearsals, in which each phrase of the dance is checked for detail. The corps de ballet must be in perfect unison, all doing the same steps, with the same port de bras and the same épaulement—everything at the same time. Painstaking cleaning rehearsals turn a group of dance students

Natalia Makarova
wearing her trademark
head scarf in rehearsal
with Anthony Dowell.

into a precise, unified ensemble of swans, wilis, sylphs, or shades that
often earns its own curtain call.

Rehearsal Etiquette

Be there. Find out the rehearsal schedule before you audition. If you can't
be at all the rehearsals, speak to the director, but understand that if you're
going to miss more than one, she may not allow you to participate. Once
you've agreed to be in a performance, honor your commitment. You
can't decide in the middle of a rehearsal period that you want to join
the soccer team.

Be on time. On time doesn't mean you arrive at the studio when a rehearsal
starts. On time means you are at the studio, in your dance attire, warmed
up, and ready to dance. If you are on pointe, have your shoes tied on
and your toes taped or otherwise made comfortable, because you can't
stop a rehearsal to adjust your shoes.

Stay until you're excused. If you must leave early, ask the director
in advance and don't allow your departure to be disruptive.

Pay attention. No one should have to show you the steps twice because
you weren't paying attention the first time. And don't be surprised if,
when creating a dance, a choreographer turns to you and asks, "What

did I just do?" Mark the steps as she gives them so you can learn them quickly. If you are in the corps, and the ballet master is working with the dancers on the other side of the studio, watch what they are doing because you may be expected to mirror it on your side of the stage. If the director tells you that she won't be working with you for a while, it's okay to do homework or another quiet activity somewhere out of the way, but be on the lookout for when you'll be needed again.

Be cheerful. Cleaning rehearsals in particular can be tedious and make dancers crabby. If you've done a step on count six for a month and someone else insists it's on count five, one of you has to change what you've been doing for the past four weeks. That's part of the process; keep a positive attitude.

Inside the Theater

The choreographer and ballet mistress are responsible for your steps, but the technical director is responsible for the theater and for your safety. The stage manager assists the technical director by coordinating and running the entire production. At "load in," the technical crew goes to the theater with the lights, scenery, costumes, and other equipment. They set up the stage, hang and focus special stage lights, lay and tape down the dance floor. As magical as the theater is, it is also full of hazards: lamps, lighting booms, trees, cables. Stay out of the technical staff's way so they can prepare the theater for the performance and for your safety.

Shortly after load in, someone, usually the stage manager, meets with the cast members to point out where they need to be careful. If the stage manager gives you an instruction, follow it, no questions asked. One basic rule: the theater, backstage, dressing rooms, and hallways are never the place for running around or horseplay.

If something goes wrong, be sure you know who to contact to get it fixed. Usually it's the stage manager. In a complicated production, the ballet mistress may act as a liaison to the technical staff, so go to her about a slippery spot on the dance floor or a cold dressing room.

The dressing room is just that, the place where you put on your costume and makeup. In large productions like *The Nutcracker* you may be asked to come to the theater fully made up to ease crowding. Keep your area of the dressing room tidy, don't hog other people's space, and clean up after yourself.

Julie Kent, principal dancer with American Ballet Theatre, in her dressing room before a performance of *The Snow Maiden*.

Rehearsing in the Theater

The first rehearsals acquaint you with the stage, and acquaint the stage crew with your production. At a technical (tech) rehearsal the crew works out the coordination of lighting and scenery changes with what the dancers and the music are doing. A spacing rehearsal, which may take place along with the tech rehearsal, determines how the dimensions of the stage affect the choreography. If the stage is wider than your studio, you may have to enter a count or two earlier to cover the extra distance. Establish how you enter and exit and which wings to use. Be mindful of other dancers using the same wing at the same time.

The stage crew marks center stage, quarter stage, and sometimes eighths with small tape markers on the floor. When you are part of a group, you use these marks to adjust your spacing for the distance from side to side; you use the panels of dance flooring to adjust from front to back. For example, if a dancer on the other side of the stage needs to mirror your position when you stand in B plus, you might agree that you two are "splitting quarter and center, third panel, toe on tape." This means you stand right between the quarter and center marks with your back toe touching the tape holding down the dance panels. You run through the entire dance this way, stopping each time there's a question about where on stage you should be.

North Carolina School
of the Arts and American
Ballet Theatre Studio
Company dancers
getting notes from
Melissa Hayden after
rehearsing Balanchine's
Symphony in C.

Dress Rehearsal

Dress rehearsal is a complete performance in makeup and costume but
without an audience. Afterward the director gives corrections and comments, called notes, and you are expected to stay for them. The costume
designer or wardrobe mistress, as well as the lighting designer, the set
designer, and the technical staff, may also give notes. Make sure you
know exactly which notes are meant for you, and ask about anything
you don't understand. In some productions, directors give notes after
every performance.

Dress rehearsal can be a shock. What works just fine in the studio can
feel completely different on stage with lights and costumes. A light may
be right in your eyes as you're turning; a costume or headpiece may
change your balance. That's why you have a dress rehearsal, to work
out those kinks. Keep your cool, and find some time on the stage to work
on problematic sections.

Curtain Up!

The first performance can be a shock, too. Everything's fine and suddenly
the curtain opens and there are all those people out there in the dark,
waiting. And they laugh or clap when you don't expect them to. Many
dancers get rubber legs and stomach butterflies before a performance.

Stage Makeup

Dancers, like all other stage performers, wear special makeup to counter the effects of stage lighting and distance, ensuring that the audience can see their faces and expressions clearly. Whether you are creating the special characteristics of a dramatic role or simply need to exaggerate your own features so they do not wash out in the lights, you need makeup. Unfortunately, at many a dance recital, well-meaning backstage helpers can have a disastrous effect on dancers' makeup—black lines drawn on the tops of cheekbones to accentuate eyes, for example, turn cygnets into monsters. Makeup suitable for a stadium will look ghastly if you are dancing in a small theater or school auditorium. Pay heed to whatever look your director is going for, and consider the size of the performance hall. In addition to any variations required by your director, follow these simple steps for basic stage makeup.

Apply foundation to a clean face. The foundation or base color, whether chosen to suit the mood of a particular ballet—pale and ethereal for *Swan Lake*, darker and ruddier for *Don Quixote*—is intended to even out your complexion and reduce shadows caused by stage lights. Blend foundation under the chin and onto your neck, as well as around your ears right up and into your hairline, otherwise it looks as if you're wearing a mask. Be sure to cover the tops of your lips as well.

There are different types of foundation, from self-setting pancake makeups that do not require powder, to cream makeups that work well with cream blushes and shadows, but then need to be "set" or finished with powder. Either of these is preferable to the liquid foundation that one might ordinarily wear—it rarely has the staying power needed for performing. If using pancake foundation, apply dry or pressed shadows and blushes; cream makeups on top of pancake don't hold. You will have to experiment to determine which foundation works best for your skin. Use a greater concentration of foundation on areas that need contour, such as cheekbones and chin.

For **eyes,** use a concealer a shade or two lighter than your foundation to reduce the appearance of dark circles under your eyes. Use concealer as a shadow base on lids. Remove any excess base or concealer before setting the foundation with powder. Powder is necessary for preventing smudges and smears, as well as for not looking shiny under the lights.

To bring out your **eyebrows,** use a dark eyebrow pencil and highlight the natural line with small strokes. Concentrate on the upper brow, and try not to make a solid line, which can look fake.

Apply base eye shadow over the entire **eyelid,** darker near the eyelash line and fading toward the brow. If you want to use two or more complementary colors, use the darkest color nearer your eye, a medium color just above the crease of the eyelid, and the lightest color underneath the brow. Smooth the colors together.

To line eyes, line the top of your lashes, beginning at the inner corner, pressing firmly but gently along the lash line. To line the bottom, start at the outer corner of your eye with the tip of the liner under your lower lashes. Gently press along the lash line. Liner should start where the lashes begin and stop where the lashes end, on top and bottom. Avoid harsh, solid lines, and make sure top and bottom lines meet in the outer corner. Professional dancers usually wear false eyelashes. You may be able to forgo these glamorous encumbrances by using an eyelash curler and then applying at least two coats of lash-lengthening mascara. A clear mascara underneath dark mascara can help prevent smudges.

Blush or rouge adds definition as well as color to your face. Smile and apply blush to the apples of the cheeks, sweeping upward and outward toward your hairline. For **lips,** line with color and fill in with lipstick.

If a makeup artist is designing a particular look for your performance, lip and rouge colors may fall within the specialist's domain. Otherwise, choose colors that complement your costume and flatter your face. During dress rehearsal, be sure to ask if your makeup is working under the intensity of the stage lights.

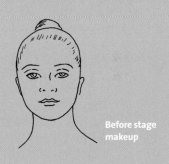

Before stage makeup

After stage makeup

The best way to handle stage fright is not to obsess about it beforehand. If you continually worry about forgetting choreography, you're going to forget the choreography. Spend a little time on your own before the performance imagining what your part looks like when you do it absolutely right, as if it were a movie. If you are a Soldier in *The Nutcracker*, say, envision yourself marching in perfect unison with the others; if you are a Flower, picture perfect balancés and waltz steps; if you are the Sugar Plum Fairy, see a flawless variation. Don't allow yourself to imagine mistakes— no bumping into the Mouse King or slipping on snowflakes. When you get to the stage, "play back" that movie and do the part the same way.

Take jitters in stride; the more you are on stage the more comfortable you will be there. Remember to breathe. Over time you will be able to transform those nerves into positive performing energy—they actually help you become a more exciting dancer.

Just because you can't see the audience, don't think they can't see you. When you are meant to be offstage, be totally out of sight. Standing too close to the edge of the wings when waiting for your entrance makes you visible to part of the audience. And when you exit, exit completely. A closed curtain must stay closed, with no peering out from behind it.

The audience can hear you backstage, too. It doesn't matter whether you're having a good time; it matters that they are. There's nothing that says "amateur" more than hearing the cast whooping it up when the curtain closes. Go to your dressing room quietly and cheer there, not on stage.

Taking a Bow

Your reward for a job well done, the bow, is set shortly before the show, and needs to be rehearsed as carefully as the performance itself.

A standard bow for a corps of women:

Line up across the center of the stage in B plus with the right foot back. When the lights come up, take four steps forward together, so you are again in B plus with the right foot back. Lift your right arms to fifth position en haut, and curtsy to the audience. Start on the right foot and take four steps back, then put the right foot back into B plus. If the audience is still applauding or the stage manager motions you from the wing, repeat. In order to do this all together, agree to follow one person in the center of the line and watch her. When she goes, you go.

Soloists and principal women do a similar bow, although you may see more elaborate variations in big theaters, such as walking to one side of the stage to acknowledge that side of the house, then crossing the apron to acknowledge the other. In European theaters there is often a royal box, to which the dancers direct a special bow if royalty is in attendance.

If you are presented with flowers, you (and the onstage presenter) should hold the bouquet as if holding a baby. It is traditional to withdraw one especially lovely flower from your bouquet and offer it to your partner. I once saw a touching display of appreciation: the ballerina—it was Gelsey Kirkland in her *Giselle* debut—withdrew the single stem but then impulsively held on to it and handed the rest of her enormous bouquet to her partner, Mikhail Baryshnikov.

A man usually stands in a small first position with one knee slightly bent and bows a little from the waist, bringing his right hand to his chest. With a partner, a man escorts her forward and stays a step behind to present her to the audience while she curtsies, then walks forward to escort her back.

Audience Etiquette

Just as you have a responsibility to your audience, so they have one to you.

No noise. Once the performance has begun no one should speak, unwrap candy, or otherwise make a sound. Be sure your cell phone is turned off. Cell phone noise during a performance of any kind is infuriating, and answering a call is completely unacceptable.

Be on time. You may not be seated after the show starts. Ballet audiences, and opera audiences, too, do not tolerate latecomers who might step over them, block their sight lines, or force them to stand or move. It spoils the moment. If you are late, you may have to wait out the entire first act. Sometimes there is a pause or other opportunity for the usher to find you a spot discreetly. But it may not be the seat your ticket indicates if getting there would distract or disturb anyone.

No photography or recording. In many theaters this is actually a law, in part because of legal protections for intellectual property but, more important, because a flash from a camera could cause injury to a dancer if it threw off his spotting or blinded him for even a second.

Louis XIV, the "Sun King," as Apollo in *Ballet de la Nuit*, 1653.

Tour de Force

LOUIS XIV AND THE FRENCH TRADITION

Court ballet existed in France as far back as the sixteenth century, but King Louis XIV (1638–1715) ensured its solid toehold on the aristocracy and, ultimately, the people. Under Louis XIV court spectacles reached new heights of magnificence. Louis, a skilled and enthusiastic dancer, was an avid participant. Ballet was astute politics for an absolute monarch: he would be on the receiving end of constant bows and curtsies, and could portray a deity like Apollo, the role that earned him his nickname: "le Roi Soleil," the Sun King.

Under Louis XIV ballet was codified and a system of professional dance training created. In 1661 Louis founded the Académie Royale de Danse, and in 1669 he established the Académie Royale de Musique, forerunner of today's School of the Paris Opera Ballet. In 1681 the first professional female dancer performed in a public theater.

Louis's talented team, in charge of court productions, included the composer and dancer Jean-Baptiste Lully, the ballet master Pierre Beauchamps, and the playwright Molière; they created the comédie-ballet. Their successors, Jean-Philippe Rameau in music and Louis Pécour in dance, developed even more proficient dancers and devised a new form of entertainment, the opera-ballet. (See page 46, Ballet's Courtly Origins.)

Paris presided over the rise of Romantic ballet with the historic premieres of *La Sylphide*, 1832, and *Giselle*, 1841. But by the latter part of the century the cult of the female dancer had become so strong that the men's roles were danced by pretty women. Yet even in the midst of this period of decline, called *la décadence*, Saint-Léon and Délibes produced *Coppélia* (1870), albeit with the character of Franz danced by a woman.

Carlotta Grisi, the first Giselle. The premiere of *Giselle* in 1841 was a triumph for the Paris Opera, and the ballet became one of the best-loved of all time.

Serge Lifar, one of Diaghilev's star dancers, became ballet master of the Paris Opera Ballet in 1929. He choreographed numerous works, brought a new energy to the company, and helped restore the place of the danseur.

Marie-Agnès Gilloet and José Martinez of the Paris Opera Ballet in William Forsythe's *In the Middle, Somewhat Elevated.*

When Rudolf Nureyev became director in 1983, Claude Bessy's impeccably trained students at the Paris Opera Ballet School gave him the raw material he needed to renew the company. Nureyev spotted, and promoted, stars in their early stages. Rank did not matter to him as much as talent; he ignored the institution's rigid hierarchy and pushed promising dancers forward. Among his "children" were Isabel Guérin, Laurent Hilaire, Manuel Legris, and especially Sylvie Guillem. He reigned for only six years, and not without controversy. As the French say diplomatically, Nureyev's choreography "can be discussed." But he propelled the Paris Opera Ballet back into worldwide recognition, and the momentum he gave the company is felt to this day.

Brigitte Lefèvre now runs this large (over 150 dancers) and venerable institution that performs in two theaters in Paris. The present repertory places a strong emphasis on contemporary European choreographers. The ornate Opera House, with its ceiling painted by Chagall, is one of the most splendid buildings in Europe.

Summer Intensives

School's out and there's no better time to immerse yourself in dancing. Summer programs present wonderful opportunities. Your technique improves literally by leaps and bounds when you take several classes a day, provided they are substantive and well structured. New teachers, who see you with fresh eyes, can help you overcome hurdles or polish what you think you have already mastered.

Not only do summer programs offer the chance of a technical break-through, they also allow you to experience some of the breadth and diversity of ballet, and of dance in general. You can branch out and explore modern, jazz, or ethnic dance to complement your ballet train-ing. I studied classical Chinese dancing one summer. You may be able to take variations, advanced pointe, or partnering classes, or perhaps develop new skills in composition and improvisation.

Many year-round ballet academies offer special summer programs; other programs exist only in summer, sometimes at spectacularly beautiful places. They can be day programs or sleepaway. You may be away from home for the first time. There are new friends to make, new places to see, new things to experience, and a new sense of independence to gain. You're on your own, dancing from dawn till dusk with other dancers your own age.

For some, a summer intensive is also the place to make decisions about dancing. You can see if you really like dancing all day, and determine where you stand in comparison with equally serious-minded peers.

Many summer intensives offer performing opportunities, and a few make performing the emphasis, with multiple, even weekly, shows. Other programs run in conjunction with summer festivals: you attend perfor-mances almost every night and take class alongside professional dancers.

To get the most out of a summer intensive, start by doing some research. Ask your teacher for advice, and ask older students about their recent experiences. Most programs have informative Web sites. Your parents have to be in on this decision, because there's more to summer programs than dancing: tuition, transportation, and your family's summer plans must be considered. Don't wait until the last minute; the application deadline may be sooner than you think, and you may need to submit a letter of recommendation along with photographs or a video.

A student at the School at Jacob's Pillow performs on the Inside/Out stage during a summer workshop.

Choose a program that suits your goals and needs, ideally one that will expose you to what you don't get at home. If your town offers few choices for training, look for a program with top-quality classes. If you've got strong training at home but never get on stage, consider one that emphasizes performance. If you are contemplating a professional career, you can try for one of the top competitive programs affiliated with a major company but it is not essential. Companies sometimes choose trainees or apprentices from their summer programs but not always.

It takes time to adjust to being away from home. Everything's different—the environment, the teachers, even the food (*especially* the food). It can be confusing if your summer teachers use different terminology or seem to contradict what your regular teachers say. Do as you are asked even if it is different from the way you do it at home. Then, perhaps after class, find a good moment to (politely!) query your teacher about the discrepancy.

Dancing all day can be a bit of a shock both mentally and physically. Your feet may be unaccustomed to so much dancing, so take blister protection and treatment. Your pointe shoe size can change when you dance a lot in hot weather, so consider having a spare pair in a larger size and a fitting kit to adjust it.

The summer intensive experience isn't always perfect. You may discover just how good your training is at home. Or how bad. You may find out that famous dancers aren't always great pedagogues, or you may come back with a bunch of mannerisms that will annoy your regular teacher. If it's your first time away from home, perhaps you can enlist a friend from your studio to go with you. But if you are on your own, rest assured you're not the only one who is feeling lonely, shy, or insecure. Go ahead, be outgoing, make a friend. If mealtimes have a certain "Where shall I sit?" anxiety, use those moments in the studio before and after class to cultivate new acquaintances.

In the past many studios shut down or went on reduced schedules in summer, forcing serious students to go away. Now many local studios offer their own intensives. They're worth considering. And there's also no rule that says you must go to only one program. You can split your time, attending one program at the beginning of the summer and another at the end of it.

Most intensives have a suggested packing list, but in addition to your dance wear and daily clothing, take along one dress-up outfit, a bathing suit, and a towel. Sew name tags on your clothes. Don't forget toenail clippers. Books, a fan, and a reading lamp are lifesavers on summer nights. Have music to listen to and a way to listen to it, both for pleasure and because you never know when you may have an opportunity to choreograph. Take writing paper for letters home, and a journal so you can record the corrections your teachers give you and new things you learn, as well as your ideas, observations, and adventures.

Evaluation

Some schools offer written evaluations at the close of the summer. This may be the first time you receive anything like a report card on your dancing, and it can be quite helpful to see your teachers' assessments in black and white. In addition to handwritten comments on how to improve something as specific as adagio or pirouettes, here are the kinds of things summer intensive teachers may observe and rate on a scale from excellent to good, satisfactory, or needs improvement.

Attendance. Has the student had regular attendance?

Behavior. Does the student comply with school and class regulations? Is the student respectful to teachers, staff, and fellow students?

Attitude. Does the student show interest and enthusiasm? Does the student exhibit discipline?

Concentration. Is the student focused and attentive during class?

Promptness. Is the student prepared and on time for class?

Flexibility of the torso. Does the student understand movement of the torso?

Flexibility of legs. Does the student understand movement and use of the legs?
Turnout?
Stretch?

Flexibility of feet. Does the student understand movement and use of feet?

Coordination. Does the student understand and exhibit basic coordination skills for his or her level?
Does the student combine steps to follow basic combinations for his or her level?

Musicality.
Does the student understand phrasing?
Does the student understand tempo and mood changes?

Ballet's Courtly Origins

Popular entertainment in the Middle Ages included jugglers, minstrels, and jousters. Over time their performances became more structured and rehearsed, culminating in exquisitely choreographed horse ballets, with streamered riders guiding their mounts in intricate patterns in an arena. "Dancing" Lipizzaner horses can still be seen today in Vienna's well-known riding academy, the Spanish Riding School.

Ballet de cour (court ballet) grew out of Renaissance pageantry and evolved further inside royal palaces, mainly in France. Eventually, dancing moved to the proscenium stage, and brought a change in choreographic emphasis: the dancers were seen from only one direction instead of three. Turnout already existed but became more important. Costumes were restrictive but splendid, and port de bras evolved in part to show them off. For example, the slight turn of the wrist as the arms open to second position—a detail still practiced today—displays a large lace sleeve to best advantage.

When ballet moved to public theaters, society, especially the Church, held professional dancers in low esteem, but in ballet de cour's heyday, its aristocratic amateurs were much admired. These were some of ballet's earliest forms:

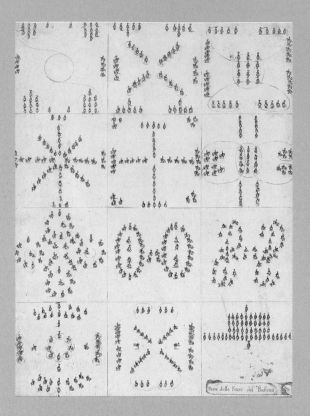

Diagram for a horse ballet performed at night in Florence, Italy, 1652.

Ballet Comique: A spectacle in which a dance performance contained a unifying story or theme. The most famous was *Le Ballet Comique de la Reine*. (See Catherine de Medici and *Le Ballet Comique de la Reine*, page 14.)

Masque: England's version of ballet de cour. It featured music and dance but emphasized the spoken word. Shakespeare's colleague Ben Jonson wrote numerous masques, many with ingenious scenery designed by the architect Inigo Jones, but Puritanism put an end to ballet in England for many years.

Comédie-ballet: A genre created during the reign of Louis XIV. Dance was united with words and music and became an integral part of the whole—often comic—entertainment.

Ballet à entrées: An entertainment featuring dance divertissements, presented between courses of a meal or between acts of a play or concert (and allowing other performers a chance to rest or change their costumes).

An outgrowth of ballet à entrées achieved success on the professional stage: the *opéra-ballet*, in which song was added to a series of dance scenes. Jean-Philippe Rameau's (1683–1764) *Les Indes Galantes*, 1735, was a hit with its exotic locales and controversial use of the jumping intensive danse haute, or danse d'elevation, rather than danse basse.

46

Dancers audition in
New York City for the
American Academy
of Ballet.

Auditions

The most riveting words in ballet: "Will number 5, number 33, and number 18 please stay. The rest of you can go. Thank you very much."

That's a headline that Gaynor Minden decided not to use on a poster because it made our focus group cry. (We later softened it for a catalog.) For professional dancers whose careers depend on them, auditions can be heartbreaking. They need not be traumatic for the amateur dancer, but they certainly are a rite of passage, proving you ready for a new level, a new school, or a new role. Even if you never intend to dance professionally, you will probably audition for placement within a school or for acceptance to a summer intensive. In most cases, the audition is a ballet class.

Auditioning is a skill of its own. It's as much a test of how you perform under pressure as of how you dance. You should learn to handle auditions, but a crucial opportunity for you may not be the place to do that learning. It is a good idea to attend some auditions to gain experience, but it isn't a good idea to put yourself through the ordeal repeatedly for that reason. Yes, the audition may be a class, but not all audition classes are worthwhile.

What to Bring, What to Wear, What to Expect

Check the application materials carefully and heed every requirement. If you're asked to wear a black leotard and pink tights and to have pointe shoes ready, that's exactly what you should do. Be sure you have the application form and fee, if any. You may need a photograph as well. If the audition is large, the auditioners will give you a slip of paper with a number to wear on your leotard. Fasten it securely and place it where the auditioners can see it clearly, but where it distracts you as little as possible. Most dancers safety-pin it on their chests right where they'd gather their leotards.

Don't panic about what to wear, but do choose carefully. If the audition has no dress code, keep it simple. If you shouldn't wear it in class, don't wear it here. Within those guidelines, make an effort to pick an outfit you feel good in. Wear your favorite leotard. It's not bad to wear something slightly uncommon that distinguishes you: it doesn't hurt to be "the girl in the red leotard."

Be prepared. If the audition requires pointework, have a good pair of shoes ready and a backup as well. This isn't the time to be breaking them in. The audition may be crowded, so keep your dance bag to a minimum and put it where you can see it.

Good dance photographs are expensive, but you may need them if you're doing a lot of auditioning. You can get "head shots" showing only your face or "dance shots" of your full body. Dance shots are a must if you cannot audition in person; a head shot helps auditioners connect a face with a number after they have seen you. Photography, especially full-body dance shots, is expensive and time-consuming, but you can save money by making color copies rather than multiple prints. If you do need body shots, invest in a good photographer with dance experience. A regular photographer, no matter how talented, won't know when a shot isn't acceptable because your line is incorrect or your foot is sickled. All photographs should show you at your best without being misleading. Don't use dim lighting or shadows; keep makeup soft and natural-looking.

Audition etiquette is similar to classroom etiquette, but an audition is a highly competitive situation. You have to go in with confidence, and, most important, you have to present yourself. This doesn't mean shoving other dancers out of their places, but if you hide in the back, you won't get "taken"—dancer slang for being selected. Competition doesn't always bring out the best in people, so be ready for a cold environment. Be prepared, be alert, be polite, be self-assured, and show yourself to best advantage.

The auditioners may excuse, or "cut," dancers during the class. In an especially crowded audition, there may be several cuts, or even one after each exercise to winnow down the numbers. At the end of the audition, a few lucky dancers are left. Alas, making it to the end of an audition doesn't necessarily mean acceptance. Much of the time it means that you are in the final pool of applicants and a decision will be made later, possibly after more auditions.

Audition by Video

If you can't be there in person, you may be able to audition by video. Professionals send tapes of themselves in performance; students send tapes of themselves in a variation or a class done specifically for video.

▶ Keep it brief—under ten minutes—auditioners must often review hundreds of tapes.

▶ If you are not told specifically what to do, include excerpts from barre doing only one side per exercise, but switching sides after each one.

▶ Video yourself in profile: it shows most clearly your turnout and the line of your feet. After that, show short combinations in center en face: simple pirouettes, then petit and grand allegro.

▶ Women should include pointework; men should include tours en l'air.

Staying Positive

You won't be selected every time you audition, but that doesn't mean you're a bad dancer. The competition is fierce. Success depends on technique, but timing, connections, and plain old luck are involved as well. An auditioner is often seeking something specific: your height or even the color of your hair can matter. Don't automatically assume that your rejection was based on lack of talent. Don't let it dent your self-esteem. Think about what you can learn from how you handled the audition and what you can improve for the next time. Remember that you can't

Marie Taglioni
with Antonio
Guerra in
l'Ombre, 1840.

Tour de Force

ROMANTICISM

Long-haired poets celebrating beauty, nature, passion, and the
redeeming power of love. Artists and writers rejoicing in the liberation of the true self from repressive codes, rules, and social hierar-
chies. Ballet was well suited to the issues and ideals of the Romantic
era (early to mid-1800s). What better symbol of loveliness and freedom than the ethereal ballerina?

Her characters are free from gravity, free from society, free from
reality. Her unattainability makes her all the more desirable. The
Romantic ballerina is seldom of this world: the sylph in *La Sylphide*,
the wilis in *Giselle*, the water nymph Ondine, the fairy in *La Peri*.
The appeal of ballerina-as-supernatural carried over into the late

Lucile Grahn in
Eoline ou la Dryade,
1845.

nineteenth century: swan maidens in *Swan Lake*, more fairies in *The Sleeping Beauty*, shades in *La Bayadère*.

Romantic ballet tragedies are born of the conflict not only between man and woman but between flesh and spirit, natural and supernatural, real and ideal. *La Sylphide* (1832) and *Giselle* (1841) epitomize Romantic ballet. In both, a mortal man encounters a supernatural woman. His human weakness leads to heartbreak and disaster. But in *Giselle*, which was an instant success and remains one to this day, the supernatural woman forgives our poor cad and, with love from beyond the grave, saves him from death.

More than just characters, these supernatural creatures were womanhood idealized—icons of grace, delicacy, love, virtue, immortality. In depicting them, the nineteenth-century ballerinas had three enormously helpful assets: the Romantic tutu, the gaslit stage, and their newly developed pointe technique.

The flowing, gauzy Romantic tutu was starkly simple compared to the opulent costumes of previous eras. Its light, billowy skirts looked weightless as they floated independent of the wearer, and its whiteness signaled her purity, virginity, and goodness.

Enhancing the effect was the novelty of gas lighting. People did not yet have gaslight in their homes, and it had only been in theaters since about 1820. It looked like moonlight, and gave a ghostly glow to the diaphanous costumes.

Further heightening the illusion was the other-worldly grace achieved by dancing sur les pointes. The ballerina could appear to hover or float, her feet just skimming the stage. Gravity lost its pull on her. An image of Taglioni shows her en pointe, poised on a flower (actually a sturdily constructed bit of scenery); the man beside her recoils at the sight of a ghost but is enthralled by its beauty.

Pointe dancing elevated the ballerina figuratively as well as literally. The middle class began to adore ballet; audiences had favorites whom they followed with devotion. For the first time the female dancer was more important than the male. The cult of the ballerina had begun.

Nina Ananiashvili,
a modern-day Giselle.

control an audition. You can work to do your best, but you can't make someone choose you.

Stay positive when you audition, and be yourself. Believe it or not, the auditioners hate auditions as much as you do. They don't want to pass judgment on anyone; they're just trying to find good students for their school. They need to know who you are as much as how you dance. Show them.

Advanced Classes: Partnering and Variations

Partnering

Two people dancing together generate a particularly exciting—and beautiful—dynamic. The synergy of partnering creates some of ballet's most poignant, thrilling, and rapturous moments. A partnership can take on a life of its own, and its felicitous chemistry can become ballet legend: Karsavina and Nijinsky, Alonso and Youskevitch, Fonteyn and Nureyev, Sibley and Dowell, Fracci and Bruhn, Kirkland and Baryshnikov.

During the era known as *la décadence,* when ballet fell into decline in nineteenth-century Paris, male dancers were often mere *porteurs,* their roles limited to presenting the ballerinas and lending a supporting hand. The original production of *Coppélia,* for example, would not have had the lifts we see today. Often women donned men's costumes and did the parts themselves.

In the past century a great deal of choreographic creativity has gone into partnering, and its possibilities have greatly expanded. A "shoulder sit" is no longer considered indecent; men are no longer limited to supporting their partners only at the waist or hand. Nowadays partnering includes such daredevil acrobatics as the Soviet style one-arm overhead lift, or the breathtaking catch of an airborne dancer midleap. It can be starkly sculptural as in many of Balanchine's "leotard ballets" or charged with erotic tension as in his exotic *Bugaku.* It can express the most powerful emotions: Kenneth MacMillan's pas de deux in *Romeo and Juliet* ache with heartbreak and passion. The avant-garde troupes Pilobolus and Momix redefine partnering with their multiperson, cantilevered human totem poles that cleave and merge to produce fantastic effects.

Partnering does not begin for either men or women until they have
trained for several years. Like a pointe class that focuses only on pointework, or a variations class that teaches actual ballet repertory, partnering
is a separate, stand-alone class—one taken in addition to several weekly
technique classes.

It's a luxury to be in a school where there are enough men to partner each
woman. In some schools students pair off and form regular partnerships;
in others they switch partners from class to class or even from exercise
to exercise. Ideally you will study partnering with teachers of both sexes
and gain both perspectives. If you have the opportunity to take class
from a couple who have actually performed together, seize it.

For women, technique and pointework must be secure; if you can't do a step correctly, a partner won't help. You can get away with being slightly less advanced technically if you are a man, but you still need to understand how a step is done, both from your point of view and from the woman's. A man must be sufficiently developed physically to support the ballerina. In Russia boys practice terre à terre work for a long time before they attempt straight up and down lifts. A time-honored exercise for building strength is push-ups. Supervised training with light weights is also effective, but intense body-builder regimes can make muscles tight and bulky. Be sure your weight lifting is right for dancers.

You won't learn a fish dive on the first day. Partnering begins with basic moves such as supported promenades and single pirouettes en dehors. As you learn how to work together in different positions, using different grips, being supported at the waist or by the hands, partnering progresses to more complicated maneuvers and finally to learning a pas de deux from the classical repertory.

The heightened sense of timing required of good partnering comes out of your own musicality. When two people don't hear music the same way, everything is harder. The tiniest sparrow of a ballerina feels like a ton to her partner if she seems to be descending at the moment when he wants to lifts her up. Talk about your timing and work out your musical cues. Let the music help you to move fluidly and happily together.

It takes time to get used to the intimacy of partnering. There you are in class, wearing just a leotard and tights, touching and being touched in places where you'd slug someone if it happened when you weren't expecting it.

If you're a man, you're usually the one doing the touching. Remember, this isn't a personal intimacy; it's professional. She needs to trust you, and you need to work to earn that trust. Generally the attractiveness of your partner's body becomes less of an issue once you are concentrating on the technicalities of a tricky lift or turn.

For men, excellent partnering skills can be even more important than strong technique when it comes to getting a role or a job. It's old-fashioned, but one of the loveliest aspects of ballet is that when a ballerina reaches out her hand, the male dancer's hand is there to receive it. You're there, not just to support her, but also to make her look beautiful. And in doing so, you look better yourself. Take pride in that skill.

Women, be patient with your partner and allow him to do his job. You're in danger of getting hurt during a lift if he feels he must approach you timidly. Understand that he may need some time to figure it all out. Even if it means you have to endure the precarious feeling of being "off your leg" for a while, let him go through his learning process.

Experienced male dancers can usually spot a woman who comes from a school without many men, because she tries to do all the work herself. It's important to overcome this tendency. After developing enough technique to do a step on your own, you must then learn how to allow the man to help you. Try not to do it for him. When he's supposed to be supporting you, relax and let him. That's what makes partnering look gracious as well as graceful.

For both men and women, successful partnering is built on trust and cooperation. Considerate partners are considerate people. Your attitude is paramount; put ego aside. When you begin with a new partner, make it clear that you are delighted to be working together and confident of your partner's abilities. Half the battle is won when two people want to dance together. As Peter Boal, a renowned dancer and teacher, once said, "Just like a stimulating conversation, it is the energy, electricity, or simply the care between the two people that is rewarding."

Variations

Variations class is an opportunity to develop and refine yourself as a dancer as well as to learn some great choreography. Instead of the relatively brief combinations you do in technique class, you now learn more extended pieces, often from the classic repertory. You may also work on known pas de deux in a partnering class, but men's and women's variations classes are most often separate.

You will probably practice styles as well as steps. If you are learning a variation from *La Sylphide*, *Pas de Quatre*, or *Giselle*, for example, you would work on Romantic port de bras. Variations class offers a chance to inflect your dancing, to acquire subtlety, to broaden your range dramatically as well as technically, to go beyond technique.

Men's Training

Men have some real advantages in ballet. They can start later and continue their careers longer. They have an easier time getting scholarships and jobs. After they retire from performing they often transition to offstage positions of great responsibility and prestige; look at who is directing so many of our major dance companies.

It takes tremendous athleticism and strength to jump up, turn twice in the air, and then land with precision, and it takes even more to lift a woman over your head. Because of both anatomy and destiny, there are differences in training for girls and boys. A male dancer is taller and heavier, has less flexibility in the spine, and is straighter in the shoulders and narrower in the hips. All these attributes affect placement. Turnout and flexibility may be more difficult to achieve. A man doesn't need to go on pointe but does need to become a solid partner, and he must concentrate on developing the strength for that as well as for the virtuoso turns and jumps that are expected of a male dancer. He can get excellent training from a female teacher, but there's an incalculable value to having a good male teacher as a role model.

In large schools or companies, daily class may be segregated by sex, or there may be a special men's class in addition to mixed technique classes. When he was a student at the School of American Ballet, Peter Boal, a future star of the New York City Ballet, was in a class with four boys and about twenty girls. "The imbalance of girls to boys was a drag. Ten-year-old boys don't want to even be in a room with twenty girls, let alone a ballet class. I was talking to my parents about dropping out. One day a new teacher came to remove the four boys and begin a separate boy's class. This absolutely saved me. It heightened my interest and helped me to understand what was unique about male dancing."

In recent decades, for both men and women, the "ideal" body has become more flexible and elongated. Boal describes one of the changes he has observed during his career: "When I joined the New York City Ballet, I was the only man in class but one who could lift my leg in a développé past ninety degrees. Today every male dancer in the company can do that."

Men's Class and Men's Steps

Much of ballet is the same for both men and women, but there are special differences. Certain steps such as double tours en l'air or double sauts de basques are generally male dancer territory. Mens' jumps are bigger and higher in grand allegro, and strive for "ballon"—that exciting combination of bounciness and "hang time"—in petit allegro. Men are expected to turn multiple pirouettes, not just doubles, and to work more on grand pirouettes in large poses with the leg extended front or back, straight or in attitude, or à la seconde.

The different look of men's movements—broader and weightier— becomes clear when you are among your peers. Friendly turning competitions always seem to happen when you get a bunch of men in a studio. Men's class is an opportunity to dance where you're no longer the only guy in a roomful of girls.

Margot Fonteyn and
Rudolf Nureyev in *The
Sleeping Beauty*, 1977.

Tour de Force

EXTRAORDINARY PARTNERSHIP: FONTEYN AND NUREYEV

Margot Fonteyn, an acclaimed ballerina who had had an illustrious career with the Royal Ballet in London for nearly thirty years, was on the verge of retirement and troubled by an injury when Rudolf Nureyev arrived in a spectacular defection from the Soviet Union in 1961. The bold young dancer's reputation as a rising star had preceded him; Fonteyn (with the astute approval of Ninette de Valois, the Royal's founding artistic director), invited him to dance with her in *Giselle* in February 1962, in what she called an experiment. But as even non-ballet fans know, it was the beginning of a legendary, seventeen-year professional relationship.

Fonteyn (1919–1991) and Nureyev (1938–1993) had a yin-and-yang rapport based on contrasting strengths. He danced with passion and power. His leaps and turns, if occasionally rough around the edges, were thrilling—he was compared to Nijinsky. His commanding, forthrightly sexy stage presence bordered on arrogant hauteur. Fonteyn's dancing, on the other hand, was the epitome of refined elegance, with exquisitely nuanced emotional

gestures and a trademark arabesque of just 90 degrees—a soaring extension would have seemed vulgar. Their pas de deux were unforgettable, being paired with an opposite type highlighted the distinctive genius of each.

They danced the classic repertory as well as more modern ballets such as the achingly romantic *Marguerite and Armand*, made expressly for them in 1963 by Frederick Ashton. Even when Fonteyn was near the end of her career and no longer capable of her former technical virtuosity, her acting talent and dramatic presence in the role of the dying Marguerite created performances of tremendous poignancy. Nureyev was equally moving as her ardent lover.

Offstage, too, they made headlines. Nureyev was a regular part of the international jet set. Fonteyn was arrested over a political incident involving her husband, a Panamanian diplomat. Like golden age Hollywood idols, they exuded mystery and glamour, and their partnership helped spark an unprecedented ballet boom in the years that followed.

Competitions

Local and international ballet competitions draw thousands of participants every year. The Royal Academy of Dance's Adeline Genée Awards in London and the International Ballet Competitions in Varna, Bulgaria, and Jackson, Mississippi, are world famous. Winners often go on to major careers. A few competitions are about more than winning. At one of the most respected, the Prix de Lausanne in Switzerland, medals are awarded as much for a dancer's potential as for her performance. The top prizes are scholarships to major international ballet schools.

Ballet competitions are controversial, however. Many teachers and dancers, even those who are past winners, do not encourage students to compete. Most high-level competitions base their awards mainly on how dancers perform certain preapproved variations from the classical repertory. It's impossible to gauge a dancer's taste or refinement from a single variation or two, and ballet is, after all, an art not a competitive sport.

For serious dancers in preprofessional schools or well-known dance programs, even the most prestigious competition is likely to be a detour, and it would be better to concentrate on training. Performance experience can often be gained from a summer intensive or from your school's productions, without the pressure. The preparations involved in competitions—extra rehearsals, costume-sewing and fittings, private instruction, travel to and from the events themselves—require a significant commitment of time and money.

On the other hand, for serious dancers from smaller schools who have the technique, elite competitions can be a chance to see and be seen and get on a faster track. Competitions offer an opportunity to learn about performing as a soloist through an intense preparation and coaching process that you don't get in class, or even in a corps de ballet. You meet and work with other talented dancers and are exposed to styles of dance you might not see otherwise. Even on the more commercial, less elite, circuits, it's another way to enjoy dancing, meet new people, and see new places.

Part Two

Ballet Basics

Major Schools of Ballet

They all look alike to you, but one teacher calls it a tendu jeté, another tendu dégagé, still another tendu glissé. One teacher wants your arms allongé, another insists on classically rounded positions. One asks for fifth arabesque, another refuses to acknowledge its existence. Different terms, different styles, and different emphases—in ballet's family tree the descendants of ballet de cour are like cousins who resemble one another because of their common heritage, but who differ, and sometimes bicker, as well.

Ballet evolved along divergent lines when it spread beyond Italy and France in the eighteenth and nineteenth centuries. Training systems and performing styles absorbed the characters of new homelands. Certain outstanding teachers developed highly influential methods. Variation crept into the pedagogy. Several different national "schools" are the result—each with its own look and its own approach. Each produces glorious dancers.

Isolation—especially the geographical isolation of Denmark and the political isolation of the Soviet Union—kept these styles and teaching methods distinct. Today the distinctions are blurring. Russia is now open, and dancers and choreographers tend to move around rather than stay with one company. For the student, the downside of this cross-pollination is inconsistent terminology and some conflicting stylistic ideals; the upside is the richer dance education that hybrids can offer.

Training a body handpicked for the demands of ballet is different from training a dedicated amateur. This is an important difference between systems like those of England's Royal Academy of Dance and the Cecchetti organizations on the one hand, and those of the national ballet academies in Paris, Copenhagen, or St. Petersburg on the other. At the

Fish dive.

national academies the school takes over all aspects of its carefully screened and selected students' education, academic as well as dance.

In the United States you may encounter training that is informed by any combination of the major schools. Fine teachers do not always follow a particular school to the letter; they may start with a firm grounding in one approach and add details from other styles. The quality of the teacher matters more than his or her syllabus.

The French School

In the seventeenth century, under King Louis XIV, ballet teaching became standardized, its steps codified, and the five positions of the feet defined. The French school officially began in the 1660s when Louis founded royal academies of dance and of music, forerunners of the School of the Paris Opera Ballet. But even before that Pierre Beauchamps had begun to codify and standardize teaching; we continue to use his terminology. France produced great dancers, choreographers, and ballet masters who migrated to Russia, Denmark, and elsewhere throughout Europe. Marius Petipa, creator of so many of the classic ballets still performed today, is the most famous.

The hallmark of the French school is a clean and sophisticated style—ballet with elegance, with chic. Positions are perfect every time. The cleanness comes from an insistence on scrupulous placement, on hips correctly aligned with shoulders and on legs that move independently of the pelvis. The training concentrates on port de bras and épaulement from the earliest stages. First-year students do their exercises facing the barre and holding it with both hands, sometimes doing nothing more than moving their heads properly. Claude Bessy, who directed the school for more than thirty years beginning in 1973, expanded the curriculum, adding character, mime, gymnastics, and partnering classes to traditional ballet technique.

Admission to the School of the Opera Ballet begins with a medical examination, which now includes X rays to warn of any anatomical malformations or potential problems. It's possible to push such carefully screened students much harder, to insist on 180-degree turnout and perfect fifth positions—not something that can safely be done with the average student. Body types may have changed over the years, but the French traditions of technique and training are proudly maintained. Former étoile Elisabeth Platel became director in 2004.

Bournonville (Denmark)

Bournonville technique exemplifies modest grace without apparent effort. It emphasizes brilliant petit and medium allegros but never in a showy, bravura style. It is rounder and softer—kind, not proud. It has a dancy quality that never compromises the integrity of lithe, seamless phrases for the sake of a flashy step.

Its famous elevation, ballon, and batterie are virtues born of cramped studios and cluttered stages: there was scarcely any room to travel, so the dancers had to go up instead. The distinctive port de bras is clean and low, often more in front of the torso than in other styles—a remnant of the old French school. The arms may look somewhat held but they are never rigid; they breathe and the bras bas position has a swingy quality that, along with the use of the head, helps the dancer's momentum.

Limiting the contribution of the arms in jumping means that the legs must be especially powerful and the plié particularly efficient. To this end Bournonville training includes long, hard endurance-building exercises that repeat not just left and right but in all orientations. The plié gets enormous attention, with fine distinctions made among various types, not just demi and grand. The grand plié is used extensively: grand plié into grand battement or into pirouette, grand plié as a landing from big jumps. Vestiges of Bournonville's mid-nineteenth-century origins are still apparent in the low position of the working foot in pirouette—the skirts were too long for turning in retiré—and in its emphasis on brilliant jumping rather than on brilliant pointework.

Bournonville technique formed the basis of Danish training for many decades and is still taught in Denmark, but the Danes have now incorporated other teaching methods as well.

Dance Notation

Dance has always resisted recording, but there's been no lack of trying by ballet masters over the centuries. In 1588 Thoinot Arbeau published *Orchesographie*, a reference for court musicians and dancers that included a notation system and written descriptions of basic dance steps. Because the steps themselves were not complicated (women's feet and ankles couldn't even be seen under the costumes), the notation consisted mainly of floor patterns.

Pierre Beauchamps and his compatriots at the Académie Royale, the dance academy founded by Louis XIV, codified ballet positions and specific steps, and throughout the seventeenth and eighteenth centuries, ballet masters described dances with floor drawings and symbols for feet positions. In 1700 Raoul-Auger Feuillet, a dance master, published *Choréographie, ou l'Art de décrire la danse par caracteres, figures et signes démonstratifs, avec lesquels on apprend facilement de soy même toutes sortes de dances*, incorporating Beauchamp's work on positions and steps. In a 1713 book of the choreography of Louis Pécour, another celebrated dance master, Beauchamps is recognized as the inventor of notation and Feuillet as the one responsible for completing the system.

In 1926, Rudolf Laban, a modern-dance teacher, established the Choreographic Institute in Germany, where dance research and notation were the primary focus. Labanotation, a system described and published in 1928, is a widely recognized method still in use. The other major system is Benesh Movement

Notation, also known as choreology, invented by Joan and Rudolf Benesh and established in 1955 in London. Benesh is used by recorders for the Royal Ballet and the Royal Academy of Dance, among others.

Crucial as notation is, it is in the memories of dancers themselves that choreography is often most faithfully preserved. Traditionally, dance steps are passed down from one generation to the next in person. Today, video is a great asset as well. But Laban, Benesh, and video came too late to save one of the most important ballets ever made: Nijinsky's original *Rite of Spring*. Although the Joffrey Ballet pre

sented an excellent reconstruction based on what little was left, it's lost.

Feuillet Notation

Below is a sample of Feuillet notation for one of Louis Pecour's dances, 1713. The continuous lines represent the circling paths of four dancers. Short perpendicular lines divide the paths into sections that correspond to measures of music on the staff above. Steps, jumps, turns, and arm and foot positions are among the many instructions that could be encoded in Feuillet's system.

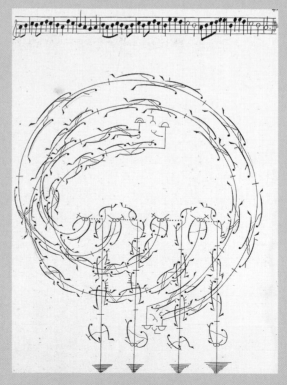

Feuillet

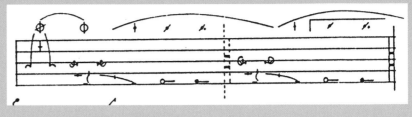

Benesh

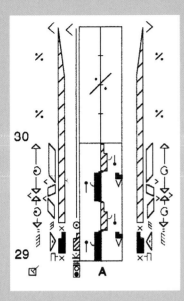

Labanotation

Labanotation

This Labanotation sample represents measures 29–30 of Aurora's wedding variation from Marius Petipa's *The Sleeping Beauty*. Labanotation is read from the bottom of the page up. The staff is vertical as opposed to horizontal (as in the Benesh or the music staff).

In this excerpt, the ballerina is performing delicate forward steps on pointe traveling diagonally downstage right. The center line of the staff represents the center line of the body. The symbols immediately on the right and left sides of the center line represent the right and left supports—in this case the feet (the forward steps on pointe). Farther out from the center line are symbols for leg gestures, then the torso, and outside the staff are indications for the arms and parts of the arms; in this case the whole arm, the wrist, and the hand are written. The length of a symbol tells us how long it takes to complete a step or gesture. In the second measure, repeat signs are used for the footwork and wrist/hand gestures as the arms and torso continue slowly to rise.

Benesh Movement Notation

This Benesh sample represents exactly the same two measures but in Benesh notation. Benesh is read from left to right in a series of consecutive frames. Movements of the limbs and body appear within the staff; rhythm and phrasing, above the staff; and orientation and travel below. The staff lines, from top to bottom, coincide with the height of the top of the head, shoulders, waist, knees, and floor respectively. In this case, the signs for stepping and closing the feet in fifth position rest on the bottom line of the staff, the actions of the hand and wrist are in the middle, and the head action appears in the top staff space. In both Benesh and Labanotation, measures in the staff correspond to measures in the music staff.

67

Cecchetti (Italy)

Enrico Cecchetti moved from his native Italy to St. Petersburg at the height of his career as a principal dancer, ballet master, and teacher. A virtuoso, he was the original Bluebird in *The Sleeping Beauty*. As a teacher, at the Imperial Ballet and later at Diaghilev's Ballets Russes, he influenced the greatest talents of the day—Pavlova, Nijinsky, Karsavina, Spessivtseva, Lifar, Balanchine—and his legacy is still apparent in Russia in the training of men. His method was the first to address proper placement in order to avoid strain and injury. Not forcing turnout, correct use of the barre, distribution of weight during transitions—concepts we now take for granted started with Cecchetti.

Properly taught, the method builds great strength: the Cecchetti-trained Nadia Nerina once famously substituted thirty-two entrechat six for the thirty-two fouettés in *Swan Lake*. Rigorous, repetitive classes are based on a strict syllabus. According to the Cecchetti Council of America, "The imposition of a Spartan unalterable regimen, according to which every day in the working week has its own particular set exercises, is an essential part of the system." Spartan but also complex, rich, and detailed.

After St. Petersburg, Cecchetti emigrated to London where, in 1922, Cyril Beaumont published the *Manual of Theory and Practice of Classical Theatrical Dancing (Cecchetti Method)*. Beaumont founded the Cecchetti Society that same year to ensure the propagation of the technique, among its first members were Ninette de Valois and Marie Rambert—future founders of major English ballet companies. The Cecchetti method flourished in England—Darcy Bussell, Vivianna Durante, Monica Mason, and Anthony Dowell are among the many trained in it—and Cecchetti continues to be taught throughout the world today.

Royal Academy of Dance (England)

The Royal Academy of Dance (formerly the Royal Academy of Dancing), developed a graded syllabus to train all students, not just preprofessionals. In 1920, Philip Richardson, editor of the *Dancing Times* of London, brought together representatives of each of the five great styles of the time: Adeline Genée of Denmark, Tamara Karsavina

Through the Ranks

Ballet companies often rank their dancers in a hierarchy emulating the court structure that first produced ballet. Casting and salary decisions are made according to those designations. The system is most practical for large companies staging the classical ballets in which roles are identified by different levels. For example, in *The Nutcracker* the Sugar Plum Fairy is a principal role, "Spanish" is usually a soloist, Flowers and Mice usually corps de ballet.

The Paris Opera Ballet is an example of a many-tiered system:

▶ Étoile, "star," the leading dancers of the company

▶ Premier danseur or premiere danseuse, principal dancers who do top soloist parts as well as leads

▶ Sujets, soloists (formerly divided into grand sujet and petit sujet)

▶ Coryphées, leading dancers in the corps de ballet

▶ Quadrilles (also formerly divided into two ranks), corps de ballet

▶ Stagiaire, the newest dancers, equivalent to an apprentice or trainee

The Royal Ballet has fewer levels:

▶ Principal

▶ First Soloist

▶ Soloist

▶ First Artist

▶ Artist (equivalent to the corps de ballet)

American Ballet Theatre and New York City Ballet, like most major American companies, are even more streamlined. Both also have apprentices.

▶ Principal

▶ Soloist

▶ Corps de ballet

Prima ballerina is rarely an official title; it is sometimes used to refer to a prominent female principal dancer. *Prima ballerina assoluta* is an old-fashioned term that means the highest-ranking ballerina. This honor was bestowed on only a very few. The title was first used by Italian dancers, less as an honor than as an assurance in contracts that another dancer didn't get top billing.

69

of Russia, Lucia Cormani of Italy, Edouard Espinosa of France, and Phyllis Bedells of England. The goal was to combine the best of all the major schools to improve the quality of training in England. It began as the Association of Teachers and was granted a Royal Charter in 1935. R.A.D. training produces a strong, clean dancer, well trained and well placed. An R.A.D.-trained dancer would never sacrifice proper form for extra extension. The gentle use of head and arms also distinguishes R.A.D. style.

R.A.D. students study character dance and "free movement" as well as classical ballet technique. They are also instructed in proper terminology, and often become real sticklers about it. The syllabus is continually reevaluated and refined by the academy. Certified R.A.D. examiners evaluate students' ability and progress in special examination classes.

The academy expanded to member schools in many countries, including the United States; the influence of the R.A.D. is strongest in countries that were once part of the British Empire. It is not the same as the Royal Ballet School, which trains dancers for England's Royal Ballet. The R.B.S. follows its own syllabus.

Vaganova (Soviet Russia)

Soviet training produces powerful, expansive, and expressive dancers: Baryshnikov, Nureyev, Makarova. Their grand allegro is truly grand, with immense, soaring leaps. Soviet training favors a line made possible by a very pliable upper back and high extensions. Especially at the Bolshoi, they go for bravura.

Agrippina Vaganova documented the Soviet system of training she helped develop in *Basic Principles of Classical Ballet*, published in 1934. She was a dancer whose teaching method developed from sharp observations of her own shortcomings and from her dissatisfaction with the older, Imperial style of Petipa's day.

The roots of the Imperial style were in the French and Italian schools. Vaganova worked to synthesize the strength and aplomb of the Italian school with the more flowing French port de bras. Her careful analysis of movement, identifying the particular muscles involved, helped create the distinctive technique and style of the Soviet ballerina.

Soviet technique developed after the Russian Revolution. The Imperial Russian tradition continued in the West—but not in the U.S.S.R.—because of the many highly accomplished emigrés who brought their pre-Vaganova training and technique with them. The popularity of Russian ballets and Russian dancers throughout the rest of the world is in large part due to this diaspora.

Olga Preobrajenska, a student of Cecchetti's, moved to Paris and taught Igor Youskevitch, a star of the mid-twentieth century, as well as two of the three celebrated "baby ballerinas," Irina Baronova and Tamara Toumanova. The third, Tatiana Riabouchinska, studied with Mathilda Kchessinska, the Maryinsky's *prima ballerina assoluta*. Seraphine Astafieva taught Margot Fonteyn in London, and Pierre Vladimiroff and Felia Doubrovska joined the School of American Ballet. After the Soviet era, Rudolf Nureyev revitalized the Paris Opera Ballet Company, and an offshoot of the renowned Kirov Academy opened in Washington, D.C. Many schools base their syllabi on Vagonova's method, but no centralized organization exists in the United States to govern teaching or certify teachers.

Balanchine

In the United States, George Balanchine's teachings have had a significant impact. Balanchine did not write a syllabus, but he influenced the way dancing and dancers look today. Balanchine used his company class at the New York City Ballet to help his dancers develop the speed, timing, and musicality that his choreography demands. His technique is an extension of nineteenth-century classicism: it's faster, with cleaner, clearer, more articulate footwork and a more windswept and elongated look.

There are specific differences, too, between Balanchine's and other techniques. For example, his arabesque has longer lines because the working shoulder and hip are more open. Dancers often spot to the front, regardless of the direction in which they are traveling. The timing of glissade shows second position in the air. For catlike silence and control in jumps, Balanchine trained dancers are very particular in the use the feet, landing first on the ball of the foot, then rolling down.

Originally Balanchine taught his technique and style to his company members while students at his school studied a more traditional syllabus. Now that so many of his former dancers have become teachers both at the School of American Ballet and around the world, his influence will surely increase even further. Over the years, many have gone on to found or direct companies as well: Lew Christensen and later Helgi Tomasson in San Francisco, Barbara Weisberger in Philadelphia, Todd Bolender in Kansas City, Francia Russell and Kent Stowell and later Peter Boal in Seattle, Patricia Wilde in Pittsburgh, Arthur Mitchell in Harlem, Jean-Pierre Bonnefous and Patricia McBride in North Carolina, Edward Villella in Miami, Ib Andersen in Phoenix. Prominent teachers include Mclissa Hayden at North Carolina School of the Arts and Violette

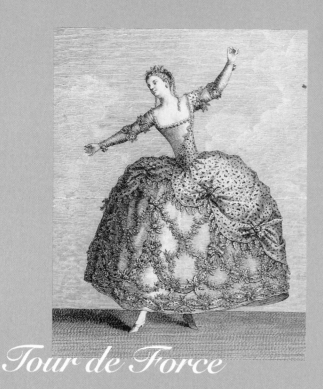

Female courtier costume.

Male courtier costume.

Tour de Force

TUTU MUCH: BALLET COSTUMES

The earliest ballet costumes matched the ornate, splendid attire of the royal courts, where ballet was first performed in the sixteenth and seventeenth centuries. Women wore long multilayered gowns, encrusted with jewels, often supported by hoop skirts as large as six feet in diameter. They would have felt naked without their heavy wigs and enormous, elaborate headdresses. For female dancers, it was a challenge to walk and breathe at the same time, let alone dance. Men, on the other hand, wore silk hose and short breeches, with fitted doublets or jackets to display their turned-out and nicely muscled legs. Both men and women danced in their party shoes, with buckles or bows and fairly high heels. In France courtiers were allowed to paint their heels red, a status symbol and the origin of the phrase "well heeled."

Modesty Panties

In the eighteenth century, Camargo and Sallé (see Rebels, Rivals and the "Shakespeare of Ballet," page 22) led the rebellion against restrictive, cumbersome clothing with loosened gowns, shorter skirts, and flat slippers. To preserve their modesty they wore a new article of clothing under their skirts: *caleçons de précaution,* "modesty panties." Made of muslin and adjusted with a drawstring, they covered the area between the top of the ballerina's stockings and her waist.

Following fashion as well as function, in the early nineteenth century ballerinas adopted gowns that were simpler and lighter still. The Romantic era tutu was perfectly suited for the ethereal qualities they sought in their dancing (see Romanticism, page 50). Men replaced their knickers with fitted hose that went all the way up to their waists and wore their own form of modesty brief. (This garment changed ballet history: Nijinsky deliberately did not wear his at a major performance. For this he was fired—perhaps just what he wanted—and thus free to join Diaghilev's troupe.)

Virginia Zucchi in a shortened tutu.

73

Revolt of the Granddaughter

By the late nineteenth century, skirts had shortened once again, culminating in the costume we most identify with ballet: the tutu. In 1885, in St. Petersburg, the Italian ballerina Virginia Zucchi ("The Divine"), defiantly declared that she would not perform in a skirt fit for a grandmother. She appeared in what was essentially a tutu, much to the chagrin of the Imperial Theater authorities, who had tried to force her to lengthen her skirt.

Tutu building is an art and a science. A tutu is a one-piece garment with the skirt attached to the bodice. It takes more than a dozen layers of a very fine, mesh material called tulle, which can be silk or synthetic, to achieve the flouncy yet semi-rigid quality of a tutu—not to mention steel hoops, steel spiral boning, hooks, eyes, bars, cording, elastic, ribbon, and more, depending on the nature of the design. National differences exist: the methods of the costume shop at England's Royal Ballet are not the same as those in Russia. The Russian-born Barbara Karinska became legendary for the exquisite tutus she designed for the New York City Ballet. Their costume shop carries on her legacy, sewing tutus at an average cost of $3,500.

It's Not Just Tutus Anymore

Modern-day costumes reflect the upheavals in ballet since the classical period. In the early twentieth century Léon Bakst designed for the Ballets Russes; his voluptuous exoticism and opulent palette made "orientalism" all the rage in Paris. Diaghilev was among the first to tap the fashion world; he hired Coco Chanel; later, Halston, La Croix, Mizrahi, and many others also designed for dance. Balanchine's iconoclastic "leotard ballets" were revolutionary

sartorially as well as choreographically: the costumes are based on spare, simple studio attire.

The twentieth century broke all the rules. Today, costumes for dance can be anything at all or, quite literally, nothing at all. Twenty-first-century technology will surely produce new materials that will inspire exciting and unexpected costume design of the future.

A twenty-first century version of the tutu: Christina Johnson in the Oakland Ballet's production of Robert Henry Johnson's *Thirsting*, 2001.

74

Verdy at Indiana University. Suzanne Farrell and Jillana direct their own programs in Washington, D.C. and Taos, respectively.

Not only are Balanchine's aesthetic and training methods finding new homes, most of his choreography is carefully preserved and managed, protecting it from future ambiguity of the "after Petipa" kind. The Balanchine Foundation was formed in 1983; its goal is to utilize the Balanchine legacy to advance the development of dance through a broad range of activities and programs. The Balanchine Trust was formed in 1987 to foster public awareness and understanding of Balanchine and to facilitate the licensing of his works, trademarks, and servicemarks. To preserve the artistic integrity of his works, the trust provides Balanchine-trained répétiteurs to stage his ballets for qualified companies and requires periodic reviews of the productions.

In the years after Martha Graham and Michel Fokine died, bitter disputes arose over the performing rights to many of their works, sometimes preventing the works from being staged. The Balanchine organizations set an important precedent for the management of a choreographic inheritance.

Fundamentals of Technique

Time and geography produced variation among the major teaching systems, but underneath the surface differences the fundamentals of ballet are universal. You can always spot ballet dancers no matter where they trained. They're the ones with regal posture, beautiful muscles, and turned-out legs. Even walking down the street most dancers can't help it: they stand lifted and tall. Many retain their distinctive "duck foot" stance outside the studio as well—even after they've retired. Turnout, along with alignment, also called placement, and lift, also called pull-up, are so fundamental to ballet technique that they are the first things you learn. Once you learn them, your body absorbs them so completely that they often stay with you forever.

Battement tendu à la seconde.

Alignment

Align yourself by starting with your feet and working your way up.

▶ All ten toes are on the floor. Your weight is evenly distributed on both sides of the foot. The ankle rolls neither inward, "pronating," nor outward, "supinating."

▶ Your knees are over your toes.

▶ Your legs are turned out at the hip with the knees straight.

▶ Your hips are in line with the center of your feet.

▶ Your shoulders are wide and flat, with your shoulder blades gently pulled down to support your arms.

▶ Your torso is slightly forward so your armpits align with your hip bones.

▶ Your chest is lifted but your ribs do not protrude.

▶ The back of your neck is long and relaxed, your chin neither juts forward nor tucks under.

The alignment of your supporting side is crucial when you stand on one leg. You must be "on your leg," with your weight neither sinking into the supporting hip nor shifting away toward the working foot. In par terre exercises such as tendu, you should—as a test—be able to lift the working foot off the floor without adjusting your hips.

Don't allow your pelvis to tuck underneath and forward. Don't position your feet so that you cannot straighten your knees or so that your knees are forward of your toes.

Lifting your chest does not mean that the pelvis tilts back or the ribs protrude.

Lift

Placement alone is not enough; to move with speed and precision you must also be "pulled up." You engage and lift, but do not clench, the muscles of your feet, legs, and torso. The arches of your feet, your calves, the muscles that lift your kneecaps, your inner thighs and hamstrings, your buttocks, and your abdominals are all activated. Pull-up is not rigidity. It does not restrict you to verticality—your body still bends with freedom and fluidity. You still feel and use the floor.

Pull-up lifts you forward as well as upward. Ballet requires forward momentum: in a big center floor combination it's tremendous. Think how fast you get out of the way of the people coming across the floor. When standing still you prepare for and assist that momentum by pushing forward with the muscles on the backs of your legs, by keeping more weight on the balls of your feet than on your heels, and by lifting your chest.

Don't sink into the supporting hip.

Correct alignment.

Turnout

Ballet dancers have been turned out since the time of ballet de cour, well before the days of ear-high développés. Turnout enables the dancer to move easily from side to side, to jump, and to pose without ever turning away from the audience. Dancers have always believed that it looks better that way. Back in the days of court dancing, women wore huge, concealing skirts, but men showed their well-formed legs in elegant silk hose. Turnout displayed those handsome calf muscles to better advantage.

Turnout is what enables a dancer to raise the leg elegantly to the side without displacing the hips or torso. Try to do this without turning out and you'll find that when your leg reaches waist height, your hips become uneven and your alignment is lost. Turnout facilitates everything you do in ballet, and batterie would be quite impossible without it: absent good turnout the heels get in the way of the beats.

Proper turnout starts deep in the hip socket and continues all the way down the leg to the knee, ankle, and foot. Led by the inner-thigh muscles, the entire leg rotates. A few lucky dancers have a full 180-degree turnout, but it's possible to dance well with less. Work fully with what you have—your imperfect turnout properly used looks better than perfect turnout on someone who can't control it. You can and should stretch gently to help open your hips. Turnout should be carefully coaxed, never forced. Working in incorrect, overly turned-out positions can cause injury.

Your knees are aligned directly over your toes at all times; position your feet accordingly and do not allow your knees to roll inward, especially when you plié.

▶ Turn out both legs equally at all times.

▶ Don't let the pelvis "tuck under" in an effort to increase turnout.

▶ It's a rotation within the hips, not a clenching of the buttocks.

▶ Don't force your feet into a perfect toe-to-heel-heel-to-toe fifth position if it means the slightest compromise of straight knees or a properly placed pelvis.

▶ Never force your feet to turn out in a plié and then try to straighten your legs—it could injure your knees.

Now you have achieved an almost perfect state of readiness; your body is properly placed and lifted, correctly turned out, free of tension. There's just one more thing: a pleasant, intelligent expression on your face.

Sickled foot.

Don't "sickle" the foot, allowing the big toe to point inward.

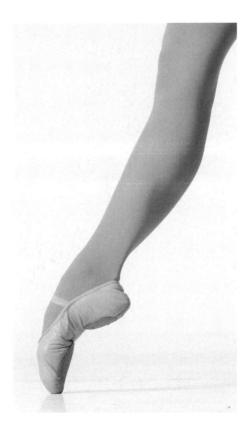

Correctly pointed foot.

A note on feet: When you point your foot in tendu or in any extended position, the big toe should align with the ankle, pointing neither inward, "sickled," nor outward, "winged."

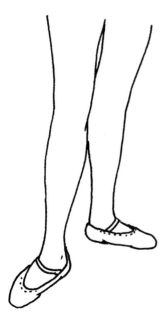

Winged foot.

Don't "wing" the foot, allowing the big toe to point outward.

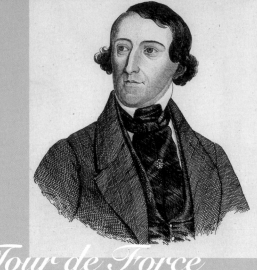

Tour de Force

BOURNONVILLE AND THE DANISH TRADITION

At the Royal Theater in Copenhagen the words "Not for Pleasure Only" appear above the proscenium. Auguste Bournonville believed that dance should ennoble and uplift as well as please.

Bournonville (1805–1879) trained in Copenhagen with his father, Antoine, a pupil of Noverre's and director of the Royal Theater, and with Vincenzo Galeotti, his father's predecessor. Young Bournonville then studied in Paris with the renowned Vestris and went on to partner Marie Taglioni. Memories of his training form the basis of one of his best-known ballets, *Konservatoriet* (*The Conservatory*).

On his return to Copenhagen Bournonville succeeded his father at the Royal Theater, while continuing to dance and choreograph. In his forty-five years there he created scores of ballets, some still performed today, which provide a living link to the Romantic and even the pre-Romantic tradition. Among the most beloved are *A Folk Tale, Napoli, The Flower Festival at Genzano* (pas de deux), and *La Sylphide*. Except for the latter, his ballets are usually charming, happy tales. Bournonville believed that dance could come only from joy; his characters do not dance when they are sad, they mime.

And the Danes are celebrated mimes. In Bournonville, dance seamlessly blends with pantomime to create narrative. Students at the School of the Royal Danish Ballet become exceptionally well-rounded performing artists. They study mime extensively, as well as theater history, ballet history, and a musical instrument. Dance spans generations; as in Russia, children participate in productions at a young age, and older dancers play important parts in character and mime roles.

When male dancing was withering in France, Bournonville kept it alive in Denmark. The technique and training methods he developed produced some of the twentieth century's great male dancers. Some stayed at home: Niels Kehlet, Henning Kronstam, Arne Villumsen; others achieved success abroad: Erik Bruhn, Peter Martins, Ib Andersen, Adam Lüders, Nikolaj Hübbe, Peter Schaufuss, Johan Kobborg.

The men may be more famous, but Denmark has always had its ballerinas. Lucile Grahn was Bournonville's adored muse, his first Sylph, and one of the superstar ballerinas of *Pas de Quatre*. Subsequent stars included Margot Lander, Margrethe Schanne, Toni Lander, Kirsten Simone, Anna Laerkesen, Lis Jeppesen.

Bournonville's influence made its way to Russia and eventually to America. His pupil Christian Johansson taught at the Imperial Theater in St. Petersburg; Johansson's pupil Pavel Gerdt taught Pavlova, Vaganova, and Balanchine. Balanchine was briefly ballet master at the Royal Danish Ballet; he later hired Stanley Williams to teach at his own school and invited Andersen, Lüders, and Martins to join his company. Meanwhile, Russian influence made its way to Denmark when Vaganova's pupil Vera Volkova joined the faculty of the Royal Danish Ballet School in the 1950s.

The company has expanded its repertoire to include other choreographers, among them past directors Harald Lander and Flemming Flindt, as it strives to balance its extraordinary Bournonville legacy with a contemporary European sensibility.

Erik Bruhn and Carla Fracci in *The Flower Festival at Genzano*, circa 1969.

Bournonville's Choreographic Creed

Dance is an art because it presupposes calling, knowledge, and skill.

It is a fine art because it strives for the ideal, not only in sculptural ways but also lyrically and dramatically.

The beauty to which dance ought to aspire is not dependent on taste and fashion but is based on the unchangeable laws of Nature.

Mime includes all the emotions of the soul; dance, on the other hand, is most importantly an expression of joy, a desire to follow the rhythms of music.

It is the mission of art and particularly of the theater to sharpen thought, elevate the mind, and freshen the senses. Dance should above all beware of flattering the preferences of a blasé public for effects foreign to true art.

Gaiety strengthens; intoxication weakens.

The beautiful always retains the freshness of novelty, the amazing bores in the long run.

Dance, with the help of music, can raise itself to poetry but it can also sink to buffoonery through an excess of gymnastics. The so-called difficult has numerous adepts, while the apparently easy is only achieved by a chosen few.

The high point of artistic skill is to conceal mechanics and effort under a harmonious calm.

Mannerism is not character and affectation is the decided enemy of grace.

Every dancer ought to consider his difficult art as a link in the chain of beauty, as a useful adornment to the stage, and this in turn as a meaningful element in the spiritual development of the Nation.

Positions and Orientations

A syllabus is never carved in stone. The syllabi of the major schools evolved as they traveled or underwent reinterpretation. Disciples can disagree, and disputes can arise over what the Cecchettis of the world really intended. This happens with choreography as well as teaching: exactly how did Fokine want the dying swan to die? Which version of *The Sleeping Beauty* is authentic? It happens outside ballet, too, as anyone who's studied Pilates with more than one instructor well knows.

The major schools of ballet all use Beauchamps's original positions of the feet and, for the most part, the same French terminology. All maintain ballet's traditions of courtesy and dignity; all prize grace and elegance. On the most fundamental aspects of technique there is no disagreement.

However, the schools do diverge on, among other things, which arm positions are codified and how they are identified. In some cases there are variants along with "official" positions. And just because an arm position is not recognized with an official name does not mean that it is not used. Sometimes two or even more terms exist for the same position. Arabesques and sur le cou-de-pied positions are also identified differently among the major schools.

Positions of the Feet

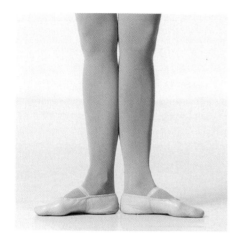

First Position

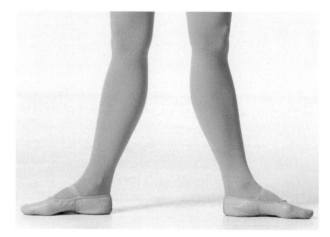

Second Position

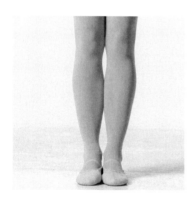

Parallel First Position, also
called Sixth Position

B plus, also called Attitude à
Terre (Soviet) and Preparatory
Position (R.A.D.)

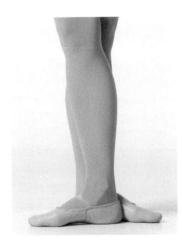

Third Position

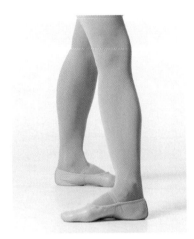
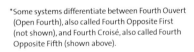

Fourth Position*

*Some systems differentiate between Fourth Ouvert
(Open Fourth), also called Fourth Opposite First
(not shown), and Fourth Croisé, also called Fourth
Opposite Fifth (shown above).

Fifth Position

Positions and Orientations

Positions of the Arms

Bournonville: Bras Bas
Cecchetti: Fifth en Bas
French: De Départ, Preparation, Au Repos, or Première en Bas
R.A.D.: Bras Bas
Soviet Russian: Preparatory Position

Bournonville: First Position
Cecchetti: First Position

Bournonville: Bras Arrondis Devant or First Position en Avant
Cecchetti: Fifth Position en Avant
French: First Position
R.A.D.: First Position
Soviet Russian: First Position

Bournonville: Demi-seconde

Cecchetti: *

R.A.D.: Demi-seconde†

*Not an official position, but it's called Demi-seconde of Allegro when the palms face the body and Demi-seconde of Adagio when the palms are higher and face slightly upward.

†For women the fingertips should just touch the edge of the tutu. The R.A.D. also uses a similar position called demi-bras, in which the arms are more in front of the body and the palms face upward as if offering, much like the position used with grand jeté in Bournonville technique (see page 160).

Bournonville: Bras à la Ligne or Second Position

Cecchetti: Second Position

French: Second Position

R.A.D.: Second Position

Soviet Russian: Second Position*

*Men hold the arms at shoulder height, women slightly lower.

Note on Cecchetti: In his own manual of the Cecchetti method, Cecchetti's son, Grazioso, identifies Fourth en Haut as Third, Fifth en Avant as First, Spanish Fourth as the official Fourth, Fourth en Avant as Fourth Low, Fifth en Haut as Fifth, and the positions with both arms lowered as De Repos Normal and De Repos Wide. The names listed above with the pictures are more widely accepted.

Positions and Orientations

Bournonville: Third Position en Haut
Cecchetti: Fourth Position en Haut
French: Third Position
R.A.D.: Fourth Position‡
Soviet Russian: Big Pose

Bournonville: Fourth Position
Cecchetti: *
French: Fourth Position
R.A.D.: Fourth Position
Crossed‡

*As a "softened" rather than an official position,
with head turned, gaze up and épaulement, it is
called Spanish Fourth.

Bournonville: À la Couronne
or Fifth Position
Cecchetti: Fifth en Haut
French: Fifth Position or Bras
en Couronne
R.A.D.: Fifth Position
Soviet Russian: Third Position

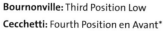

Bournonville: Third Position Low
Cecchetti: Fourth Position en Avant*
French: †
R.A.D.: Third Position‡
Soviet Russian: Small Pose

*Cecchetti Third Position, not shown, is like this but both
arms are lower—one en bas, one demi-seconde.

†Not an official position but sometimes called "Sixth."

‡In Third and both Fourth Positions, the R.A.D.
distinguishes between regular positions and those
"in opposition," depending on which foot is front or is
working. "In opposition" is when the working foot or
the front foot corresponds to the arm that is out to
the side, or in Fourth Crossed, to the arm in front.

Shapes and Distance

The oval shape the arms make when they are both overhead is exactly the same shape they make when in front of you and when lowered in bras bas. That's why Cecchetti calls them all "fifth" and just differentiates among "high," "front," and "low." Men maintain slightly more distance between the fingertips (about the width of the face), than do women (about the width of two fingertips). The French word courrone means "crown."

Hands and Wrists

Mannered, affected hands and wrists are rightly mocked. You see them on ridiculous characters like the Ugly Stepsisters in *Cinderella*, or the divas of the Ballets Trockadero de Monte Carlo, the all-male troupe who don tutus and pointe shoes for their hilarious ballet parodies. Hands and wrists should be relaxed and natural, flowing along with the arm, with space between the fingers.

Head and Gaze

Coordinate your head and gaze with your port de bras. It makes all the difference between confident, expressive dancing and dancing that looks clueless or robotic. There are several correct head positions—straight front, turned 45 degrees, turned in profile, inclined 45 degrees—but in none is the chin raised or lowered so far that the audience cannot see your face. The important thing about gaze is that you have one: look at your hand, look in the direction you are traveling, look at the audience, or look at your partner; but look.

The corps de ballet of the Bolshoi in the Kingdom of the Shades scene of *La Bayadère*.

Tour de Force

BALLET BLANC: THE CORPS DE BALLET'S TRIUMPH

Long before today's plotless ballet, ballet blanc (white ballet) existed as a form of pure dance, a set piece separate from the main action of a story ballet. The name derives from the identical white costumes worn by a female corps. Ballet blanc grew out of Romantic ballets like *La Sylphide*, gained grandeur in Petipa's revision of *Giselle*, and reached its pinnacle in *Swan Lake* and *La Bayadère*. Fokine created a tribute to ballet blanc in *Les Sylphides*; Balanchine's masterly use of his corps could be seen as a neoclassical update.

The corps, like the chorus in Greek theater, is a character itself: as important as the prima ballerina, not just her decorative backdrop. Its power lies in its uniformity and simultaneity rather than individual movements. Its patterns create forceful, sometimes even fearsome, designs: the wilis' diagonal barricade against Albrecht, the Shades' zigzag down the ramp, the snowflakes' swarm surrounding Clara, and the swans' fluttering formations.

Seeing the same shapes and movements repeatedly has a hypnotic effect; the device of ballet blanc often supports a plot involving a visit to the supernatural world, with the order and precision of the corps creating a striking contrast to the hero's passion, chaos, and upheaval.

The reality behind the ballet blanc's beauty is that the corps dancers earn every bit of their applause. Uniformity requires a lot of work and tremendous attention to detail. Members of the corps leave their individuality in the dressing room: every leg the same height, every gaze the same direction, arms and feet always together—they don't get to dance it their way. A corps dancer cannot land her pirouette wherever she ends up. Standing still for long stretches, usually with arms in a pose and often with the weight on just one leg can be excruciating. They are the junior dancers in a ballet company, with the lowest pay, the lowest status, and in many ways, the hardest work—sometimes eight shows a week. And almost without exception, every great ballerina started there.

Épaulement

Épaulement allows the classical positions to expand beyond their squared-off, academic confines to become more expressive and more exciting. Many lively character dances and demi-caractère variations derive their flavor in large part from épaulement.

It can add the illusion of height to a jump or extra yearning to arabesque in a poignant adagio. The upper body rotates—only from the waist up—so that one shoulder moves slightly forward and the other slightly back. The head and gaze turn to finish the new line.

Second Arabesque à Terre without épaulement

Second Arabesque à Terre with épaulement. In the Cecchetti system this position, facing a downstage corner and with the head tilted to the audience, is called Épaulé and considered one of the main orientations of the body.

Sur le Cou-de-Pied

Most training systems specify sur le cou-de-pied as having the working foot positioned in front of or behind the supporting ankle, with the foot fully pointed and the ankle fully stretched, *or* with the foot "wrapped" around the supporting ankle. In the pointed position devant, the toes of the working foot rest just above the supporting ankle, never sickling. In the pointed position derrière the working foot angles back away from the body, never dangling. The toes of the working foot do not contact the floor or the top of the supporting foot except in the Cecchetti system, which describes sur le cou-de-pied devant and derrière as having the working toes resting on the floor in the demi-pointe position.

The Soviet system has five positions. In addition to the three shown here, there is high-conditional, in which the working foot is midway up the shin, and low-conditional, which is used for battements battus on pointe or demi-pointe. The wrapped position, in which the working foot is forcefully stretched, is considered the basic sur le cou-de-pied position.

Note: Coupé is a movement, not a position, and is sometimes confused with sur le cou-de-pied.

Sur le Cou-de-Pied Devant
Soviet Russian: Conditional Sur le Cou-de-Pied

Sur le Cou-de-Pied Derrière

Wrapped Sur le Cou-de-Pied
Soviet Russian: Sur le Cou-de-Pied

Lucile Grahn, Fanny Cerrito, Marie Taglioni, and Carlotta Grisi in *Pas de Quatre*.

Fanny Elssler in *Le Diable*, 1837.

Tour de Force

PAS DE QUATRE (NOT PAS DE CINQ)

Imagine persuading four hugely popular Oscar-winning divas to work together in a movie with only one lead role. In 1845 theater promoter Benjamin Lumley managed the ballet equivalent in London with *Pas de Quatre*. Marie Taglioni, already a legend, was diplomatically dubbed "first among equals" and assured the most prominent part. Fanny Cerrito and Carlotta Grisi of Italy and Lucile Grahn of Denmark agreed to appear with her.

But Fanny Elssler also enjoyed a huge following; her fiery, sensual dancing—famously characterized as "pagan" to Taglioni's "Christian"—represented the other end of

the Romantic spectrum. There was no chance of her accepting second billing to her archrival; a *Pas de Cinq* was not to be.

Jules Perrot's choreography highlighted the distinct styles and fortes of each dancer. In a brilliant stroke, Perrot also diffused a potentially disastrous argument over who would have the coveted position of appearing just before Taglioni: he decreed that their order be from youngest to oldest. The original cast appeared only four times, but *Pas de Quatre* continues to be staged to this day.

Tour de Force

Marie Taglioni and her rivals dominated the Romantic age of ballet. The leading contender for superstar of the next generation was Taglioni's protégée, Emma Livry. The daughter of a soloist in the Paris Opera, Livry displayed such talent at such a young age that a brilliant career seemed assured.

At sixteen, in 1858, she debuted as the Sylph—the role that made Taglioni famous—in the Paris Opera's revival of *La Sylphide*. In 1860 Taglioni herself created *Le Papillon* (*The Butterfly*), her first and only choreographic effort, expressly for Livry. With her strong technique and delicate épaulement Livry was splendid as Farfalla, a girl-turned-butterfly whose wings are burned when she gets too close to a lighted torch. The ballet was eerily prescient.

Theaters and stages in Livry's day were illuminated with open flame gas lighting. The

hazards were well known to performers; dancers' skirts caught fire easily, and ballerinas had been burned. Fireproof material was available, but Livry, like most dancers, refused to wear it. Skirts made of safer fabrics such as muslin were heavy and dull-looking; fireproof coatings made costumes lose their billowy, diaphanous qualities.

During a rehearsal for *The Dumb Girl of Portici* in November 1862, Livry's skirt ignited backstage. Livry was badly burned and suffered horribly for months before dying in 1863 at age twenty-one. Paris wept at her untimely death, and critics wrote of white butterflies escorting her coffin—an ethereal shroud. France would soon cede ballet supremacy to Russia. Livry's death was like a final curtain on the glory days of Romantic ballet.

Passé or Retiré

In the United States the position in which the toe of the working leg touches the knee of the supporting leg is very often called passé, but the correct term is retiré.

Passé is a movement: the working leg passes the supporting leg. Retiré is sometimes defined as a movement as well as a position: the leg is drawn up to the bent-knee position and returned to its starting place.

Schools also differ on the exact placement of the working foot: some say at the side of the supporting knee; others slightly in front, just under the kneecap.

Arabesques

The major training systems differentiate among arabesques in different ways. The French school considers orientation: which leg is raised relative to the audience. R.A.D. and Bournonville consider the positions of the arms; Cecchetti does, too, and adds variations facing a corner with a bent supporting leg (fourth and fifth arabesques). The Soviet system incorporates both orientation and port de bras.

The working leg—always long and stretched—may range in height from arabesque à terre, in which the working toes touch the floor, to a "six o'clock" arabesque penchée in which the upper body leans forward to allow the working foot to point straight up to the ceiling.

▶ The pelvis tips to allow the leg to rise above 45 degrees, and the shoulders must move forward as well, but the back is strong and arched at all times.

▶ The working hip resists opening until the height of the working leg requires it.

▶ The upper back, from the bust up, is always upright and slightly arched.

▶ Be careful not to let the ribs protrude or the shoulders hunch or twist.

Bournonville: First
Cecchetti: First
R.A.D.: First
Soviet Russian: First

The arm of the supporting side is in front.

Cecchetti: Fourth

Faces corner and supporting leg is in plié.

Soviet Russian: Third

Faces the audience.

Bournonville: Second*
Cecchetti: Second
R.A.D.: Second
Soviet Russian: Second†

*The arms are softer and lower
than shown.
†The head turns to the audience.

Bournonville: à la Lyre
Cecchetti: Third
R.A.D.: Third
Soviet Russian (Variant):
à deux bras

Cecchetti: Fifth

Faces corner and supporting
leg is in plié.

Soviet Russian: Fourth

The body twists, and the
head turns in opposition, so
both the back and the face
are toward the audience.

French: Ouvert

French: Croisé

Positions and Orientations

Attitude

The well-known Renaissance statue of Winged Mercury by Gian de Bologna was the inspiration for the position attitude. Carlo Blasis, an early nineteenth-century ballet master and author of *The Code of Terpsichore*, was the first to describe it. Ballet's attitude, unlike the famous statue's, requires that the working knee never turn in and drop lower than the foot.

The position has evolved. In the past the working knee was bent at a 90-degree angle, and there was also a 90-degree angle between the thigh of the working leg and the thigh of the supporting leg. Attitude today is often higher and more open, the ideal angles are now 135 degrees. You should be able to do both.

Attitude is not codified as extensively as arabesque, but it sometimes is defined according to the orientation of the body— attitude effacé or attitude croisé derrière, for example—or according to arm and head position.

Attitude Devant

Attitude (also called Attitude Derrière)

Orientations of the Body

Ever conscious of how the body is presented to the audience, ballet has specific terminology for the dancer's orientation. The impact of steps and positions changes greatly depending on how the body and head are angled; for example, arabesque done facing the audience conceals its beautiful lines, arabesque done in profile displays them. Many steps look best oriented along the diagonal.

Shown here is tendu, with lowered arms, in each of the major orientations.

Croisé Devant

À la Quatrième Devant

Effacé Derrière

Effacé Devant

Croisé Derrière

À la Quatrième Derrière

Écarté Devant

À la Seconde

Écarté Derrière

Part Three

Ballet Class

Before Class

Ballet class progresses deliberately so that your body is prepared for dancing, but you get a lot more out of class if you arrive ten minutes early to warm up and to stretch. A regular preclass warm-up and stretch—and they are not the same thing—maintain and increase your flexibility. A long, lean, balanced musculature is not only a part of ballet's aesthetic; it facilitates ballet technique. The muscles that work so hard in ballet can become tight, bunchy, and overdeveloped if not properly and frequently stretched. And it is easier to coax the body into ballet's positions without strain when the muscles are warm and the joints have had some advance notice.

Finally, a good warm-up and stretch, even if you do a long, slow, careful barre, is important for preventing injury, especially the tiny injuries, strains, and small tears that are just serious enough to keep you from improving your technique and enjoying class.

Human nature makes us want to practice what we are already good at and avoid practicing what needs work. We like to be comfortable. At the gym you often see the person with beautifully developed arms doing biceps curls; in the ballet studio the good turners are often doing pirouettes before class, and dancers with great extension are stretching their already flexible legs and hips. Be proud of what you do well, but at the same time be willing to put your ego aside and, without being too hard on yourself, work on overcoming your weaknesses. This is true not just of stretching but throughout your ballet training. It is particularly important in stretching because of the great temptation to stretch only the parts that are willing, and to avoid addressing those that are not.

Warm Up

Warming up is just that; it elevates tissue temperature, which in turn makes the muscles more pliable, coordinated, responsive, and resistant to injury.

Prances are an ideal way to warm up. Keep your knees soft and articulate your feet, pointing them not just at the ankle, but also through the toes and metatarsals. Light prances, forward, backward, and even around the room increase tissue temperature—it's like lubricating the joints. Two or three minutes should suffice.

Rises at the barre, in parallel position and ideally with a tennis ball between and just below your ankles, help you find your placement for the rest of class so that you are properly aligned even before the first plié. Think of distributing the weight equally on both feet over all ten toes, and allow the body to move forward as a unit with each rise.

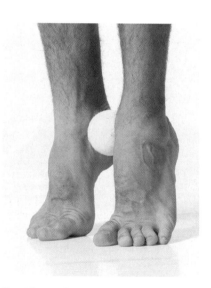

Rise with tennis ball between the ankles.

Stretch

Only when you feel warm is it appropriate to begin stretching. Once warm, be guided by the idea of "gently dynamic." Small, controlled movements are safer than either big, ballistic movement or no movement at all. Resist the urge to hang out in a static stretch position, especially in a big straddle stretch such as à la seconde on the floor. The other extreme—sudden, forceful movement—can cause tears, sometimes the "uh-oh" kind you notice immediately, sometimes the more subtle and insidious kind that heal by forming scar tissue that creates a permanently vulnerable area prone to reinjury. Before class is not the time to test your full range of motion; a low, slow, mini battement cloche before class is okay, but whacking your leg up to a full extension might pull a muscle.

How you arrive at and how you leave a position are as important as the position itself; this is just as true for stretching as it is in the rest of ballet. Your transitions into and out of a stretch should be slow, controlled, and graceful.

Ambition, discipline, and zeal—all admirable traits—can get in the way of listening to the body. Put them aside for long enough to tune in and take an inventory of what feels tight. Try to distinguish between the salutary discomfort that indicates productive effort and the pain that warns of injury. If a movement feels "pinchy" in the joints or causes residual pain, don't do it. It's not self-indulgent to heed your body's messages. It's prudent.

Finally, the mirror is not just for primping. Try to find a spot where you can see yourself to check for symmetry and alignment.

Most of the stretches described here use the barre, but all can be adapted for floor stretching at home. Stretching on vacation, weekends, and sick days contributes to maintaining flexibility, avoiding soreness, and making the return to class much easier.

Quadriceps

These big muscles along the fronts of your thighs are continually called upon. They contribute to pulling up when you stand, and they are strongly engaged when you jump. Stretching prevents them from becoming tight or overdeveloped. This quadriceps stretch and the lunge stretch that follow are great for your arabesque, too.

Quadriceps stretch:

▶ Stand with your back to the barre, and with both hands holding it.

▶ Bend the knee of your stretching leg completely.

▶ Rest stretching leg against the (lower) barre, toes pointed upward.

▶ Keep the thigh of your stretching leg perpendicular to the floor.

▶ Make sure your pelvis is neutral, not tilted forward or back; tailbone down.

▶ Engage your abdominal muscles.

▶ Do little pliés on your supporting leg.

Anterior Hip: Hip Flexors and Psoas

Every retiré works the muscles in front of the hip joint, as do your extensions.

Lunge stretch:

▶ Face the barre with both hands holding on to it.

▶ Stand with your feet and legs parallel.

▶ Place the arch of your foot on the barre.

▶ Keep your spine, pelvis, and supporting leg aligned in a straight diagonal.

▶ Keep your shoulders square to the barre and aligned over hips.

▶ Gently incline farther toward the barre.

▶ If you feel pinching in the working hip, you are too close to the barre or your hips are not level.

Hamstrings

These muscles on the backs of your thighs enable you to bend your knee in positions such as retiré. They work in concert with the front thigh muscles to control plié and jumps. They must be flexible to permit the elongation needed in front and side extensions.

Hamstring stretch:

▶ Stand facing the barre with feet parallel, *not* turned out.

▶ Place one leg on the barre, foot flexed.

▶ Keep your pelvis square and hips level.

▶ Slightly hinge your torso forward at the hips, without rounding.

▶ Feel the stretch all along the back of your thigh, from the knee to the ischial tuberosity, where the hamstring muscles attach to the sitz or "sitting" bones.

Adductor/Groin

The muscles of the inner thigh elongate in all movements à la seconde. The adductor muscles also draw the legs together when closing in fifth position.

Inner thigh stretch:

▶ Stand with your side to the barre, one leg on the barre à la seconde, and slightly in front of center; keep both legs turned out and the foot on the barre flexed.

▶ Plié supporting leg.

▶ Cambré side over the working leg.

▶ Hold your turnout and keep your hips level.

External Rotators

These six muscles around the hips work together constantly when you turn out and can easily become tight if you are dancing a lot.

External rotator stretch:

▶ Stand facing the barre with the working ankle on the barre and the working knee bent. Your legs are turned out.

▶ Hold your hips square to the barre and don't let the working side creep in toward the barre.

▶ Bend forward at the hips. Feel the stretch across the buttocks.

Flexor Hallucis Longus

Most athletes never notice this muscle, but dancers give it a tremendous workout because it's the muscle that points the big toe and stabilizes the inside of the foot in relevé and on pointe. It runs from deep in the back of the calf, past the underside of the inner ankle bone, along the bottom of the foot to the big toe.

Flexor hallucis longus stretch:

▶ Gently press the bottoms of your toes against a wall, with the ball of your foot as close to the wall as possible. The knee is bent.

▶ The other leg is in a lunge with the knee straight and foot parallel.

▶ Don't do this stretch if you feel pain or stiffness around the joint of the big toe.

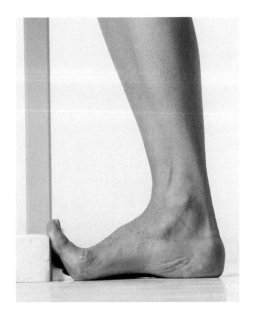

Calves

Every relevé, every balance on demi- or full pointe engages your calf muscles.

Calf stretch:

▶ Face the barre.

▶ Stagger your feet as if in a turned-in fourth position, keeping them parallel. On each foot the second toe aligns with the heel.

▶ Keeping the back leg straight, bend the front knee and tilt your upper body slightly forward.

▶ Ease back if you feel any restriction at the front of the ankles.

Calf and shoulder

Your upper back and especially the shoulder blade muscles—not your upper arms—support your port de bras. This stretch helps lengthen those muscles as well as your calves.

Calf and shoulder stretch:

▶ Face the barre with feet parallel.

▶ Bend your knees completely while holding firmly onto the barre.

▶ Feel the stretch in your shoulders, upper back and calves.

▶ Don't do this stretch if you feel pinching in your shoulder joints.

Pierina Legnani on pointe in *Swan Lake*, circa 1895.

Marie Taglioni and her brother Paul in *La Sylphide*, 1832. She danced the ballet on pointe wearing satin slippers.

Tour de Force

PIONEERS OF POINTE: TAGLIONI AND LEGNANI

The credit—or blame—for inventing pointework goes to Marie Taglioni. She wasn't the first, but she was the pioneer who transformed toe dancing from mere trick to genuine artistry.

Taglioni (1804–1884) was an unlikely star. As a child, she was plain, with unusually long arms, and shoulders so stooped her classmates called her Hunchback. The ballet master at the Paris Opera suggested she become a dressmaker. Her father, Filippo Taglioni, a well-regarded choreographer, trained Marie mercilessly. She overcame her limitations and developed extraordinarily strong legs and feet. In 1832 she starred in her father's production of *La Sylphide*, the first full-length ballet on pointe.

Taglioni was a marvel. She enthralled audiences with her feathery step, her soaring leaps, her ballon, and her impossibly light landings.

Her signature port de bras—arms bent at the elbows or across her chest (her father's inventions for concealing the length of her arms)—became classic poses associated with Romanticism. Although the stories of adoring fans cooking her slippers and eating them with a sauce are probably apocryphal, in status and popularity she was a rock star of her day.

Ballerinas had been made to fly and execute aerial maneuvers in the past with the help of wires; now they could do it on their own. Although negligible by today's standards, even minimal toe dancing exhilarated nineteenth-century audiences. It was, as Lincoln Kirstein called it, "the speech of the inexpressible." Not just another crowd-pleasing feat like the first entrechat quatre, pointe dancing added to a ballerina's drama as well as to her technique.

Emma Livry's slippers.

Pointe virtuosity was limited to the briefest of balances. The dancer was not "over her feet" as are today's dancers—her flimsy shoes did not permit it. Her alignment was less vertical: the hips released back and the upper body tilted slightly forward.

Sturdier shoes afforded the placement and support for pointe dancing to reach the next level. The dancer who led the way was Pierina

Legnani (1863–1923), the first *prima ballerina assoluta*. Trained by Carlo Blasis at La Scala, Legnani made a sensational debut in St. Petersburg in *Cinderella* in 1893, performing an unheard-of thirty-two fouettés on pointe. Young Michel Fokine had a part in the production and was severely reprimanded for forgetting himself and clapping wildly onstage.

Other dancers had managed to turn fouettés before that, but none had pulled off quite so many quite so prominently. Soon intricate multiple turns, hops, and sustained balances on pointe were in every ballerina's vocabulary. *Swan Lake* had been a flop in 1877. With Petipa's choreography and Legnani in the lead, it was a smash in 1895.

The Romantic ballerinas had used pointe work for drama, for making their characters more vivid, and so did Petipa. Odile turns those thirty-two fouettés because she is a wicked temptress hypnotizing Siegfried. Aurora sustains those balances in *The Sleeping Beauty* because she is a poised, regal princess. Later choreographers, notably Balanchine, explored pointework's nonnarrative possibilities, and it became an important and enduring feature of the ballerina's newly elongated line.

Marie Taglioni's slipper.

At the Barre

Ballet class begins at the barre, and so does ballet technique. Barre develops the strength, speed, balance, flexibility, turnout, alignment, extension, articulation, and coordination that ballet demands. Barre exercises are not separate steps from a separate world, nor is barre simply a stylized warm-up for center floor; it's where you learn and maintain your skills. Whether a fast barre or a slow one, a set barre or one that changes every day, barre work is the sustenance of ballet technique.

The steps at the barre provide direct preparation for the steps center floor, in the second part of class, which in turn become choreography performed on stage. Those glorious, soaring leaps and turns all start at the barre with perfect pliés and tendus. Pliés may look like nothing more than knee bends, but that exquisitely controlled bending is the origin of every jump and turn. And that humble battement tendu, practiced constantly at the barre, initiates every step you do center floor in which a leg moves away from the body and every step you do in which the leg returns to the body—whether it's a simple glissade or a virtuosic brisé volé.

A well-designed barre achieves two purposes. Short term, it prepares you for dancing immediately afterwards. Your body grows warm and limber; your muscles become nicely stretched and ready to attempt center floor work, rehearsal, or performance safely. The relative simplicity of barre exercises allows you to focus on the fundamentals so that they are there for you later when your attention must be on bigger steps and more challenging combinations. A proper barre sets you up to sustain balances, turn pirouettes, and perform a clean, sparkling allegro.

In the long term, barre work builds and refines your technique. Barre constantly reinforces the basics; it also offers the time to think about details: your gaze, the tightness of your fifth position, the pressure of your toes on the floor, how you hold your fingers. The repetition and concentration in barre work engraves correct details into your technique, so that even if the rest of class doesn't go well on a particular day, you progress nonetheless.

Extension à la seconde.

Finally, barre is your repair shop for anything that is not working center floor. If you are having difficulty with a particular step or family of steps, don't just practice the step itself—go back to the barre and examine its components. If, for example, pirouettes are the problem, examine your placement in pliés, your position in retiré, and your balance on demi-pointe. If your glissades are sloppy, or your assemblés don't assemble, work on your articulation and your finishing positions during battements tendus and frappés. Barre is more introspective and meditative than center floor work. You can—and should—be inwardly focused. Center floor is the time to perform and project.

The Set Barre

Some teachers give the same barre in every class; this is called a "set barre" and it is a feature of several teaching methods, notably that of the Paris Opera School, Bournonville, and Cecchetti. The advantage lies in learning by repetition.

Patient, correct repetition of barre exercises makes dancing properly as natural and automatic as riding a bicycle or touch-typing. Mindless rote learning is emphatically not the point: your brain engages completely in observing and correcting the body, and does so all the better for being unencumbered with the task of remembering steps. And, because the teacher need not explain each exercise, the set barre saves precious class time. Naturally the set barre for a beginner class differs from that of an advanced class.

The set barre's disadvantage: the muscles of the mind miss out on some conditioning. Picking up combinations quickly (a crucial audition and professional skill) and adapting to different styles require versatility and overall mental agility, both of which develop better when challenged by variety and by the occasional "brain twister" combination that moves in irregular patterns or rhythms.

Many teachers try to achieve the best of both approaches. One strategy is to change the barre weekly so that by the end of the week students will have learned the combinations and can devote themselves to perfecting them. Another approach is to give the same barre for several days in a row, gradually increasing its difficulty with extra challenges. Yet another is to vary certain combinations but not others.

Center floor combinations and even entire classes can also be set. Hans Beck, who succeeded Bournonville at the Royal Danish Ballet, compiled Bournonville's greatest combinations into a series of classes named for the days of the week. Students at the Royal Theater in Copenhagen would study Monday's class for several days, regardless of the actual day of the week, moving on to another day only when they had mastered Monday's combinations.

Cecchetti also had set classes. I remember the apprehension I felt on hearing my Cecchetti-trained teacher announce that we would be doing the Wednesday Adagio, no matter what day of the week it was. But the Cecchetti Method also specifies a *temps à plaisir*, in which the teacher is at liberty to introduce combinations of his or her own invention.

The Long, Short, Fast, or Slow Barre

The duration of the barre varies greatly from class to class. Some teachers keep you at the barre for as long as an hour, with lots of slow, careful combinations gradually working up to full speed. Others get the whole thing done in a brisk half hour. Balanchine was known to polish off the barre in a blistering twenty minutes or less, and many dancers would do a barre themselves before taking his class just to have their muscles ready. A slow tempo helps injured dancers recover and prevent reinjury; a quick tempo warms up the muscles faster and helps develop speed.

Sequence of Exercises

There are as many different barres as there are teachers, but the overall structure of barre varies little from class to class. The order in which the exercises are done progresses logically to meet the body's needs. Pliés everywhere are at or near the beginning of barre; grands battements and adagio are near the end. Battements tendus dégagés come after battements tendus à terre and so on. Some exercises may be combined (développé and grand rond de jambe for instance), but they almost all appear. Go anywhere in the world and you may find that although class is in a different dialect, the grammar of barre is the same.

Barre exercises often move in a pattern called en croix, from the French meaning "crosswise." You do the step or sequence of steps four times: to the front, the side, the back, and again to the side. The Russian school has its own pattern, which can include switching the supporting leg mid-exercise and adding épaulement. In most classes you do each exercise beginning with the left hand on the barre and the right leg as the working leg, but some teachers alternate beginning sides on a weekly basis. When the combination is finished, you turn in toward the barre to repeat it on the other side. (Don't turn away from the barre to change sides unless specifically directed.) In some classes changing sides is a choreographed motion, often with a demi-détourné or soutenu turn and no break in the music; in others it is done informally.

Holding the Barre

The barre itself, that wooden dowel or metal pipe, is meant to help you maintain balance and alignment as you perform the exercises. You hold the barre, but it should not hold you; it's not a crutch. Correct grasp is a requisite for correct placement. Your hand rests gently on the barre, never gripping, grabbing, or leaning on it. Most teachers insist that the thumb rest atop the barre alongside the fingers rather than wrap around underneath, thus making it impossible to grip. If your studio has barres of different heights, select one too low rather than too high. A high barre is great for stretching your legs, but can encourage shoulders to hunch up. Maintain a comfortable distance from the barre, with the barre hand slightly in front of your body. Keep your elbow lightly bent and relaxed and maintain a space between your upper arm and torso.

If the class is crowded and you risk hitting another dancer, face outward an eighth of a turn, or 45 degrees, away from the barre when working to the front; face forward when working to the side; face 45 degrees in toward the barre while working to the back.

Beginning and Ending Each Exercise

Each exercise begins and ends deliberately. Execute the preparation and the conclusion with as much focus and discipline as you apply to the steps themselves. A preparation of some sort precedes every combination. For some it is fairly elaborate, involving both arms and legs; for others, it is a simple port de bras. Your teacher will probably use the words "prepare," "present," or just a simple "and . . . " Whether you have an accompanist or a recording, the preparation usually has its own music, a two-bar introduction indicating the tempo and dynamic of the combination.

When you finish an exercise, hold the final position for a moment before releasing it. R.A.D. students are expected to show a clear, strong conclusion by gracefully lowering the working arm, turning the head and gaze 45 degrees outward, then standing absolutely straight and still.

Being Classically Trained

Being classically trained, whether in ballet or in music or in a martial art, requires that you break down movements into their smallest components, practice and perfect those components through repetition, then reassemble them. Barre is the opportunity to work on ballet movements at the smallest, most elemental level. Center floor is where they get put back together. The newly reconstructed whole is always greater than the sum of its polished parts.

Mathilda Kchessinska
in Petipa's *Esmeralda*,
St. Petersburg, 1899.

Marius Petipa

Tour de Force

PETIPA AND THE TSARS' BALLET

From remote St. Petersburg, Russia's nobility looked to the West
as a window on culture and civilization. Ballet as a court entertainment
had been imported since the mid-1600s; formal dance training had
begun in 1738 under the patronage of the royal family. The tsars
of Russia established great theaters and financed them well; many
of Europe's best dancers, attracted by the fine stages as well as the
pay, stayed in Russia for long visits. Marie Taglioni, Christian
Johansson, Jules Perrot, Fanny Elssler, Arthur Saint-Léon, Lucile
Grahn, and Carlotta Grisi—all danced in Russia.

By the time he, too, went to Russia in 1847, Marius Petipa (1818–1910),
the son of a ballet master, was already well traveled as an itinerant

soloist, had danced opposite Fanny Elssler and Carlotta Grisi, and was a principal dancer at the Paris Opera. He arrived in St. Petersburg on a one-year contract, but he stayed the rest of his life, first as a principal dancer, then choreographer in chief, and finally as head ballet master for almost three and a half decades.

For Petipa the dance came first; he used plot and drama in the service of pure dance rather than the reverse. He was a master of the classical set piece: the grand pas, the divertissement, and the ballet blanc. He championed Tchaikovsky's music—then considered too symphonic and not sufficiently "dansant" for ballet. His works—*Swan Lake, The Sleeping Beauty, The Nutcracker, Don Quixote, La Bayadère, Raymonda*— are beloved and for many the very definition of the word "ballet."

By the 1890s, with ongoing support from the royal coffers and a steady influx of well-trained and hugely popular Italian dancers to supplement the local talent, Russia ruled ballet. Petipa's choreography showcases virtuosity; the level of technique rose to provide it. Cecchetti, Legnani, Zucchi, Carlotta Brianza, and Antonietta Dell'Era brought Italian bravura; Russian stars included Pavlova, Olga Preobrajenska, Mathilda Kchessinska. Ballerinas were often favorites of the nobility, sometimes proudly performing in the jewels their admirers had given them. Kchessinska, Legnani's successor as *prima ballerina assoluta*, wrote of her romance with Tsarevitch Nicolas and subsequent marriage to a grand duke.

Questions of authenticity haunt any Petipa production. Lev Ivanov, Petipa's assistant ballet master, is generally thought to have created Acts II and IV of *Swan Lake*. The choreography credit often reads "after Petipa."

This could mean choreography very close to the original, or it could mean that the steps are quite different but the costumes and intentions are similar. Ballets were passed down from memory from one generation to the next; ballet masters often changed the steps. Nicholas Sergeyev, the régisseur of the Maryinsky, worked with Diaghilev and later with the fledgling Sadler's Wells company to faithfully re-create the ballets from notebooks. But whether the choreography is exact or approximate, Petipa's ideals and principles shape classical ballet to this day.

Alina Cojocaru and Johan Kobborg in the Royal Ballet's production of *La Bayadère*.

Plié

Plié means "fold" or "bend"; in ballet it is to bend the knee or knees of your standing leg or legs. The barre usually begins with demi- and grands pliés, but just because they are first doesn't mean they are simple.

Purpose

Pliés warm the muscles and joints of the legs, as well as those crucial muscles that control your turnout. They help establish correct placement and are the foundation of every turn, every jump, and every safe landing.

Getting the Most Out of Plié

▶ Work your turnout properly from the hip, and maintain the alignment of your ribs and pelvis.

▶ Be aware of all ten toes on the floor, and of controlling your ankles and knees so they don't roll in.

▶ Keep your heels on the floor at all times during demi-plié; during grand plié lift them at the last possible moment going down and replace them as soon as you can coming up. Lift them as little as possible. In second position the heels remain on the floor

▶ A word from two legendary ballet masters, Enrico Cecchetti and George Balanchine: Don't sit at the bottom of the plié; start the ascent immediately and keep the timing consistent: if it's two counts going down it's two counts coming up.

▶ Plié means bend, but the straightening and stretching of the legs is even more important than the bending. Rrrrrrresist! Do your pliés as if moving through peanut butter.

▶ Grands pliés in fourth and fifth positions really challenge the control of the turnout, so they are sometimes omitted from beginners' classes.

Relevé

Relevé means "raised." You raise yourself onto demi-pointe, or full pointe. Many schools distinguish between a rise, in which you press up with straight knees, and a relevé, in which a tiny demi-plié precedes the movement to provide a little spring.

Purpose

Although not the main purpose of the exercise, the distinctively beautiful dancer's leg is the result of innumerable relevés. Relevés develop the leg muscles, especially the calves and inner thighs. They challenge you to maintain your turnout, your alignment, and your pull-up when your heels are off the ground; they strengthen your ankles so you can safely sustain long balances, and they prepare you for pointework.

Getting the Most Out of Relevé

Think of pressing down to rise up. In fifth position, squeeze the legs together as you rise to make a tighter, cleaner position— an excellent opportunity to discover and develop inner thigh and gluteal muscles. As a student I was advised to hold an imaginary quarter between my inner thighs and never let it drop.

Cambré

Cambré means "arched." The French term also means "to throw out one's chest," but that's the wrong way to do the exercise. A cambré is a bending to the front, side, or back, or in a circular motion. Cambré front bends from the hips, cambré side and back from the waist. Cambré is not the same as port de bras. (See Glossary.)

Purpose

Cambré provides a wonderful stretch for the backs of the legs, and for the entire torso. It loosens the spine and helps develop flexibility in the upper and midback. It trains the lower body to maintain its placement while the upper body enjoys a wide range of motion.

Getting the Most Out of Cambré

▶ Move your chest up, out, and away from your legs, not just downward.

▶ Keep your hips firmly in place.

▶ Hold your turnout.

▶ Be aware of your shoulders; they may try to hunch up when you arch backward.

▶ Cambré feels delightfully elongating, but you should resist the temptation to sacrifice form for extra stretching.

Battement Tendu

Balanchine said, "If you just do battement tendu well, you don't have to do anything else." It's an exaggeration, of course, but it makes the point that battements tendus—often shortened in class to just tendus—are, along with pliés, the very foundation of your technique.

Literally "stretched beating," the straight working leg brushes out to its longest, stretched position, toes always in contact with the floor. It returns to its original position or to a new one, sometimes with a plié, sometimes with an additional variation in the extended position.

Purpose

Tendus teach you how to move your feet and legs correctly. They develop a supple, articulate foot and a strong, flexible ankle. They build the strength and control you need to stand on just one leg while the other leg works in all directions around you. The tendu has a fairly small range of motion, but mastering it is crucial for executing bigger movements.

Getting the Most Out of Tendu

▶ Always be aware of your supporting side.

▶ Lead with your inner thigh to really work your turnout.

▶ Use your toes and work through the ball of your foot. Pointing happens at both the ankle and the metatarsal joints.

▶ Keep the inner thighs actively engaged; even at a slow tempo, the working foot never just drifts in and out.

▶ The return is essential; close your tendu precisely into a perfect first or fifth position.

Variations on Tendu

This all-important exercise usually merits two or three different combinations at every barre, with at least one slow version and one fast one. Here are some typical variations, all of which can be further embellished by the addition of épaulement:

▶ Tendu flexing the foot in the extended position and repointing it before closing.

▶ Tendu lowering the ball of the foot in the extended position then repointing it before closing.

▶ Tendu lowering the heel to the floor and in the extended position with or without a shift of weight then repointing it before closing.

▶ Tendu with a change of supporting leg and a transfer of weight: for example, the right leg does tendu front then the left does tendu back.

▶ Tendu with pas de cheval. (See Glossary.)

▶ Tendu with temps lié. (See Glossary.)

▶ Battement tendu dégagé (also known as battement dégagé glissé in the French school and battement tendu jeté in the Russian). The terminology reveals subtle differences: dégagé means "disengaged," "open," and "airy"; glissé means "gliding"; but jeté means "thrown." In the Russian school the working leg is "thrown" up to 45 degrees; in other schools the working foot leaves the floor slightly and finishes just an inch or two in the air.

▶ A variation on dégagé is tendu jeté pointé or tendu jeté piqué, in which the foot sharply taps the floor in the extended position.

Anna Pavlova in *The Dragonfly*, 1914.

Tour de Force

PAVLOVA

"Leave acrobatics to others, Anna ... You must realize that your daintiness and fragility are your greatest assets. You should always do the kind of dancing which brings out your own rare qualities instead of trying to win praise by mere acrobatic tricks."

That was Pavel Gerdt's advice to his pupil when she tried multiple turns. At a time when fouettés were fashionable but Romanticism was not, when strong Italian ballerinas were favored and dainty Russian girls weren't, Anna Pavlova resurrected the ethereal, delicate qualities of the Romantic ballerina and imbued them with her enormously expressive style.

Born in 1881 outside St. Petersburg, Pavlova saw a performance of *The Sleeping Beauty* as a child and resolved that some day she herself would be Princess Aurora. It was several years before the Imperial School of the Maryinsky Ballet would accept her, and even then her weak feet, poor turnout, and spindly body made a ballet career dubious.

But Pavlova took advantage of what she did have: extension, ballon, a pliable torso, feminine delicacy, and expressiveness. She had the best teachers—Gerdt, Christian Johansson, Nicholas Legat, Enrico Cecchetti—and she worked assiduously.

She excelled in the classical repertory at the Imperial Theater. Petipa even reworked *Giselle* to showcase her Romantic qualities, but it was the choreography of Michel Fokine that immortalized her. *The Dying Swan* (originally, *The Swan,* 1905), a solo depicting the last moments in the life of a swan, was technically a mere matter of bourrées and highly stylized port de bras, but Pavlova's genius transcended the sentimental melodrama of the piece, and her emotional, ecstatic style thrilled audiences.

She performed with Diaghilev's Ballets Russes in 1909, then formed her own company in 1910, and toured the globe for nearly two decades, becoming ballet's most influential ambassador and inspiring balletomania thousands of miles away from her native Russia. Frederick Ashton saw her in Peru and decided to devote his life to ballet.

Enchanting in roles that required beautiful line and fluid moments—a flower, a dragonfly, a swan—Pavlova was the most famous ballerina of her time. She chose not to have an operation that could have saved her life because it would have meant giving up dancing. Her last words before she died of pleurisy in 1931: "Prepare my Swan costume."

Rond de Jambe par Terre

Rond de jambe par terre means "circle of the leg on the ground." A straight working leg moves in an arc while the toes lightly touch the floor.

Purpose

With its circular, rather than linear, range of motion, rond de jambe really warms up the hip joints while further challenging and developing control of turnout. The circular movement of the leg, from front to side or from back to side, is the building block of more complicated steps such as fouetté turns or pas de basque.

Getting the Most Out of Rond de Jambe par Terre

- Think of lengthening your working leg.
- Keep your hips level and really work your turnout.
- It's easy to forget your supporting side; don't let it go.
- Keep your foot well pointed and follow a clean path that's the same every time you go around.
- Bear in mind that the movements through first position from the back to the front, and vice versa, are the same as a battement tendu and require the same articulation of the foot and the same attention to turnout.

  Note: The range of motion does not exceed a semicircle; the working foot must not "*over*cross" to describe an arc greater than 180 degrees. In some schools, in order to develop speed and ensure level hips, the range of motion is smaller: not a whole semicircle, but a more limited "two o'clock" to "four o'clock."

Fondu

Fondu means "melted." It is a bending of the supporting leg. As a barre exercise, properly called battement fondu, the bending and straightening of the supporting leg is coordinated with the bending and straightening of the working leg, with the working leg starting sur le cou de-pied and extending à terre. Battement fondu développé extends to 45 or 90 degrees, but no matter how high the working leg, both legs straighten smoothly at the same moment.

Purpose

Fondu builds the strength in your supporting side that is essential for controlling your turnout in jumps that land on one leg.

Getting the Most Out of Fondu

▶ Resist the downward motion; don't collapse!
▶ Work with equal turnout on both legs.
▶ Watch the weight distribution on the supporting foot to avoid rolling in at the ankle.

Variations on Fondu

Fondus may finish with the supporting leg en relevé. Rond de jambes, fouettés, and/or tombés often appear in fondu combinations as well.

In the Soviet syllabus, in a variation called fondu double, the supporting leg bends twice. The working leg extends with the second fondu, in which the plié should be deeper to stretch the Achilles tendon even more.

Battement Frappé

Here is an especially marked difference among the schools. Frappé means "to strike or knock," and in all battements frappés, the working leg starts sur le cou-de-pied and moves out directly to the same slightly lifted position as in battement dégagé. In most schools, the working foot starts in a flexed position sur le cou-de-pied, brushes the floor to the extended position, and then returns without brushing. The accent is on the "out." In the Soviet syllabus, however, in an adoption from the French, the working foot starts from a fully stretched position sur le cou-de-pied and barely grazes the floor before extending to an angle of 22.5 degrees. The accent is on the "in," and the working foot "strikes" the supporting ankle to rebound out for the next one.

Purpose

Frappé is an essential exercise for developing a bright, speedy petit allegro. Its strong, brisk outward motion trains your legs and feet to initiate jumps with speed and force. A clear "stop and hold" at the end of the movement trains them to maintain correct, photo-op positions in the air.

Getting the Most Out of Battement Frappé

▶ Do battements frappés with speed and attack. As the name implies, they are forceful.

▶ Hold your supporting side as you extend the working foot. Engage your inner thighs and don't jiggle!

Variations on Battement Frappé

▶ Battement Frappé a Terre. Your working leg extends without brushing but finishes with the toes touching the floor. In a further variation the supporting leg pliés.

▶ Battement Frappé Double. The working foot beats sur le cou-de-pied back and then front before extending (then it alternates, the next one beats front to back and so on). This variation develops fast, strong legs for entrechats and other beats.

▶ Battement Frappé Fouetté. In this variation, unique to the R.A.D., the leg starts at 45 degrees à la seconde and moves forcefully to a modified retiré in which the working foot is below and crossed in front of, or behind, the knee of the supporting leg.

Alternate preparation.

Développé

Développé means "developed." In a développé, your working foot travels up the supporting leg, clearly showing the intermediary sur le cou-de-pied (pointed) and retiré positions, out to a sustained extension, to the front, side, or back. After the beginner level, développé is usually incorporated into a more complex adagio at the barre.

Purpose

Développé is a fundamental adagio step. Both at barre and center floor adagio's big, slow movements build strength and control. You've been concentrating on your turnout and placement throughout the entire barre; this is the test. You're warm enough to lift your leg to full height and work on your extension and your line. Développés can, and should, also be practiced at a quick tempo.

Getting the Most Out of Développé

▶ Work on alignment first, then extension; don't sacrifice form for height.

▶ Keep your supporting side solidly rooted into the floor.

▶ In développé back your upper body adjusts forward, not downward, to achieve the arabesque position. Be sure to slide your hand forward along the barre so you can manage this without twisting your shoulders.

▶ If you find barre adagio difficult, frustrating, or tedious, try what one of my own teachers, Rochelle Zide-Booth, quoting her teacher Robert Joffrey, recommended: Psyche yourself up for it; think, "Oh, yippee! adagio!" It's silly and surprisingly effective.

Grand Rond de Jambe

As in rond de jambe à terre, the foot
describes an arc from front to back or
back to front, but now your foot is off the
floor; the working leg is at 45 degrees,
90 degrees, or higher if you can maintain
your alignment.

Purpose

Often performed on stage, especially by the
woman during a pas de deux, grand rond
de jambe is a spectacular step, not just an
exercise. It requires, and builds, tremendous
strength and control in the hip joints. It
trains you to realign yourself correctly and
keep your balance during big movements
of the fully extended working leg.

**Getting the Most Out of Grand Rond
de Jambe**

▶ Don't go for extension alone; focus on
maintaining a strong, pulled-up supporting side and proper—not lifted—placement of the hips.

▶ Keep the working leg at a consistent
height, especially during that tricky
moment as the leg passes from à la
seconde to arabesque, and as it returns
from arabesque to à la seconde.

▶ Move your upper body slightly forward,
not downward, to accommodate
arabesque. The hand on the barre slides
forward, too.

Petit Battement Sur le Cou-de-Pied

Literally this means "little beating on the cou-de-pied," or "neck of the foot." Petits battements are an entire family of small, quick, beating movements in which the working foot moves repeatedly sur le cou-de-pied. In Cecchetti's method it's done standing flat; the ball of the working foot stays on the floor while the heel moves back and forth in front of and behind the supporting ankle. In other schools, both standing flat and in relevé, the working foot maintains a pointed or wrapped shape as it moves front-back-front-back.

In a different step, traditionally called petits battements serrés (petits battements battus in the Soviet syllabus), the working foot beats the ankle of the supporting foot in relevé, without alternating front and back. (Some schools beat the arch of the supporting foot.) It creates the fluttering effect famously used by Odette in *Swan Lake*.

Purpose

Like battements frappés, petits battements work on the speed you need for petit allegro and beats.

Getting the Most Out of Petit Battement Sur le Cou-de-Pied

▶ Keep the movements of the working foot small, brisk, and free.

▶ Recruit your turnout muscles and keep them strongly engaged in order to hold the working thigh and knee as still as possible.

Rond de Jambe en l'Air

Rond de jambe en l'air is a cousin to rond de jambe par terre, but it is not grand rond de jambe. In a rond de jambe en l'air, the working leg remains à la seconde as the foot moves in toward the supporting knee and back out à la seconde, tracing an oval or a "D." Both men and women perform ronds de jambe in solo variations on stage, some-times with two "circles" of the leg (infor-mally called a double rond de jambe) instead of a single one.

Purpose

Rond de jambe en l'air helps with strength, coordination, and speed, and it fortifies the knees. The knee's natural rotary capability can make it vulnerable; strengthening the surrounding area is protective.

Getting the Most Out of Rond de Jambe en l'Air

▶ Keep your working thigh lifted and turned out.

▶ Move your thigh and knee as little as possible.

▶ The path of the foot is not a circle and should not extend behind the knee. Although the Russian school calls for an oval-shaped path, most schools prefer that it be curved on one side and straight on the other, like the letter "D," with the curved part toward the front.

Barre Stretches

Many teachers dedicate a few minutes of class time to a barre stretch. Some leave you free to stretch yourself; others give a combination. Barre stretch usually involves lifting—not hoisting— your leg gracefully onto the barre, perhaps with a développé, to the front or side extension (and sometimes arabesque). Often you cambré toward and away from the working leg, sometimes sliding the foot along the barre for even more stretch, sometimes adding pliés and relevés as well.

Purpose

You're working on developing your extension and your placement when your body is warm enough to coax the muscles and connective tissue into greater length and flexibility.

Getting the Most Out of Stretching at the Barre

Even though you're focusing on your stretch, stay in proper alignment and work on keeping your hips level. Stretching should be relaxed and restful. Breathe. Enjoy it.

Grand Battement

A grand battement is a controlled throwing of the straight leg to its full extension, usually to a march or other music with a strong tempo. The step is also done "en cloche," in which the leg swings back and forth like the clapper of a bell.

Purpose

The beginning of every large jump is a grand battement. These biggest of the barre movements prepare the body for grand allegro and train the supporting side to remain still, strong, and properly aligned even when challenged by great force and momentum from the working side.

Getting the Most Out of Grand Battement

▶ Strive for height, but not at the expense of alignment or control of the hips.

▶ Resist the temptation to relax the working foot.

▶ Apply the principle of pushing down to go up; use the brush against the floor to build the force that will lift your leg.

▶ In grand battement devant the hips stay absolutely level. Concentrate on holding the pelvis and abdomen.

▶ In grand battement à la seconde the working hip must displace slightly to allow an extension greater than 90 degrees, but you should resist it as much as possible.

Remember that the side trajectory is actually slightly in front of your hips.

▶ In grand battement derrière don't let the working knee soften. Allow the upper body to move slightly forward, but be sure to keep the chest and chin lifted and the shoulders square.

Grands battements usually conclude the barre, but many teachers go on to practice pirouettes or small jumps before moving to center floor. Although the sequence of exercises listed above is typical, there are many exceptions. I once observed a professional class in Denmark in which the first exercise was a grand plié right into a grand battement.

Martha Graham, 1944.

Tour de Force

MODERN DANCE

Modern dance arose at the end of the nineteenth century in rebellion against the strict constraints of both classical ballet and Victorian society. Pioneering women like Loie Fuller and Isadora Duncan eschewed ballet vocabulary and abandoned the binding corsetry of the tutu for draperies that allowed freer, more natural movement. Fuller was almost invisible within the yards of fabric she manipulated with long sticks; Duncan danced in a flowing silk tunic to evoke the nobility of Greek architecture and the motion of ocean waves. Her rejection of "ballet music" in favor of "serious" composers like Chopin, along with her unfettered movements, greatly influenced Fokine, who went on to transform ballet.

Another trailblazer, Ruth St. Denis, was fascinated by Eastern culture and mythology; her dances were a Western reimagination of Indian and Asian dance. With her husband, Ted Shawn, she founded Denishawn and toured vaudeville. Students at their Denishawn School in Los Angeles included future pioneers Martha Graham, Doris Humphrey, and Charles Weidman. Shawn bought a farm, Jacob's Pillow, in Massachusetts as a retreat; it became one of the foremost summer dance centers in America. In 1933, to combat the stereotype of male dancers as effeminate, he formed a touring company: Ted Shawn and his Men Dancers.

Humphrey and Weidman cultivated a more lyrical style of dance, and like all modern dance it worked with the floor. Ballet denied gravity; modern dance embraced it. Graham founded her own company and developed her own technique. Her iconoclastic works remain powerful and dramatic to this day. She championed modern art, collaborating with the sculptor Isamu Noguchi for her striking décors, and commissioned scores from American composers like Aaron Copland.

Katherine Dunham and Pearl Primus drew on African and Caribbean dance, fusing them

Ted Shawn's Men Dancers rehearsing *Polonaise* at Jacob's Pillow, 1936.

with ballet and modern dance to form the roots of African American concert dance. Alvin Ailey's determination to create a multiracial dance troupe and to truly popularize modern dance led to the major company and school that bear his name.

In Europe, modern dance had its origins as much in theory as in theater. Émile Jaques-Dalcroze became interested in dance through his work in education and music, and he developed the idea of Eurythmy, which influenced Nijinsky's choreography. Rudolf Laban, of dance notation fame, taught Mary Wigman and Kurt Jooss, pioneers of expressionism in dance.

Like ballet, modern dance has a family tree, but there's more reinvention from generation to generation. It is something of an honored tradition in modern dance to learn from your teacher, then rebel and go off to create your own slant on choreography and technique. St. Denis taught Graham, who taught Merce Cunningham and Paul Taylor. Taylor taught Twyla Tharp and David Parsons. St. Denis also taught Humphrey, who taught José Limón. Wigman's student Hanya Holm taught Alwin Nikolais. Jooss's pupil Pina Bausch transformed Jooss's expressionism into Tanztheater, where dramatic effect is as important as the steps.

151

Isadora Duncan, age twelve.

Center Floor

Center floor rewards all your patient, disciplined work at the barre. Not that center floor work requires any less effort—quite the opposite—but class becomes exhilarating when you are truly dancing. While barre work usually concentrates on one exercise at a time, center floor combinations link various steps—enchaînement. They are not confined to the en croix pattern and they often travel, allowing you to move freely through space. The combinations feel "dancier": they are more likely to emphasize musicality and épaulement, the expressive use of the head and shoulders.

Every ballet class should include at least one combination from each of these broad categories: adagio, petit allegro, grand allegro, and pirouettes. In addition, center floor often begins with a separate battement tendu (yes, more tendus) combination. It may be an adagio with lots of port de bras, or an up-tempo preliminary pirouette combination. You will probably practice, both slowly and quickly, tendu en tournant, in which your body changes direction during the tendu—training the supporting side not to let go during a pivot. Balanchine eloquently demonstrated how such "simple" tendus can become a choreographic masterpiece: in the majestic opening of *Theme and Variations* the dancers execute impeccable tendus, while changing direction with precision and in perfect coordination with their elegant port de bras.

Other steps from the barre may be done center floor as well—an instant test of overdependence on the actual barre itself. Turning steps may appear in any combination, at any tempo, but most classes include at least one exercise specifically aimed at pirouettes. Révérence, the ritual of elaborate bows and curtsies that concludes most classes, is a traditional, gracious acknowledgment of your teacher, accompanist, and fellow dancers, and a final chance for you to practice your dancer's mien.

Extension croisé devant, arms allongés.

Adagio/Adage

The interchangeable terms adagio and adage describe slow, lyrical dancing. The French term "adage," preferred by English schools, derives from the Italian musical term "adagio," which means "at ease" or "at leisure." Your line, extension, balance, and turnout control are put to the test as you move with slow, fluid serenity from one elegant position to the next—all the while trying to look and feel at ease.

Adagio in the Great Ballets

Often romantic, often with themes of love sought, love found, or love lost, in adagio dancers move the audience with exquisite line, eloquent phrasing, and musical sensitivity.

Odette's first tender pas de deux with Siegfried in *Swan Lake,* in which he wins her trust, is one of ballet's most poignant adagios. Princess Aurora's Rose Adagio in *The Sleeping Beauty* is one of the grandest—her astounding series of balances with four ardent suitors a truly regal display of elegance and poise. In *Giselle,* the heroine rises from her grave, and with a slow, sustained développé à la seconde chillingly communicates the heartbreak and the horror of her fate. In the Kingdom of the Shades scene in *La Bayadère,* the hero in his desolation hallucinates; not one but multiple ghosts of his beloved appear. Their mesmerizing entrance down a ramp, in which ghost after ghost steps again and again into identical arabesque allongé in plié, creates one of the most powerful spectacles in ballet. Adagio stirs the emotions even in the absence of a story: the second movement of Balanchine's *Symphony in C,* a plotless, "pure dance" ballet, reveals the exquisite passion in Bizet's music through dance alone. Even if you don't aspire to these roles, you can enjoy the challenge of ballet at its most expressive during the adagio. Here is an opportunity to project your musicality and lyricism as well as your rock-solid stability and composure.

Extension à la seconde,
écarté.

Adagio Steps and Technique

The beauty of your line and the fluidity of your movements are every bit as important as the steps themselves, many of which are exactly what you practiced at the barre: plié, développé, grand rond de jambe, fondu, attitude, arabesque, and arabesque penchée. During center floor you connect steps and practice them in different orientations: croisé, écarté, effacé, and so forth. You often change direction with promenades, typically in attitude or arabesque, rotating your whole body by turning only the supporting heel and resolutely maintaining your position.

Improving Your Adagio

▶ The audience may be watching your working leg, but you must focus on your supporting side; your adagio depends on it. Your supporting leg and hip must be as solid as a tree trunk and, like a tree, feel rooted in the ground.

▶ If your arabesques are wobbly, practice on your own. Step into an arabesque, with the leg at a height you can control, and hold the position for a count of five. Repeat several times, always stepping onto the same leg, and make your way across the studio. By the time you reach the other side, your back muscles will be highly engaged and your arabesque more secure. Practice on both sides.

▶ Hold, hold, hold your turnout. It is better to sacrifice a little height in your extension than to distort your placement.

▶ Use the adagio to work on phrasing and on maximizing the expressive potential of the arms, head, and gaze as well as that of the legs. Your line is not just your extension, and even a spectacular extension is meaningless if not coordinated with the rest of the body.

▶ Extension is the product of strength and flexibility. To improve yours, do all you can to develop a strong supporting side, a strong back for arabesque, and strong abdominal muscles. Stretch frequently when you are warmed up (but not during class unless the teacher asks). Barre stretches and splits are excellent, but don't neglect the rest of your body. Tight, gripping muscles in the quadriceps, hips, or back, for example, can hinder your extension.

▶ Take a cue from jazz dancers and the Rockettes about front extension: practice front grands battements center floor with the supporting leg in plié. The momentum of the kick, and the freedom from the constraint of a straight supporting leg, will send your leg way up high. Once you've experienced that, you can try to recapture it in a balletically correct position. Warm up carefully and thoroughly first.

Arabesque penché en pointe.

Allegro: Petit and Grand

In music allegro means "at a brisk tempo"; in Italian it means "merry." As a ballet term, sometimes spelled the French way with an accent, allégro is "grand" when it includes big, traveling jumps and turns and "petit" when the steps are smaller and faster. Petit allegro terre à terre is the fastest of all—a merry challenge.

Petit Allegro in the Great Ballets

From La Camargo's daring eighteenth-century entrechats to Balanchine's quicksilver twentieth-century gargouillades, petit allegro has always charmed the audience. Nineteenth-century choreographers used it to communicate the dainty and even magical attributes of their characters. Most of ballet's wilis, sprites, ghosts, fairies, and nymphs dance a petit allegro to demonstrate their gravity-defying, supernatural qualities. The ethereal Sylph in Bournonville's *La Sylphide* barely touches the ground as she floats and hovers with fluttering batterie. Bournonville's style is particularly noteworthy for the clarity, buoyancy, and brilliance of his petit allegro.

Petipa, too, choreographed legendary examples: the four little swans in Act II of *Swan Lake* displayed synchronized dancing well before the Rockettes. With their arms interlocked, the cygnets skim the floor and beat their legs with every look and tilt of the head in perfect unison. In *The Sleeping Beauty* Prologue, the fifth fairy's "finger" variation includes a daunting series of pas de chats that go where men don't dare: taking off and landing on pointe. And every holiday season, throughout the land, Mirlitons, Candy Canes, and other treats bounce briskly through *The Nutcracker*'s Kingdom of the Sweets.

Grand pas de chat développé.

Grand jeté, Bournonville style, with
back leg bent and arms open.

Petit allegro showcases both male and female virtuosity. In Act II of *Giselle*, Myrtha, Queen of the Wilis, forces Albrecht to dance petit and grand allegro until he dies of exhaustion. The "killer" steps are entrechats or brisés volés. Often it's a friendly competition between the sexes, such as *Tarantella* (either Balanchine's or Bournonville's), or Petipa's "Bluebird Pas de Deux," a showpiece of dueling petit allegros at their most bravura and one of the most challenging pas de deux in ballet.

Grand Allegro in the Great Ballets

Those moments in performance that are so thrilling and unexpected that the audience gasps, or even breaches decorum to applaud midvariation, those moments when dancers devour space, attain and maintain amazing elevation, change position midair, and land with effortless precision—those grand allegro moments are ballet at its most electrifying.

Men get to shine in grand allegro. The performances of dancers like Nijinsky, Nureyev, and Baryshnikov are legendary. Male dancers are expected to perform double tours en l'air, sometimes landing on one knee, sometimes—like the sailor in Jerome Robbins's *Fancy Free*—into a split. Basilio's variation in *Don Quixote*, with its soaring double sauts de basque en dedans, never fails to draw applause. At the end of a variation the man often executes a series of jumps en manège, circling the stage while arcing through coupé jetés en tournant, his legs in a split at the apex of each jump.

Women's grand allegro has come a long way since the days when it was shocking for a ballerina to perform a cabriole. In the nineteenth-century classics, the man's tours are often complemented by the woman's fouettés, and matching his manège is her circle of turning steps—often lickety-split chaînés and double piqués. In the *Don Quixote* variation mentioned above, Kitri replies to Basilio's leaps with a signature jump of her own, a grand jeté with her back leg bent to graze the back of her head. In *Giselle*, the Queen of the Wilis commands the stage as well as her subjects with her huge, sailing grand jetés. Balanchine emphasized female prowess and gave women double sauts de basques and double tours en l'air, among other challenges. As more choreographers recognize the virtuosity, strength, and stamina of the ballerina, more of the so-called men's steps may go the way of the cabriole.

Saut de basque.

Pas de poisson

Allegro Steps and Technique

The vocabularies of petit and grand allegro, as well as the midsized "medium" allegro, overlap. The scale of movement and the briskness of the tempo differentiate them. Jeté and pas de chat, for example, can be either small, delicate filigrees or flying leaps that cover almost half the stage—or something in between. Most allegro steps have both petit and grand versions. Because ballet's jumps can change personality depending on tempo, and change further when done battu (with beats) or en tournant (while turning), it's useful to think of them as families of jumps, families defined by how you push off and how you land.

Changement and soubresaut push off from two feet and land on two feet. Because they are relatively simple and easily mastered, beginners usually study them first. Changement, which also makes a good warm-up for advanced steps, starts and finishes in fifth position, but the feet switch places in midair. One of my teachers liked to make us do sixty-four at a time and would insist that we smile through the last thirty-two.

In soubresaut the feet do not change position; it is both a warm-up step and—with a *slightly* arched back, knees *slightly* bent, and arms in third arabesque—a featured one made famous in *Giselle*. It is also an example of treacherous terminology: some schools define it as a traveling step, some as one that stays in place. Some would just call it a sauté in fifth position.

Assemblé pushes off from one foot while the other brushes out, then lands on both feet; the legs "assemble" in the air. Assemblé is not only a major step in its own right, it is an important exercise for developing the strength and speed in the inner thighs that you need for batterie and the more advanced ballonné.

Jetés brush one leg outward then land on that leg. Jetés and assemblés come in all sizes, travel in all directions (or remain in place), and lend themselves to numerous beats, turns, and other variations.

Sissonne pushes off from two feet and lands on one. It also offers a multitude of variations, including "ouverte" (open) and "fermé" (closed). The leg that remains off the ground can be fully extended or in a bent position; if it closes right away, it is sissonne fermé. In the Cecchetti system sissonne is called "temps levé" if one foot finishes in sur le cou-de-pied. Temps levé is another tricky term, however; in certain lexicons it is a jump that takes off from and lands on two feet, and in others it takes off from and lands on just one. This version really challenges that one foot; your elevation relies on how powerfully you can point it to push off.

Pas de chat, or step of the cat, is a light jump from one leg to the other, each passing through retiré— like galloping but turned out. The photo-op variation is grand pas de chat développé, in which the leading leg extends fully in the air. You don't add beats to a pas de chat, but you can add a double rond de jambe for each leg while you're in the air, transforming it into the notoriously difficult gargouillade.

The most spectacular—and for many dancers the most fun—allegro steps are the jumps that turn or change direction in midair. These include saut de basque, rivoltade, grand fouetté sauté, grand jeté entrelacé (also known as grand jeté entournant and abbreviated to tour jeté), and tour en l'air.

Batterie

Entrechat six.

Embellishing allegro's quick, light jumps with batterie (beats) adds much to its sparkle—and its difficulty.

To perform a step "battu" you "beat" your thighs: crisscross your legs in the air so they switch places. Certain steps don't switch feet; you separate your legs just enough to smartly close and open them again, producing the effect of clapping your legs as you might clap your hands. It's really the thighs, not the feet or the ankles, that beat.

Almost any jump can be performed battu; additionally some steps—such as brisés, cabrioles, and entrechats—are beats by definition.

Cabriole and brisé beat the legs at an angle to the body. Cabrioles can be done to the front, side, or back, with the angle of the legs ranging from very slight to above 90 degrees. Brisé is a traveling variant of assemblé battu. The effect of brisés is amplified when they are performed one after the other in quick succession. Done alternately from front to back, the step becomes the spectacular brisé volé.

Entrechats begin with the relatively simple royale. Louis XIV is said to have invented this step in his attempts to master entrechat quatre. But this is disputed, and some maintain that Louis's royale was actually an

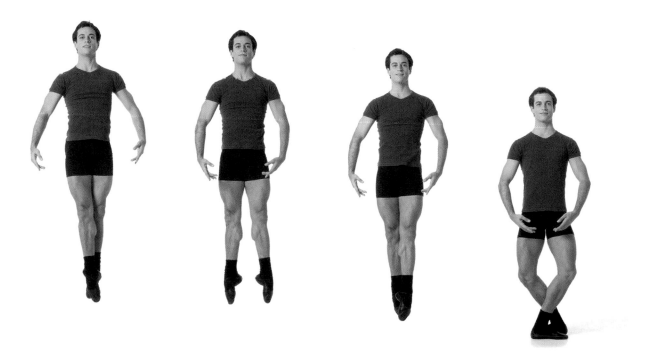

entrechat cinq. Known as changement battu in the English system, royale is most often a changement with a beat at the beginning. Getting it right, so it doesn't just look like a sticky changement, is actually more difficult than entrechat quatre because it requires opening the legs to a small but clear second position en l'air before beating.

As the numbers grow bigger the steps become harder. In entrechat quatre, or entrechat four, the legs cross twice in the air so you land in the same position you started from. Each crossing of the legs raises the number by two; an entrechat six crosses the legs three times in midair. The front leg goes to the back, then returns front, then ends in back. The terminology is not so mysterious if you think of it this way: each opening of the legs counts as one, and each closing of the legs counts as one.

Entrechats can travel (an entrechat de volée, "flying"), or land on one foot with the other in sur le cou-de-pied. In most schools even-numbered entrechats land on two legs, odd on one: an entrechat trois is a royale that ends with one leg sur le cou-de-pied front or back, an entrechat cinq is an entrechat quatre landing the same way.

Glissade shown with elevation. It is traditionally a terre à terre step
in which the toes barely leave the floor.

Pas de chat.

Connecting Steps

Anticipation—or apprehension—of a challenging featured step can make it easy to overlook the simpler step leading into it. Glissade, coupé, pas de bourré, chassé, balancé, failli, pas couru, and tombé often precede something flashier. Done neatly and correctly, connecting steps add elegance to your dancing and provide the preparation you need to launch what comes next; done carelessly they dull your polish and undermine the propulsion needed for elevation and ballon. Imagine trying to perform grand jeté from a stationary position. The successful timing and coordination of grand jeté or any difficult jump depends on the rhythm, the momentum, and especially the final plié of the connecting step that comes first.

Improving Your Allegro

▶ Push off the floor with your whole foot, all the way down to your toes. It increases your elevation and ensures that your feet will be beautifully pointed in the air.

▶ Land through your whole foot, toe-ball-heel, into an easy, elastic plié. Some teachers allow the heels to remain off the floor to achieve extra speed in certain types of allegro, but pressing the heels down provides a more secure base for your landings and a larger push for your takeoffs.

▶ Correct port de bras helps your elevation, but don't use your arms to hurl yourself into the air. Keep your shoulders down and your neck free of tension.

▶ Enlist the music to help you with timing. Let the rhythm in the music cue your take-offs. In petit allegro when it's really fast, don't panic. Instead of trying to make it through a list of steps without being late, think of matching the end of each step to the appropriate beat in the music. Concentrating on the closing, on the "down" and "in" rather than on the initiating and "out," helps keep you on top of the music.

▶ Breeeeeathe. If you hold your breath, you freeze in the air and the jump ends. In karate, students actually practice shouting; at designated points in the exercise they empty their lungs by screaming "kiaiiii." The purpose is to keep them breathing (and to add power to a movement and startle an opponent). Since dancers aren't permitted this helpful trick, you must remember to make yourself breathe.

Grand jeté.

Brisé volé.

Improving Your Batterie

You strive to move and change direction as quickly as a hummingbird, while at the same time keeping your footwork clean and precise. Speed and beats come more naturally to some physiques than to others. If you have a tight body, bowed legs, or trouble with extension, take heart: you may have an easier time than the dancer with the flexible body who excels in adagio. If you are naturally loose, you may have to work harder on batterie.

▶ Strive for clean positions and don't cut corners. Speed doesn't matter if it's sloppy.

▶ Start beating on the way up.

▶ Work on the "in" in battements tendus during barre. Close them decisively.

▶ A good after-class exercise is to face the barre, palms lightly resting on it, and stand on one leg. Flex the other foot and bring it smartly into fifth position to the front, then the back, and repeat, keeping the foot flexed the entire time. Think about the tops of your inner thighs and how they work to bring your legs together.

▶ For extra-brilliant beats and entrechats, like the ones the men of the Bolshoi do, open the legs to a small second position in the air before you beat them. The extra movement makes it harder but adds great excitement and clarity to the jump.

▶ In entrechat six, don't think of it as beating once on the way up and twice on the way down. Start beating immediately and think of the feet not as "out-in-out-in-out-in" but as "in-in-in."

Turns

The ballerina spinning like a figurine on a music box is part of ballet's enduring magic. Although even some highly accomplished dancers confess to "turn anxiety," for most who experience the glee of mastering them, turns are pure fun. And like soaring jumps, they are what the audience loves to see.

Turns in the Great Ballets

For more than a century ballerinas have been stopping the show with thirty-two fouettés. The first was Pierina Legnani, an early adopter of blocked pointe shoes and the creator of the famous series of thirty-two fouettés in *Swan Lake*. Some modern-day ballerinas, like American Ballet Theatre's Gillian Murphy, routinely insert double and even triple fouettés into the sequence, making for a truly breathtaking display.

With a few notable exceptions—the lead male in *Études*, for example— men seldom perform fouettés, which are more impressive on pointe than on demi-pointe. Not to be outdone, they do multiple turns à la seconde. Frederick Ashton used the turning gifts of the original Blue Boy, the wonderfully named Harold Turner, in *Les Patineurs* (*The Skaters*). As easily and quickly as if the stage were really ice, the young man executes tours Italiannes as the curtain falls. He spins and spins in plié with his leg à la seconde doing quick hops; the curtain then rises to show him still spinning before it closes once again.

A bravura ending for a ballerina's variation, and the counterpart of the man's virtuosic jumping version, is a manège, a series of turns circling the stage, the faster the better. For Sugar Plum Fairies in *The Nutcracker*, it's often a manège of dazzling piqués; for Aurora in *The Sleeping Beauty*, it's a brilliant coupé jeté en tournant, piqué, soutenu, châiné combination.

When it comes to piqués and pirouettes, women aren't expected to turn more than two without a partner. In *Allegro Brillante,* however, Balanchine instructed the ballerina to escalate her turns in the same way the music builds. If her first pirouette is a double, the next must be triple, and so forth. It happens when the orchestra stops playing, leaving only piano cadenzas for support. There's nothing else to look at onstage, nowhere else for the eye to go; she must do them perfectly.

The corps de ballet usually performs simpler turns, not for lack of technique (quite the opposite: many corps dancers can do thirty-two fouettés) but because it's hard for a group to turn in unison at the same speed. When it does, however, the effect is unforgettable. In Balanchine's *Serenade,* all the dancers do slow single piqué turns in a massive circle around the stage like orbiting planets in the heavens. In the finale to his *Western Symphony,* the entire cast turns single pirouettes from fifth position even while the curtain is falling. Fokine was really clever: in his *Polovtsian Dances* he wanted the ensemble of warriors to pirouette, then land on one knee with bows raised, all at the same instant; so he had them turn to the left, ensuring that nobody's pirouettes would go on too long.

Turns in the Movies

Unlike jumps, which can lose their impressiveness on film, turns look great in the movies. You can see Mikhail Baryshnikov's incredible pirouettes à la seconde in *The Turning Point* or watch him make more than ten revolutions from a single preparation in *White Nights. The Red Shoes,* starring Moira Shearer, shows turns from the ballerina's point of view as she looks out into the audience. Alfred Hitchcock used turns to create unbearable suspense in *Torn Curtain:* the hero, his life in danger, tries to hide in the audience but is "spotted" by the communist bad-gal ballerina played by Tamara Toumanova, who glares at him again and again with each turn.

Types of Turns and Turning Technique

Pirouette.

Turns can be quick and delicate, like needle-work embroidering the stage, or huge, bold, and sweeping. The term for any turn in ballet is "tour," which includes turns that travel, turns in the air, turns on one leg, or turns that change legs. You turn either en dehors or en dedans, outward or inward. En dehors turns rotate away from your supporting leg, en dedans turns rotate toward it. If you're standing on your left leg and you are turning to the right, you are turning en dehors.

Although spinning on one's heels or knees (or even head) might appear in modern choreography, in classical ballet all turns à terre are performed with the weight on the front of the foot. You turn on full pointe, demi-pointe or, for promenades and certain steps en tournant with the heel just slightly raised. You can also change position during a turn; for example, a pirouette in retiré can end in arabesque.

Following are the most frequently practiced turns, but you may also encounter emboîtés, flic-flac turns, glissades en tournant, and pirouettes sautillés (see Glossary) as well.

Pirouette, whirl, is a turn in place, on one leg en relevé. In the basic version the preparation is from fourth position demi-plié, the working leg held in retiré and the arms in front.

You can also prepare from demi-plié in first or second position, or from fifth position demi- and even grand plié. Different schools teach different preparations from fourth position. Some require that the back leg be straight, others that it be bent. Some

Alternative pirouette preparation.

want the arms to be rounded with the palms facing in; others want the arms fully extended with the palms facing down.

You can pirouette in sur le cou-de-pied, or in more open positions such as arabesque, front or back attitude, fourth front, or à la seconde—these are known as grand pirouettes.

Fouetté rond de jambe en tournant means "whipped rond de jambe while turning." Dancers usually shorten the term for these complicated turns to fouettés. After a simple pirouette or pas de bourrée en tournant en dedans as a preparation, the working leg moves to a front extension as you plié, then "whips" out to a side extension and back in to retiré as you rise. This whipping action propels you around and you repeat it, up to

and beyond that magic number thirty-two. Fouetté turns can be done in place or traveling. As any dancer can ruefully tell you, sometimes the traveling isn't planned. Legnani was happy to demonstrate her remarkable control over traveling: she could place a ruble—a Russian coin—on the studio floor, trace a circle around it, and turn her thirty-two fouettés without straying beyond the circle.

Fouettés are usually done en dehors. Fouetté turns en dedans, rarely seen and tremendously difficult, were once a requirement of the Royal Academy of Dance. You couldn't pass your Advanced Exam without mastering them.

Piqué turns, or "pricked turns," are traveling turns on one leg. Rather than relevé up

Pirouette Tips from the Pros: Gillian Murphy

Gillian Murphy is a principal dancer at American Ballet Theatre. She trained in South Carolina and then at the North Carolina School of the Arts. She was a finalist at the Jackson International Competition, a recipient of the Hope Prize at the Prix de Lausanne, and a winner of the Princess Grace Award.

"Turning is a gift, though it requires a certain dynamic and a certain fearlessness."

Gillian's breakthrough with turns came when she was practicing the Black Swan pas de deux . . . at age eleven! She was trying to build up to thirty-two fouettés and polish her multiple pirouettes. Her father was

watching and explained that centrifugal force would pull her arms away from her body and slow her down. By gradually pulling her arms in while turning, Gillian was able to resist centrifugal force and maintain the tight, compact position needed for fast fouettés and multiple pirouettes.

▷ Don't move your front heel before you turn.

▷ Push off with both legs but keep your weight forward.

▷ Relevé strongly and quickly. Pull up from the back of the leg right under your buttocks to get on your supporting leg.

▷ Use your spot. Free the head and relax the upper body.

▷ Good turns come from your work throughout the barre and center, especially from pliés, relevés, and petit allegro.

▷ You know both a good and a bad turn immediately, and in a bad turn, you know to cut your losses. A good turn feels easy.

▷ Don't sacrifice form. There's no point to lots of turns without form. In fact, everyone just wants them to stop.

▷ There's a smaller turning surface when turning on pointe but not much difference in placement. You feel higher off the ground.

▷ You gain mastery through repetition—but not repetition of your mistakes. Make sure to practice correctly.

onto the supporting leg as in a pirouette, you step out onto it, keeping it absolutely straight at all times.

Chaîné, informally, or tours chaînés déboulés, are traveling turns using both legs. Déboulé suggests unrolling, like a ball of yarn. You step from one leg to the other, back and forth, while turning one half turn with each step. You always turn in the same direction, so with each step you are alternating your half turns en dedans and en dehors.

Soutenu en tournant, short for assemblé soutenu en tournant, or sustained while turning, is a full turn in fifth position in which the feet change position as you turn. It can travel or stay in place. Most schools start from a simple tendu or tendu dégagé à la seconde with a bent supporting leg; the

French school begins the step with a demi-rond de jambe out to tendu à la seconde. Think of drawing your thighs together and gathering your legs underneath yourself. Soutenu en tournant is often used to change sides at the barre, as is demi-detourné, the simple half turn toward the back foot.

Spotting

Along with her special reinforced pointe shoes, Pierina Legnani had another secret weapon for turning multiple pirouettes: spotting, developed by the Italian school in the late nineteenth century. Supposedly the Italians guarded spotting like a trade secret and practiced their pirouettes only in locked studios with the blinds drawn. Spotting

Pirouette Tips from the Pros: Ethan Stiefel

Ethan Stiefel is a principal dancer at American Ballet Theatre. He trained at Milwaukee Ballet School, Central Pennsylvania Youth Ballet, and the School of American Ballet before rising through the ranks at New York City Ballet and joining ABT as a principal in 1997. He won a silver medal at the Prix de Lausanne in 1989 and was the star of the film *Center Stage*.

"Turning is the most mysterious skill and the hardest part of technique to talk about."

▶ Learn to turn first. Form is important, but it comes later. Get the coordination of the spot first, and then clean up your position.

▶ There's a moment of stillness essential to the preparation of a turn.

For me it's at the outset in fifth position, before the quick rond de jambe into fourth. Power and momentum in the pirouette actually originate in that moment.

▶ Relax and exhale so you can float through your turn.

▶ Get to retiré position quickly. I prefer a high retiré above the knee, but there isn't necessarily one perfect position.

▶ Success in a turn depends on a strong center. Strength and calmness come from your center; when doing air turns it's your only friend.

▶ There are turns, there are pirouettes, and then there are spins. Don't squeeze out an extra pirouette on stage; don't throw in the ugly one.

▶ The music decides when a turn is done, and the turn decides for itself; its momentum tells you to finish.

▶ My favorite pirouettes are plain old pirouettes en dehors in retiré. It's a perfect position. There's a reason we turn in this position. Clean never goes out of style.

▶ Turns en dehors felt natural to me, but en dedans did not. What helped was a change in attitude. Don't think of turning as a numbers thing. Do the right thing to set yourself up and let it happen.

▶ Repetition is the key. To improve your turns, practice them over and over again.

179

enables a dancer to turn without becoming dizzy; it is essential that you perfect spotting and make it automatic. Find a spot slightly above eye level, and hold your gaze on that spot until the last possible moment in your turn, then quickly snap your head around and find the spot again immediately. For performances there is often a light at the back of the theater for this purpose.

Practice spotting for pirouettes. Find your spot and without relevé slowly turn yourself around in place. As you turn your body, leave your head behind, eyes fixed on your spot. When you've turned too far to be able to keep your head there, snap it quickly back to the front and find the spot again. Really use your eyes to look for and lock onto your spot.

Practice spotting for chaînés. Put your right hand on your right shoulder with the elbow out to the side, left side the same way. Pick your spot and turn your body so that your right elbow points to it. Without moving your head, and keeping your eyes on your spot, turn 180 degrees to the right so your left elbow points to the spot. Quickly turn your head to the right as far as you can, and turn your body another 180 degrees to the right again. Repeat traveling across the floor. Do this first without, then with, the relevé.

Correct Turning Position

In most schools, correct pirouette position means that the toe of the working foot touches the side of the supporting knee. In others, the toe of the working foot rests just in front of and below the supporting knee. When first practicing piqué turns, Vaganova and R.A.D. students place the foot in front because it often results in a more turned-out working leg.

Improving Your Turns

▶ Think about really holding your turnout—both in the working and the supporting leg. Be "on your leg": turn in a high, perfectly aligned relevé. You should be able to balance easily in your turning position. Practice extra balances at the barre if necessary.

▶ Be definite about the position of your working leg; it goes immediately to a clean position and stays there.

▶ Keep your weight slightly forward and your chin slightly lifted.

▶ Support your torso with your stomach and back; they should feel strong and engaged.

▶ Think of initiating the turn with your back rather than your arms. Don't use your arms to hurl yourself around. Hold them neatly in position; it is tempting to overcross them in front or to let the elbows sag.

▶ Finish your turns. Ideally you sustain your balance for an extra moment at the end of the turn before the working leg moves gracefully to its clear, final position. Your demeanor is the same whether you turn nine flawless pirouettes or lose your balance before you even make it around once. You can rescue turns gone wrong by finishing with aplomb—an important survival skill for performing.

▶ Know when to leave it alone. Lots of patient practice is required, but if you feel frustrated and tired and as though nothing is working even after sincere extra attempts, then let it rest and resume the next day. The same applies to tours en l'air.

▶ If you're one of those lucky natural turners, your challenge is to work on form and go from spinning to turning. If turns don't come naturally, think of getting "up on" the supporting leg, practice spotting, and work on the feeling of turning. Some dancers need to overcome a little fear about spinning. You may need to force yourself through multiple turns. A good way to master the double pirouette is to try for a triple; naturally you don't want the extra momentum to compromise your form and make you sloppy, but sometimes you just have to go for it. Once you've got the hang of multiple turns, it's quality over quantity.

Révérence

No matter how exhilarating the final grand allegro, no matter how much you might prefer to jeté right out the door, class isn't over. The conclusion is révérence, the acknowledgment of your teacher; of your accompanist; and of ballet's own traditions of courtesy, elegance, and respect.

In some classes, révérence is an unchanging ritual; in others, the teacher may choreograph a different one each time. It can be a simple curtsy with basic port de bras—or a bow for men—or a more elaborate series of steps with sweeping, ornate port de bras and several changes of direction. Either way, don't shortchange it. Révérence is not that demanding technically, but there's still much you can learn from it. And if you did not meet the technical demands of class to your own satisfaction, you can find some redemption in the loveliness of your révérence. Practice smooth, flowing port de bras with beautiful hands and elegant épaulement; you can never do it often enough. Bowing and curtsying need practice to be graceful; in this country they are no longer a regular part of daily life. Révérence develops your good manners and prepares you for the stage and your relationship to the audience. Make it grand, as if you were already on stage.

Ballet is larger than life; it's not just about who we are but what we can become. Today you thank your teacher for helping you and you thank the pianist for the beautiful music. One day you may thank your partner for dancing with you, the conductor for the beautiful music, and your audience for their applause.

Tour de Force

NIJINSKY

Nijinsky was a superstar. His virtuosity, especially his huge, light jump, astounded audiences, who had never seen anything like him. Rumors abounded: did he have bones like a bird in his foot that enabled him to soar? Marie Rambert said of his prodigious elevation: "I don't know how far from the ground it was, but I know it was near the stars." Nijinsky's great roles were exotic or fantastic: the Favorite Slave in *Schéhérazade*, the puppet in *Petroushka*, the spectre of a rose who soars out a window.

Born to Polish parents and trained at the Maryinsky, Vaslav Nijinsky (1889–1950) danced classic roles at the Imperial Theater before joining Diaghilev's troupe. He made only four ballets, each radical in its own way. *L'Après-midi d'un Faune*, 1912, was a Greek frieze come to life and shocking for its sensuality. *Jeux*, 1913, which mixed naturalistic movements with ballet, depicted a man and two women flirting on a tennis court. His final work, *Till Eulenspiegel*, 1916, the story of the merry prankster of German legend, was created in New York.

But Nijinsky's crowning achievement was *Le Sacre du Printemps*, 1913. It caused riots at its premiere. Paris wasn't ready for Nijinsky's

brew of influences and ideas: primitivism, modernism, fauvism, and Dalcroze's theories of Eurythmy. The harsh, pounding music by Stravinsky, the primitive-looking décor by Nicholas Roerich, the very subject of human sacrifice, and the choreography that abandoned any semblance of traditional ballet—there was hissing in the audience almost from the first notes and bedlam by the climactic Dance of the Chosen One. But *Sacre* was a modernist masterpiece, predicting the future while looking at the past.

On a South American tour the same year Nijinsky married a young Hungarian woman, Romola de Pulszky. When the company returned, a jealous and betrayed Diaghilev fired him. Nijinsky suffered from schizophrenia; in 1919 he had a nervous breakdown that ended his career. He spent the rest of his life in hospitals and asylums.

Even to this day Nijinsky's legend—his supernatural jump, his feral and androgynous quality, his tempestuous relationship with Diaghilev, his madness—remains so powerful that it sometimes overshadows his artistry as a dancer and choreographer.

Musicality

There is an essential interconnectedness between music and dance. The poet Ezra Pound wrote, "Music begins to atrophy when it departs too far from the dance." Dance, especially ballet, doesn't often renounce audible music or rhythm—Jerome Robbins's *Moves,* a work performed in silence, notwithstanding—but it's easy to take music for granted, or to treat it merely as a means of keeping time. Listen to the music: it inspires, it motivates, and it actually helps you to dance better.

Music provides the fundamental pulse; its rhythm and tempo indicate where you should be at certain specific moments. In some modern-dance classes the accompaniment is almost that minimal—just a drummer. But even a lone drumbeat can suggest the quality and the character of movement; its accents can remind you to brush out forcefully or close quickly. When melody and harmony join rhythm and tempo, music offers abundant information and guidance to the dancer.

Allow the personality of the music to bring out the same in yourself. If the music is bold and big, dance bold and big. Delicate music calls for delicate dancing. Unless a choreographer is trying for a special effect, let staccato or pizzicato music inspire your own sharpness, clarity, and attack. Let legato music help you fluidly connect your steps in smooth, supple, elongated lines. Work on becoming versatile enough to do either comfortably.

Then take it to the next level and consider the phrasing. Movement phrases connect individual steps the same way that musical phrases connect individual notes. Think of your dancing as a pearl necklace: each pearl is beautiful by itself, but the whole necklace is the thing. Listen for the way the music arcs or changes dynamic; notice the climaxes and cadences. Think about what you would emphasize were you to sing the melody line and shape your dancing accordingly.

Being "on the music" means that you reach the correct position on the appropriate count. Being "late" or "behind the music" means that you are not getting where you must be on time. Musicality, however, is more than just being on the music. It's the ability to hear subtle qualities and structures within the music and then communicate them through your dancing.

Musical training and learning to read music can only help you as a dancer; at a minimum listen to music outside class to improve your musicality. You can train yourself to identify rhythm by simply allowing your hand to beat gently along with the music. It will automatically accent the downbeat, enabling you to differentiate, for example, a march, which is in 4/4 time (four beats to a measure), from a waltz, which is in 3/4 time (three beats to a measure). Next time you hear Tchaikovsky's "Waltz of the Flowers" from *The Nutcracker* listen for the "one two three one two three" rhythm that makes it a waltz. Then try Prokofiev's "Dance of the Knights" from *Romeo and Juliet* for the heavy "one two one two one two" of its rhythm. Bring that improved listening skill with you into class and graduate to more complicated music.

Musicality also helps solve problems. When a turn isn't working, or you're behind in a speedy combination, listen to the rhythm and accent of the music. You may turn better by changing your rhythm, or jump quicker by changing the accent. Music can give you the push you need to get through a long, tough combination. When you're flagging, ride the music the way a surfer rides the waves. You won't run out of breath so quickly.

Your teacher may exhort you not to rely on counting—"Count money, not music," is a favorite— in order to encourage musical sensitivity and discourage robotic dancing. While cultivating your own musicality is extremely important, don't lose sight of the fact that counting is still an essential skill for dancers. Some dancers are naturally musical, but for those who need time to develop an ear, counting helps. If you are in a group or dancing to complex music, counting gets everyone moving in unison. Some choreography just needs to be counted. Toward the end of *Concerto Barocco*, for example, the dancers hop and move their arms in fast counts of four while the music is in slow counts of three. If they didn't count, they'd be hopelessly confused.

But even counting doesn't work in every situation. The rhythms of Stravinsky's complex, exciting score for *The Rite of Spring* shift constantly, and some sections are virtually uncountable. The music gave the dancers such trouble that at the premiere in 1913, the choreographer, Nijinsky, told them to simply follow his count while he stood on a chair and shouted from the wings. Unfortunately, the ballet caused the audience to riot (see Nijinsky, page 182) and the dancers couldn't hear him above the pandemonium.

Music for Ballet

"Ballet music" was once a pejorative term. Mediocre composers producing music to order resulted in some forgettable scores. (Choreographers frequently commissioned music "by the yard" to suit their narrative needs, e.g., eight bars of Queen's entrance followed by twenty-four bars of peasants dancing, etc.) But composers such as Délibes, Glazunov, and Tchaikovsky (even when he *was* composing to order), proved that ballet music can be brilliant, and beloved of listeners far removed from its intended audience. Stravinsky's commissioned scores for *Petroushka*, *Firebird*, and *The Rite of Spring* are undisputed masterpieces of twentieth-century music.

Choreography has increased the renown of acknowledged important pieces like Debussy's *Afternoon of a Faun* and Rimsky-Korsakov's *Schéhérazade*. And it has brought recognition to music that, for whatever reason, had been underappreciated: Bizet's *Symphony in C,* for example, to which Balanchine created an enormously popular work.

In more recent times, the emergence of minimalism in music, especially in the works of such composers as Philip Glass and Steve Reich, has influenced and inspired numerous choreographers. Jerome Robbins, Eliot Feld, and Laura Dean—to name just three—have experimented with choreography that, like the music, repeats a simple step or motif over and over, with almost imperceptible changes, creating a mesmerizing overall effect.

Usually music sets the tone and the ambience, complementing and reinforcing the choreography. Like Duncan, Fokine, and Diaghilev before him, George Balanchine took it further. An accomplished musician himself, Balanchine did perhaps more than any other choreographer to elevate the music of ballet. Many of his works are without stories and without scenery, so a viewer's attention is completely on the dancing and the music—and what great music! Balanchine selected and commissioned superb works; he chose Stravinsky, Bach, Tchaikovsky, Gershwin, Brahms, Hindemith, Sousa, Ives, and Ravel, to name just a few. They range from the easily accessible to the atonal, dense, and difficult. In many ways, his works are ballets about their music. His choreography, with its nuanced grasp of musical structures, illuminates each score. It has often been said that Balanchine's dances let you see the music. He himself was known to say that if the audience did not care for the dancing, they could close their eyes and still enjoy the show.

All About Pointe

Pointework's possibilities have intrigued and inspired choreographers since its beginnings. The pointe shoe transforms the dancer and her dancing. It elongates: its conical shape extends and tapers the line of the leg. It elevates: dancers are about four to five inches taller on pointe. It creates an illusion of effortless grace and lightness as the dancer skims the floor, spins, and sustains balances. Dancers are athletes and pointe shoes are athletic shoes. But dancers are artists first, and no other athletic shoe looks like elegant lingerie, or alters its wearer's appearance so beautifully.

Pointe shoes also have a certain mystique. They are a universal symbol of ballet, a logo seen on everything from key chains to mouse pads to coffee mugs. One might think they had been around forever. Actually, dancing "sur les pointes" or "en pointe" has been part of ballet's aesthetic only since the 1830s. For two centuries before that, ballerinas wore flat slippers or low heels. Pointe dancing is a relatively new development, and the hard pointe shoes used today are newer still.

The Rise of the Ballerina

The first toe-dancing shoes were merely satin slippers, much like today's technique slippers. They had leather soles and some darning on the sides and under, not on, their pointy tips. They fitted like kid gloves and were just stiff enough for a tremendously strong dancer like Marie Taglioni (see Pioneers of Pointe, page 118) to achieve a brief, thrilling balance on pointe. It must have been a lot like dancing barefoot.

Toe-dancing slippers underwent a significant construction change toward the end of the nineteenth century when Italian ballerinas further reinforced the toes of their shoes, creating the forerunner of the modern toe box. These "blocked" toes enabled the dancer to sustain much longer balances and to turn multiple pirouettes on pointe. The shoes were less supportive than those of today, and still pointy at the tip, but the extra box strength revolutionized ballet technique, and choreography along with it.

Virginia Zucchi, of tutu fame (see Tutu Much: Ballet Costumes, page 72), Pierina Legnani, of fouetté fame (see Pioneers of Pointe, page 118), and their compatriots changed ballet forever when they traveled to St. Petersburg with their reinforced shoes. Better shoes, along with their robust Italian technique and their newly developed trick of spotting their turns, gave them an enormous advantage over their less-well-shod Russian rivals. Not to be outdanced, the Russian ballerinas quickly adopted reinforced shoes.

The cobblers of the day obliged their customers as best they could with the materials available to them. There were no durable synthetics or shock-absorbing foam cushions in the 1890s, so shoemakers had to rely on what they had: burlap, leather, paper, canvas, and glue. Anna Pavlova was probably among the first to add a reinforcing leather midsole. (This, supposedly, was part of her secret shoe preparations. She is also said to have danced on shoes with wider platforms, then later to have retouched all her photographs to make the tips appear narrower, preserving the Romantic ideal of dancing on the tiniest point.)

Over the years pointe shoes grew heavier and sturdier, widened at the platform, and evolved into different shapes and styles, but even today most are still made the old way. It was not until the late twentieth century that synthetic components made from thermoplastic elastomers and urethane foams were successfully introduced into pointe shoe design.

Advances in female ballet technique owe a debt to advances in ballet shoes. Camargo (see page 22) danced better when she removed the heels; Taglioni, by darning her slippers, furthered the ballerina's rise to preeminence; Legnani and Pavlova took female virtuosity further still with reinforced boxes and shanks. These great and resourceful dancers improved their shoes, thereby expanding their vocabularies and pushing the limits of technique. What new possibilities will today's dancers explore with theirs?

How a Pointe Shoe Works

The pointe shoe supports you with its toe box and its stiff midsole, called the shank. In engineering terms, the shoe transfers the load onto these components so that your weight rests not on your toes but on the oval-shaped platform at the end of the box. The shank presses underneath your arch and the box tightly encases the forefoot. That's why a shoe that is too wide is painful and a shoe that fits snugly is not: the shoe must hug your foot so that the box can do its job. The vamp contributes by preventing you from falling forward out of the shoe; it enables the shank to do its work by keeping the sole of your foot firmly in place on pointe.

The Inside: Shanks and Boxes

The first shanks were made of stiff leather. But leather alone proved unworkable when dancers began to ask more of their shoes: to obtain the requisite stiffness and durability, the leather would have to have been unacceptably thick.

Today most traditionally made shoes have a shank made from a thin, stiff material, usually fiberboard, cardboard, or other type of specially treated paper product. Sometimes there is an additional reinforcing strut as well. Fiberboard will break, and some dancers deliberately "crack" their shoes in a specific place in order to control exactly how and where the shoe bends. Once broken in, the shank begins to deteriorate, and many pointe shoes become unusable after only one performance. Steel has been tried and rejected for its lack of pliability.

The front of the shoe, which started out as nothing but soft satin with a little darning to reinforce it, has evolved into a substantial toe box, sometimes called the block. People often ask if pointe shoes are made of wood; the clomping of hard toe boxes on stage makes it sound as if they are.

Many pointe shoes are still blocked the traditional way: strips of burlap, canvas, or even newspaper—you can actually read the classified ads—are saturated in glue then layered like papier-mâché. With wear the traditionally made box softens and conforms to the foot, but optimum suppleness usually lasts only a short while before the box becomes too soft and deforms. This can create misalignment on pointe and may explain why female ballet dancers suffer more ankle injuries than do men, who do not dance on pointe, or than do modern dancers, who are usually barefoot. Dancers developed several ways of prolonging the life of the traditional box. By painting the insides with floor wax or shellac, ballerinas were actually plasticizing their own shoes long before synthetic toe boxes came along.

It may seem astonishing that pointe shoe design remained fundamentally unchanged for so long, given the obvious limitations of the nineteenth-century construction materials and the advent of technology that advanced other types of footwear. But—and here I speak from personal experience—introducing modern materials into pointe shoe construction is far from straightforward.

In ballet aesthetics must always be honored. Other athletic shoes have no artistic constraints. Beneficial as it might be to include an inch of padding to absorb impact, like that in a tennis shoe, it would spoil the sleek, delicate look of the pointe shoe.

The traditional shank and toe box respond to the foot in a particular way. In substituting new materials for old, the expected support, pliability, springiness, and roll-up must be preserved. Synthetics offer the advantage of retaining their shape and stiffness; the result is a shoe that can promote correct alignment and last far longer. It must, however, be fitted with more precision.

The Outside: Platform and Outer Sole

The platform on which you stand has grown larger and more oval-shaped over the years, making it more stable. The material covering the platform is crucial: too much grip and you won't be able to pirouette; too slippery and the results are easy to imagine. Wearers of traditionally made shoes often remove the satin from the tip to prevent it from fraying and dance on the exposed canvas underneath. Darning around the perimeter of the platform helps the traditionally made platform hold its shape and prevents further fraying.

The outer sole is usually suede or leather. Glue, stitching, and in some shoes small nails hold the shoe together. A drawstring running through a casing, also called the binding, helps you adjust the fit.

Although the inside of the pointe shoe will surely continue to evolve to accommodate the increasing athleticism of today's dancers, aesthetics will always win. A beautifully tapered line of the foot is not to be compromised, and therefore even this highly particular and specialized shoe is longitudinally symmetrical. There is no right or left. The classic outer material is pink satin—a ballet tradition that predates toe dancing—which can be dyed for performances. Textile technology has come a long way; certainly there are other materials more durable and more easily

Anatomy of a Pointe Shoe

Pointe Shoe Anatomy and Pointe Shoe Fitting Terms

Binding: the fabric channel through which the drawstring runs.

Box or Block: the stiff toe cup that encases the front of the foot.

Box liner: the fabric that lines the inside of the box.

Girth: the measurement around the widest part of the foot, usually at the ball of the foot.

High profile: a pointe shoe box, often cylindrical, with a fairly large space between the outer sole and the vamp.

Low profile: a pointe shoe box with a generally flat shape and a fairly small space between the outer sole and the vamp.

Metatarsals: the five bones between the ankle and the toes. Pointe shoe fitting is especially concerned with the area near the ball of the foot.

Outer sole: the bottom part of the shoe, usually made of synthetic or leather, which is in contact with the floor when the dancer stands in the normal flat position.

Platform: the part of the pointe shoe on which the dancer stands when en pointe.

Pronation: the rotation of the ankle inward so that when standing flat more weight is on the ball of the foot than on the outside of the foot.

Quarter: the part of the shoe in back of the side seam, covering the sides and heel of the foot.

Shank: the stiff midsole that provides support.

Sockliner: the fabric or cushion that lies directly underneath the foot and runs the length of the shoe.

Supination: the rotation of the ankle outward so that when standing flat more weight is on the outside of the foot than on the ball of the foot.

Throat: the opening of the shoe nearest the toes.

Upper: the part of the shoe in front of the side seam, covering the sides and front of the foot.

Vamp: the part of the shoe that covers the tops of the toes and the foot.

Vamp elastic: wide, firm elastic sewn at the throat of the shoe to extend the vamp and cover the top of the foot.

Winged box: a box with extra-long, stiffened sides.

191

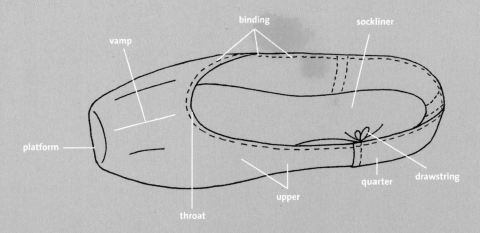

fitted, but those lustrous satin pointe shoes are the ballerina's trademark and the symbol of young dancers' aspirations. It's hard to imagine attaching such sentiment to a practical-looking shoe.

How to Select and Fit Pointe Shoes

Incomprehensibly fussy. That's how dancers seem when it comes to pointe shoes. But you must be fussy: the pointe shoe is more than just a tool of the trade, more than a tradition, more than a costume—it is an extension of your body. It is the essential equipment that takes your dancing to a higher level. The right shoe allows you your fullest artistic expression; the wrong shoe or the wrong fit can injure you so badly that you may not be able to dance. That's why so many professional dancers have their shoes custom-made. You need not go that far, but do be fussy about the fit. Dancing comfortably, correctly, and safely depends on it.

Dancers are not, as many nondancers assume, in constant pain. Amazingly, the human body does quite nicely on pointe as long as it is properly aligned, with the muscles correctly engaged, and—this is the crucial thing—as long as it is supported by precisely fitted pointe shoes. Whether you wear traditional paste shoes or high-tech modern ones, whether you are a beginner or a pro, pointe shoes must fit right.

I know one spectacular ballerina who very nearly had to stop dancing forever because of unnecessary, completely preventable bunions. Shoddy shoes (made in a formerly communist country where good materials were scarce) fitted super tight to eke out extra support just about ruined her career. Fortunately, her physiotherapists insisted she switch shoes and she did so just in time.

One pointe shoe looks very much like another, and that is as it should be to maintain harmonious uniformity in the corps de ballet. However, there is tremendous variation in the parts of the shoe that you don't see, and subtle variation in the parts that you do. Shanks range in flexibility from super stiff to utterly pliable. Boxes come in many shapes: from very square to extremely tapered and "pointy"; with high and rounded profiles or low, flat ones; with "wings" that extend support up the sides or with stiffness only at the very tip. Vamps may be very deep or very shallow; throats may be rounded and open, U-shaped, or cut in the sharp V shape typical of Russian pointe shoes. The sides may be cut down low to expose more of your foot or high for more coverage. Heels may be so low that extra elastics are needed to keep the shoes on, or extra high for greater security. Even within a given brand, there are many choices.

So many options need not be daunting. Take it one step at a time.

▶ Find a dancewear store with a knowledgeable, experienced staff and a good selection of brands and styles. Pointe shoes are readily available by mail order, but that is not a good way to buy your first pair.

▶ Your fitter should be up to date on the various foam pads, gels, and tapes that can improve comfort; there has been much innovation in these products. Don't be shy; tell the fitter exactly what you are feeling as you try different shoes.

▶ Be sure your toenails are neatly trimmed.

▶ Allow plenty of time for your fitting and expect some trial and error.

▶ Your teacher may wish to approve your choice and its fit; be sure she does so before you sew on ribbons and elastics.

Fitting Step by Step

1. Establish the correct length. If you are buying a traditionally made shoe, it should feel almost tight in the length because it will stretch out and break in. If you are buying a pointe shoe made of modern materials, such as Gaynor Minden, then you cannot expect much change in the shoe and you should allow a smidgen of extra material at the heel when en pointe.

2. Establish the correct width. The shoe should be snug but not tight around your metatarsals. The toe box must not dig into your big toe joint, nor should it end abruptly just below it so that the joint "hangs out."

3. Try a deep demi-plié on one leg; your big toe should just touch the end of the shoe. If you feel pressure on the big toe, then the shoes are too short, or possibly too wide, and they will hurt when you land from jumps.

Pointe shoes must never, ever be fitted with room to grow. Shoes that are too loose are every bit as bad as shoes that are too tight. If the box does not hug your foot, it cannot provide proper support. Your foot will slide down into it, putting enormous pressure on the bones at the front of your foot and especially on the big toe. When dancers suffer bruised or black

Foot Types

Feet vary tremendously and require different approaches to pointe shoe fitting. Most fall into one of the following general categories:

▶ Greek foot

▶ Egyptian foot

▶ Giselle or Peasant foot

Greek Foot

The second toe is longer than all the others. The width tends to be narrow to medium. Often there is a significant space between the big toe and the second toe as well. If the pointe shoe is too short and does not allow the second toe to lie flat, it can bend into a hammer toe.

Egyptian Foot

This foot type has a long first toe and the rest of the toes taper. The width tends to be narrow to medium. On full pointe that big toe is on its own; it can hurt, and its toenail can become bruised.

Giselle or Peasant Foot

This foot type, usually easy to fit, has at least three toes the same length, and the toes tend to be short. The width tends to be medium to wide.

The Compressible Foot

Many dancers have fine-boned, delicate feet to go with their slender, fine-boned bodies. Often of the Greek or Egyptian type, these feet are compressible in the metatarsal area; they are not fleshy. If you gently squeeze the sides of the foot at the metatarsal, the bones will move easily.

In order to land safely and comfortably from jumps, you should fit your pointe shoes to your feet when they are at their widest—in a deep demi-plié on one leg. But a shoe wide enough for jumping may be too wide for proper support on pointe and allow your foot to slide down into the box; this puts painful pressure on the big toe.
(See Fitting Step by Step, page 193.)

Low Arch, High Arch

The beauty of a dancer's foot need not be measured by the height of her instep. While highly arched feet are prized, they are often weaker and need extra strengthening to be ready for pointe. What makes a foot beautiful is its strength and articulation: it's the way you use it. You can stretch your feet to coax more flexibility from them, but really working them in every tendu and every jump is more effective in creating a foot that both looks good and produces lovely footwork.

Greek

Egyptian

Giselle

toenails, it is almost always because the toe box is too wide—a situation made worse if the shoe is too short.

4. Establish the stiffness and vamp length. These are both critical variables in helping you achieve and maintain correct placement. They depend in large part on your size and foot type.

The top of the shoe should completely cover your toes and metatarsals—no toe cleavage. Generally the vamp should cover a quarter to a third of the length of your foot, but not more. The shank should curve to conform to your foot. It is straighter underneath the toes, then bends underneath your arch.

Usually, the larger, bigger-boned dancer who weighs more needs a stiffer shoe than does the smaller dancer who weighs less. The dancer with long toes needs a deeper vamp than does the dancer with short toes. The dancer with a highly arched foot needs a stiffer shank and a deeper vamp than does the dancer with less arch.

If you feel pulled back when you relevé, or have trouble getting up and "over" far enough to balance easily, try a more supple shank and/or a lower vamp. If you feel that you are going "over" too far forward, or that you must clench your toes, try a firmer shank and/or a deeper (longer) vamp.

5. If you have a choice of heel height, select the one that feels most secure with the least amount of material.

Not Too Stiff

Appropriate pointe shoe stiffness is much debated. Some feel that beginners should start in hard shoes and strengthen their feet by working against the resistance of the hard shank. Others fear that hard shoes will "do the work for you" and inhibit the development of strength. Actually, it's a trade-off. A stiffer shoe makes your foot work harder rolling through demi-pointe and thus strengthens it for jumping. But the extra support it provides on full pointe could make it easier for a dancer to be lazy and not pull up out of the shoe as much as she should. Conversely, the pliable shoe makes it easy to roll through demi-pointe, but once on pointe you have to work harder. Obtaining the optimum ratio of support to flexibility is so important that professional dancers who wear traditionally made shoes painstakingly break them in until they are just right, then discard them when they become too soft.

Appropriate stiffness has nothing to do with how a shoe is made. Any shoe can be too stiff or too soft. The confusion arises because some shoes readily break in to become more pliable and others do not. As with regular cotton jeans versus preshrunk ones, the smart shopper knows what to expect. If you are buying a traditionally made shoe, then you can expect it to soften with use. It may feel overly stiff when new, and that's okay. If you are buying a shoe with synthetic shanks or boxes, then be sure you are delighted with the pliability of the shoe when it's new because you won't be able to change it.

All pointe shoes should be fitted precisely and with an understanding of the materials from which they are made.

Pads and Cushions

In the days before the advent of high-tech, impact-absorbing footwear, lamb's wool or a bit of paper towel were pretty much the dancer's only options for making her pointe shoes comfortable. Then came the first foam pads, but they were often big and bulky, and many teachers objected to them because they deprived the dancer of her essential feel for the floor. It wasn't until very recently that modern materials became sophisticated enough to meet ballet's exacting aesthetic and functional requirements.

Now you can enhance comfort without compromising the correct use of your feet: you can protect your skin from corns and blisters; you can compensate for a big toe that is shorter than your second toe; you can help stave off nonhereditary bunions—and you should. Not every foot is perfectly suited for pointe work. Painful pointe shoes distract you from concentrating on technique. Yes, your feet do have to toughen up, and there will be some discomfort, but sore toes do not make you a better dancer.

Perfecting the Fit

The inside of a pointe shoe looks very little like a human foot. There aren't even lefts and rights. You can customize the fit of your pointe shoes so they meet the needs of your own unique anatomy. Use cushioning material only where you need it, and use as little as possible.

Problem: Pain at the big toe or big toenail; bruised toenail.

Solution: Check the fit; be sure your shoe is neither too short nor too wide.

If the fit is correct, try the following:

▶ Place a small (one-inch by one-half-inch by one-eighth-inch thick) cushion made of firm gel or dense foam (most latex or E.V.A. foams bottom out too quickly) directly underneath your big toe on the inside of the platform. Be sure it lies between the sensitive outer corner of your big toe and the inside of the shoe. It helps if it curves up to just cover the top of your toenail as well.

▶ If that is not enough, place a thin (one-sixteenth-inch) liner made of dense foam on the inside of the toe box so it rests on top of and alongside, but not underneath, your foot. This prevents your foot from sliding down into the box and putting pressure on your big toe while at the same time enabling the bottom of your foot to maintain contact with the shoe.

▶ Other useful products are toe caps and the thinner pouches that encase your forefoot.

Problem: Second toe longer than big toe.

Solution: Tape dense foam or gel directly to the tip of your big toe to make it the same length as your longer toe. Or use a crescent-shaped cushion that creates a space for the second toe and removes the pressure from it.

Problem: Space between your big toe and your second toe, pain at the bunion joint. (With this foot type the second toe is often longer than the first.)

Solution: Place a toe separator made of firm gel or dense foam in the space. You may need to tape it in place. Be sure the big toe joint aligns with the bunion joint and that the separator is not too wide. Do not ignore pain at the bunion joint: be sure your shoes fit perfectly and that the edge of the toe box does not dig into the bunion or end just below it. See a podiatrist or an orthopedist if pain continues.

Problem: Sore spots, chafing.

Solution: Taping, especially with an elasticized foam tape, can protect the toes.

Problem: Heel of the pointe shoe slides off the foot.

Solution: Check the fit and be sure the shoe is not too big; if the fit is right, and if the ribbons and elastics are properly positioned and sufficiently snug, then try a heel gripper. Most have peel-and-stick adhesive that lets them adhere directly to the inside of the shoe. It's preferable to cut it in half and place the sections about one-half-inch apart, on either side of the heel seam, so that the heel gripper is not directly in back of your Achilles tendon; that way the shoe won't become too tight.

Pointe Training and Technique

No wonder she collapses: the dying swan bourrées en pointe with hardly a break for minutes on end. That kind of endurance, as well as the strength needed for bravura pointe maneuvers such as hops, multiple pirouettes, and fouettés, develops progressively, just like the rest of your technique.

Initial Training

Beginning pointe exercises focus on attaining the full pointe position correctly and on building the strength to stay up there. You work on using your feet and ankles properly, and as you do they become stronger. You learn how to use your pointe shoe without becoming overly reliant on it. You discover how the fundamentals of pulling up and engaging your abdominals enable you to support your weight on pointe. You practice making it all look easy and natural.

Pointe training sometimes starts even before you buy your first pair of pointe shoes, with special exercises for the feet, toes, and ankles: "playing the piano" with your toes by moving each one independently, and lots of pointing and flexing. Some schools train beginners in "prepointe" shoes, special slippers without stiff shanks that accustom the student to working in a blocked shoe but that do not enable her to stand on pointe.

Usually first-year pointe students wear their shoes for a short period at the end of regular technique class—ten minutes to half an hour depending on the school—for some brief, slow, basic exercises.

Often it is not until the second year of pointe training or later that dancers are ready to wear their pointe shoes for an entire class—a class devoted just to pointe. Because pointework should be practiced when you are warmed up, pointe class usually follows technique class.

Échappe à la seconde
sur les pointes.

First position on full pointe.

First position on full pointe with plié.

Pointe Exercises

The first pointe exercises are usually done facing the barre; it's more secure and it helps you to align yourself better. Some are done in parallel position; this provides a more specific sense of your own center and lets you concentrate on getting acquainted with your pointe shoes. Keep your gaze at eye level; looking at your feet could make your head drop and throw off your placement.

Beginning classes usually include slow prances and ankle circles to warm up, then some gentle stretches for the feet. Lots of pliés and relevés, both fast and slow, échappés, soussus, and then piqués, are among the first steps you practice. You also do tendus, and simple walking exercises in the center to train the feet to work against the resistance of the stiffer shoe. Slow rises, carefully rolling up and down with no plié, build strength and control, especially for the descent. Pas de bourrée works on the quick transfer of weight. Familiar barre exercises such as dégagé, fondu, or rond de jambe may appear; you do them off pointe to develop your balance standing flat in pointe shoes. You will surely do bourrées, first in place then traveling, and pas courus. Eventually you practice more challenging steps such as relevé on one leg, usually in sur le cou-de-pied or retiré. As you progress you do more holding the barre with just one hand and spend more time center floor.

An accomplished dancer is smooth, light, and effortless in her jumps and quiet in her

Second position on full pointe.

Second position on full pointe with plié.

landings. For some, allegro in pointe shoes presents a considerable challenge; the foot works so much harder to push off the floor effectively and to land with graceful control. Shoes that are too tight or too stiff just make matters worse. Adjusting to allegro nearly made me quit ballet. For jumping it's especially important that your pointe shoe be your ally, not your enemy. Start that process by wearing comfortable, perfectly fitted shoes.

You work toward being able to dance everything on pointe that you do on demi-pointe, ultimately to wearing pointe shoes for all of class. Pointe training is not only for pointe-specific movements like taqueterie (small, sharp, staccatto pointe steps) or for turns and poses that are so enhanced by the elon-

gated line of the leg. The study of pointe also greatly benefits your technique as a whole.

Steps and Technique on Pointe

Pointe technique is not different from ballet technique; it's an extension of it. It's the same, just more so. Solid fundamentals—alignment, turnout, lift, correct use of the feet—are what you need. Ballet technique evolved before pointe shoes did, so although many steps look better on pointe, few are unique to it.

Standing Flat. The most supportive parts of the pointe shoe, the shank and the bottom of the box, need a certain degree of thickness and stiffness in order to function. When you stand flat, they lie between your foot and the floor. Some traditionally made pointe shoes have more than half an inch of outer sole and shank underneath your metatarsals. This interferes with the feel for the floor that enables you to balance. Even the best-made traditional pointe shoes have pleats. When these are lumpy and irregular, it's even harder not to wobble when standing on one leg. Grand pliés and promenades can be especially challenging.

Call on your fundamentals: stay lifted, engage your supporting side, and keep your weight forward, not back on your heels.

The Ascent—Push Down to Go Up

Stepping onto full pointe, as in a piqué, feels much like stepping onto high demi-pointe because the mechanics are basically the same. Échappé and sissonne, too, have the same dynamic as they do in soft slippers. Attaining full pointe with relevé, on the other hand, requires an extra push from your toes, coordinated with the flexing of your pointe shoe as you move through demi-pointe.

There are two types of relevé. You can spring up to full pointe or you can roll. Teachers use both. The pliability of your pointe shoe, or lack thereof, is a big factor. Rolling up—achieving a high demi-pointe, then three-quarter pointe, then full pointe— is more difficult in a stiff pointe shoe. But working against a stiff shoe can make your feet stronger. Conversely, a stiffer shoe can make springing up a bit easier because the shank works like the pole in a pole vault to give you a little push. But it's your foot, not the shoe, that should do the relevé, and you won't become stronger if you rely on the shank.

▶ Press down against the floor in opposition to the lift.

▶ Relevé with control and precision, even if you are springing, or if your pointe shoes must be stiffer because you have super-high arches.

Balance

Balancing on a small oval platform one-eighth to one-quarter-inch thick feels different from balancing on the ball of your foot. There is less stability. On the other hand, there is also less friction and thus less resistance; multiple pirouettes are often easier.

▶ Pull up and out of your pointe shoes; feet should always feel long and stretched. Don't sink into the shoe and permit the shank to do all the work.

▶ Hold on to your turnout and alignment.

▶ Touch the barre very lightly; don't push on it or let it bear any of your weight.

The Descent—Pull Up to Roll Down

Coming down from full pointe actually requires more thought, training, and strength than going up does.

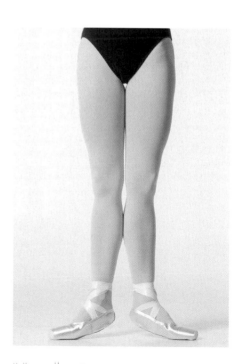

Rolling up through one-quarter pointe.

- Always control the descent from full pointe, whether you are coming down by means of a tombé, a coupé, or just a simple lowering. The heels never thump down on the floor.

- Rolling down is the reverse of a roll-through relevé; go through all the intermediary positions, resisting gravity, and really pulling up.

- Be sure that pull-up happens in your abdominals, inner thighs, and spine, not in your shoulders, ribs, or chin.

Bourrée

The swan's signature step, harder than it looks, depends on the back of the knee. You should be able to relax it without losing control of your ankles. Keep your thighs well crossed when traveling. Good bourrées are fast and quiet. It helps to think of the pressing motions of a cat kneading a pillow; although you are pulled-up, it feels more like "down-down-down" than "up-up-up."

Pirouettes

Frequent relevés into retiré on full pointe help prepare you for pirouettes. They are often practiced from fifth position to better capture the feeling of being on a plumb line that pushes straight down into the floor. Because you turn more easily on pointe than on demi-pointe, you don't need to use your arms and shoulders as much. You will probably find you need to quiet them a bit so you don't hurl yourself off pointe.

Hops on Pointe

Most of the time your pointework consists of regular steps elevated to full pointe. Consecutive hops onto the platform of your pointe shoe, however, don't really have a demi-pointe equivalent. This crowd-pleasing virtuosa step, often done traveling, involves bending the supporting knee while on pointe to push off and land. To do it you pull your heel back a bit so your ankle is not in its customary fully stretched position.

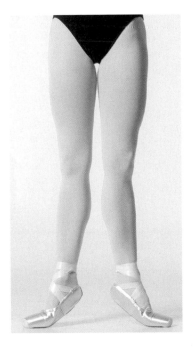

To demi-pointe.

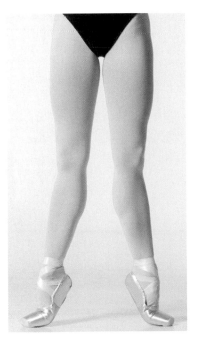

To three-quarter pointe.

To full pointe.

Michel Fokine in *Schéhérazade.*

Serge Diaghilev

Tour de Force

"ASTONISH ME." DIAGHILEV, FOKINE, AND THE BALLETS RUSSES

In the four hundred years of ballet's history nothing matches the two decades of Diaghilev's Ballets Russes for thrilling performances, groundbreaking choreography, inspired collaborations, and far-reaching influence. The Ballets Russes led ballet out of nineteenth century classicism and into the modern age, but the daring visionary responsible was neither a dancer nor a choreographer. Serge Diaghilev (1872–1929) was a Russian intellectual, art critic, editor, connoisseur, and impresario with a remarkable eye—and ear—for talent.

It wasn't just the troupes of dancers he assembled over the years—Nijinsky, Karsavina, Kchessinska, Spessivtzeva, Lifar, Markova, Danilova. Diaghilev repeatedly cultivated choreographic genius: Fokine, Nijinsky, Massine, Nijinska, Balanchine. He commissioned the greatest composers of the day, launching the career of Stravinsky and championing Prokofiev, Satie, Mussorgsky, Debussy, Ravel, Fauré, and Rimsky-Korsakov. His designers included Picasso,

Matisse, and Derain. Combining these elements like a master chef, Diaghilev served up the splendors of Russian dancing to an eager Western audience in works that revolutionized ballet's structure, vocabulary, and technique. Diaghilev's mandate to his artists was "Étonnez-moi"—astonish me—and from 1909 to 1929 they did.

Michel Fokine (1880–1942), a product of the Imperial School in St. Petersburg, was an outspoken rebel against the constraints of classicism. He discarded the multi-act, full-evening format for his expressive, single-act, "neo-Romantic" ballets. Going beyond ballet's standard steps and the rigid verticality of classical technique, he made the entire body eloquent. In *The Dying Swan*, the supple torso makes even simple bourrées heartbreaking. Ignoring the rules of port de bras, the arms in *Le Spectre de la Rose* are bent at elbow and wrist to evoke the rose, folded in like the petals of a flower. Fokine required that all the elements of ballet—choreography, music, décor—be equally strong, and rejected all restrictive or unrealistic costumes, sometimes even tutus and shoes. Putting these radical ideas into practice, the Ballets Russes scored one artistic triumph after another with

Les Sylphides, *Schéhérazade*, *The Firebird*, *Petroushka*, and *Le Spectre de la Rose*.

Socially, the ever-chic and glamorous Ballets Russes was the darling of fashionable Europe. It only got better when success became *succès de scandal*: the premiere of Nijinsky's *The Rite of Spring*, with its nonballetic movements and Stravinsky's shocking score, actually provoked a riot. (See Nijinsky, page 182.)

Subsequent choreographers—Léonide Massine (*Parade*, *La Boutique Fantasque*, *Pulcinella*, *Le Tricorne*) and Bronislava Nijinska—(*Les Noces*, *Les Biches*, *Le Train Bleu*) continued the tradition of innovation and collaboration. And the influence of Diaghilev's last ballet master, George Balanchine, continues to be immense. (See Balanchine, Kirstein, and the New York City Ballet, page 228.)

The Ballets Russes outlived Diaghilev. Successor troupes toured extensively for more than thirty years, introducing ballet to faraway places, especially in the United States. The existence of today's large and enthusiastic ballet audience is as much a part of Diaghilev's legacy as the iconoclastic ballets he conceived.

Nicholas Roerich's costumes for Nijinsky's *The Rite of Spring*. Diaghilev, though not a dancer, is third from the left.

Part Four

The Healthy Dancer

Respect Your Body; Dance Forever

Dancing is great for your body. Dancers tend to live long lives, in superb health. They maintain their strength, their suppleness, and that magnificent posture well into old age. Frederic Franklin, for example, performed with American Ballet Theatre when he was ninety. But like all elite athletes, dancers need to look after their bodies in order to perform at their best and to avoid injury.

Nutrition is fundamental. But eating well is not always so easy: ballet's very specific technical and aesthetic requirements are best met with a slender physique. Rest is also essential for the healthy dancer, as is maintaining a sensible and consistent schedule. Knowing about your own joints and muscles—and being willing to heed their warnings—is the crucial first line of defense against overuse injuries, along with proper floors and footwear.

This is all common sense, of course, but it's easy to let things slide, especially when there are many demands on your time. It can also be tempting to confuse the discipline, hard work, and occasional discomfort entailed in ballet with unhealthy patterns of thought and behavior. You won't be able to dance if you discipline yourself into illness or injury. This section examines the physical and psychological challenges of ballet training, and suggests how to meet them safely in order to realize your body's full potential for dance.

Eating Well to Dance Well

Whatever your body type—curvy or angular, perky or statuesque—your dancing and your experience as a dancer will improve if you are strong and lean. But don't stint on nutrition as you form your own beautiful dancer's physique. Real, vibrant, long-term health relies on it. Food is more than just fuel; it is the construction material with which your body builds and repairs itself. Sustained high-level athletic performance requires first-rate nutrition. It gives you the energy you need, and it

One-arm overhead lift on demi-pointe.

helps protect your body from illness and injury. Humans are highly adaptable; you might survive on a diet of junk food, but you feel better and you dance better when you eat wisely.

Nutrition and diet guidelines from "the experts" seem to change almost weekly. We do know that the dancing body requires a balanced diet. Strive for a variety of fresh, nonprocessed foods, free of additives, organic when possible, and loaded with what's good for you. Rather than count calories, make your calories count. An orange and a soda both provide sugar for energy, but one is full of vitamin C and fiber and the other is virtually nutrient-free.

Quantity matters, too. To perform or practice as hard as most dancers do every day requires calories. Insufficient caloric intake reduces muscle strength, endurance, speed, and coordination. It increases risk of injury and prolongs recovery. Low blood sugar impairs concentration, decision making, and mood. You'll feel more irritable, angry, anxious, depressed, inadequate, and alone. Undereating may also precipitate binge eating. Ultimately your performance *and* health will suffer. (See Eating Disorders, page 215.)

Why Your Body Needs Certain Kinds of Food

No one food or type of food has everything we need; it's the sensible balance that makes the body run like a well-oiled machine. Many foods provide more than one type of nutrient; a hamburger, for example, contains both protein and fat. Add ketchup, onions, and a bun, and it has carbohydrates as well. Dancers sometimes skimp on protein because they fear the fat that often accompanies it, but there are many lean sources of protein, such as chicken or fish. Protein is essential for sustained, as opposed to quick, energy; and protein at every meal also helps keep you from feeling hungry between meals. Just be aware that not all proteins, carbs, and fats are equal. For example, fats such as olive oil or the omega-3 fatty acids found in wild salmon and walnuts are very good for you, whereas the hydrogenated fat in supermarket cookies is not.

We also require water, fiber, and "micronutrients," the technical term for vitamins and minerals. Make sure your diet is rich in micronutrients, but don't overly rely on supplements to obtain them. Our bodies absorb nutrients much more efficiently and fully from real food. Excessive amounts of one vitamin or mineral can interfere with absorption of another, and some can be toxic in large doses. Fresh fruits and vegetables are the best sources for many crucial micronutrients; moreover, they are fairly low in calories and high in fiber. Fiber helps your digestion. Foods high in fiber—whole-grain breads and cereals, fresh fruit, and vegetables—are processed more slowly, helping to regulate appetite and optimizing nutrient absorption by the body.

With the exception of water, discussed separately below, the following chart outlines what certain major nutrients do for you and in which healthy foods you can find them.

Category	Why You Need It	Good Sources
Carbohydrate	Source of energy	Whole grains and cereals, brown rice, fruits, vegetables
Protein	Builds muscle; repairs muscle fibers	Meat, poultry, fish, dairy products, tofu, legumes, nuts
Fat	Fuels muscles; insulates nerves	Nut, seed, and vegetable oils; dairy products; fatty fish
Vitamin A	Antioxidant; helps muscles heal and recover; aids bone formation	Leafy green vegetables, yellow fruits, milk, cheese, egg yolks
Vitamin B1 (thiamin)	Converts food to energy	Pork, whole grains, legumes, fish
Vitamin B2 (riboflavin)	Converts food to energy	Lean meats, dairy products, leafy green vegetables, eggs
Vitamin B3 (niacin)	Converts food to energy	Dairy products, poultry, lean meat, fish, legumes, nuts, eggs
Vitamin B6 (pyridoxine)	Helps form red blood cells, which transport oxygen from the lungs to the cells of the body; helps make protein	Chicken, fish, eggs, brown rice, whole-wheat bread
Vitamin B12	Maintains healthy nerve cells and red blood cells; helps red blood cell formation	Fish, dairy products, eggs, meat, poultry

Category	Why You Need It	Good Sources
Vitamin C	Antioxidant; helps muscles heal and recover; enhances the immune system	Citrus fruits, tomatoes, berries, broccoli, cabbage, sweet potatoes
Vitamin D	Promotes absorption of calcium and formation of bone	Fortified milk, salmon, tuna; sunshine is also an important source because ultraviolet rays activate vitamin D synthesis in the skin
Vitamin E	Antioxidant; helps muscles heal and recover; helps in formation of red blood cells	Wheat germ, soybean, corn, olives, seeds and nuts, spinach, and other leafy green vegetables, asparagus, vegetable oils
Calcium	Essential for development and maintenance of bones and teeth; important for muscle contraction and nerve function	Dairy products, green leafy vegetables, tofu, fortified orange juice
Iron	Carries oxygen in the blood	Meats, poultry, fish, oysters, whole-grain cereal, fruits, green vegetables, egg yolks
Zinc	Supports immune system	Oysters, meats, poultry, legumes, nuts, dairy products, whole-grain cereal
Magnesium	Required for hundreds of different functions in the body, from metabolizing food to transmitting messages between cells to relaxing muscles	Nuts; legumes; whole grains; green vegetables, especially spinach; avocados; bananas
Potassium	Critical to muscle contraction and heart function; helps transmit nerve impulses; necessary for building muscle and for normal body growth	Fish, broccoli, peas, lima beans, tomatoes, potatoes (especially skins), leafy greens, apples, bananas, apricots

The Secret Nutrient: Water

In keeping our bodies well nourished, it's easy to forget that hydration is part of the equation. Our bodies are 50 to 70 percent water—it's vitally important.

Virtually all the body's systems require enough water to function properly. Absorbing nutrients, clearing out waste products, regulating body temperature, and even burning fat all depend on it. Dehydration can cause cramps, nausea, feeling extremely tired to the point of lethargy, even vomiting. It also affects concentration: in ballet class, dehydration can mean the inability to perform or get the hang of an intricate combination.

Because dancers and other athletes lose water through perspiration, it's especially important to stay hydrated. No one can tell you exactly how much water your body needs because it varies so much depending on the day, your activity level, the weather, and so forth, and overhydration can actually be dangerous, too. But every dancer should have access to water at all times. If your urine is dark yellow rather than clear or light yellow, this could indicate dehydration. Make a water bottle part of your regular dance kit.

Healthy Habits

Crazy eating habits and fad diets can be as dangerous to a dancer as a concrete floor. Eat well and eat mindfully. Take the time to sit down and pay attention to your meal. Eat with pleasure *and* purpose, feeding your body in kind and quantity the things you know are good for you. The French have a secret—they eat small portions, they don't eat silly snacks, and they respect good-quality food and the ritual of every meal. That's probably why they are able to treat themselves to the occasional fabulous dessert. Sounds like a good idea for us, too. Bon appétit!

Diet Don'ts

It's inevitable that any discussion of nutrition include the word "avoid." Here's my personal, not proven, list of things I avoid and recommend dancers do, too:

▶ Eating extremes of any kind

▶ Fad diets

- Food grown with pesticides, antibiotics, or hormones

- Junk food

- Refined, processed foods

- Soda, regular and diet (there is some evidence that the phosphates in sodas may deplete the calcium from bones)

- Excessive caffeine

Smoking

There are hundreds of good reasons why never to smoke—cancer, emphysema, and heart disease, for starters. As a dancer, you've got another reason: you are an athlete, and smoking will decrease your lung capacity and stamina. It's also bad for your circulation and makes your hair smell funky, your skin unhealthy, and your fingernails and toenails weak. It's very simple: if you want to dance to your full potential, don't smoke.

Body Esteem: Dealing with the Mirror

Escape the tyranny of the mirror every once in a while. For one thing, your dancing is always more interesting when your head and gaze move, too; always looking straight in front at your reflection can lead to boring habits. But more important, don't let the mirror damage your self-esteem.

The mirror can help you know when to lower your shoulder or relax your hand, but it can also make you think that you are less competent or less attractive than everybody else in class. While you cannot ignore the mirror's vital feedback on your technique and your line, you can limit it to constructive criticism.

When it comes to the inevitable comparisons with others, remember this: everyone develops at a different pace, and that goes both for body development and for technical prowess. Some people are turners, some get gorgeous feet, and some have ideal proportions. Most dancers have at least one asset; no one has them all. Remember that you are comparing yourself to other dedicated specialists, not to ordinary people, and that what you are trying to do with your body is really very hard and not particularly natural. Allow yourself to take pleasure in what you do well while you work on the rest.

Besides inviting comparison (and every dancer knows pink tights show no mercy), the mirror invites—demands—that you examine your body more frequently and in more detail than the nondancer does. You're basically looking at your body all the time, so it's easy to lose perspective. Sometimes, the mirror can truly distort your reflection and tell you that you are overweight when in fact you are not.

Our culture is obsessed with thinness. Even people of normal weight think they should be thinner. You need only watch television, open a magazine, or visit a store to be deluged by the multibillion-dollar diet industry and its images of thin, "happy" people. For dancers, ballet's aesthetic of slenderness intensifies the cultural obsession. Dancers often believe that they will earn the artistic director's approval, be cast in a better part, be accepted by a company—if only they were thinner. Do not compromise your health in the misguided belief that excessive thinness is the key to success. If your artistic director demands or encourages excessive thinness, you may be dancing in the wrong place. Be kind to yourself and remember what Eleanor Roosevelt said: No one can make you feel inferior without your permission. That goes for the mirror, too.

Eating Disorders

Over the past forty years, increasingly thin body ideals have produced increasingly unhealthy eating, both in and outside the ballet world. Ballet dancing itself does not cause eating disorders, but dancers are susceptible to them. In the past, eating disorders could flourish in parts of the dance world because of ignorance and denial; now there is awareness, acknowledgment, and help. But a lot of misinformation still floats around studios and dressing rooms. Here are the facts.

Eating disorders are actually a spectrum of illnesses involving extreme attitudes toward food and unhealthy behavior relating to it. Once ignored and misunderstood, eating disorders are now recognized as grave problems. They include anorexia nervosa, bulimia nervosa, and binge eating. Anorexia is an intense, irrational fear of weight gain that leads to self-starvation. Bulimia is a cycle of binge eating in short, secret bursts, followed by purging the ingested calories through vomiting, laxatives, fasting, or excessive exercise. While anorectics are usually very thin, bulimics may be normal, over- or underweight. Many have a combination of some anorexic and some bulimic behavior. Binge eaters, also known as compulsive overeaters, experience episodes of uncontrollable eating—past the point of feeling full—often followed by feelings of shame and self-loathing.

The most widespread eating disorder, less severe but still serious, is called disordered eating. Symptoms include engaging in some of the behavior associated with a full-blown eating disorder but sporadically or to a lesser extent. Symptoms also include altering eating habits in response to stress, repeatedly going on extreme diets, exercising too much, using supplements to reduce weight or boost metabolism, and experiencing significant weight fluctuations.

Why You Should Be Concerned

Left untreated, eating disorders can cause a myriad of medical complications and, at their worst, loss of life. They can wreck your bones, muscles, skin, and internal organs, including your reproductive system.

Anorexia Nervosa. When the body faces starvation, it does all it can to conserve energy; everything slows down. This is what can happen:

▶ Blood pressure and heart rate drop, resulting in fainting, fatigue, and even heart failure.

▶ Bones become dry and brittle because bone density is lost (osteoporosis), making them far more vulnerable to fracture.

▶ Menstrual periods cease (amenorrhea) or onset of menstruation does not occur. Prolonged amenorrhea results in low hormone levels that cause a loss of bone density and can lead to early osteoporosis. Amenorrhea can also cause infertility if left untreated and may lead to an increased risk of cardiovascular disease.

▶ Muscle mass is lost.

▶ Hair and skin become dry. Hair loss occurs.

▶ General breakdown of organs and systems occurs.

Signs of Anorexia Nervosa

Behavioral signs

▶ Restricted eating

▶ Odd food rituals (for example, counting bites of food, cutting food into tiny pieces, preparing food for others while refusing to eat)

▶ Intense fear of becoming fat

▶ Avoidance of situations where food will be present

▶ Extreme exercise regimes

▶ Wearing baggy clothes to hide weight loss

▶ Binge eating

▶ Use of laxatives, enemas, or diuretics to get rid of food

Physiological signs

▶ Weight loss

▶ Cessation of menstruation (amenorrhea)

▶ Pale complexion

▶ Often feeling cold

▶ Fainting spells, dizziness

▶ Distended abdomen

▶ Fatigue

Psychological signs

▶ Mood swings

▶ Withdrawal from friends and family

▶ Perfectionist tendencies

▶ Insecurity

▶ Self-worth determined by food choices

▶ Distorted sense of reality

Bulimia Nervosa. The entire digestive tract can be damaged by the purging aspect of the bulimic cycle.

▶ Frequent vomiting can inflame and even rupture the esophagus. It can decay and stain the teeth with stomach acids and may lead later to ulcers and possibly to esophageal cancer.

▶ Laxative abuse can cause chronic bowel problems.

▶ Other consequences include peptic ulcers (sores in the stomach lining), pancreatitis (inflammation of the pancreas in which enzymes actually start to digest the pancreas itself), and electrolyte imbalances (potassium, calcium, sodium and magnesium naturally found in the body are not at proper levels) that can disrupt the heart and even cause heart failure.

Signs of Bulimia Nervosa

Behavioral signs

▶ Binge eating

▶ Sneaking food and eating in secret

▶ Preoccupation with food

▶ Self-hatred when too much food is consumed

▶ Bathroom visits after meals

▶ Vomiting, laxative abuse, or fasting

▶ Extreme exercise routines

Physiological signs

▶ Enlarged salivary glands, bloated cheeks ("chipmunk cheeks"), or broken blood vessels under the skin

▶ Frequent sore throats

▶ Tooth decay

▶ Muscle aches

▶ Weight fluctuations

▶ Fatigue

Psychological signs

◗ Mood swings

◗ Self-loathing and self-criticism

◗ Self-worth determined by food choices

Female Athlete Triad: *A Special Alert for Girls*

Dancers and other athletes should be aware of a syndrome recognized only recently: the female athlete triad. This three-part condition consists of disordered eating, lack of menstruation (amenorrhea), and loss of bone density (osteoporosis). The culprit is poor diet, which, when combined with extreme amounts of exercise, disrupts the hormone balance essential for menstruation and for maintaining healthy bones. Some girls might think that not getting their period is a blessing. Actually, it can interfere with your dancing now and cripple you later in life. Amenorrhea sets you up for osteoporosis. Osteoporosis creates thin, weak bones highly vulnerable to fractures—stress fractures of the feet that can sideline a young dancer, and catastrophic fractures of the hip that devastate older women. Left untreated, the loss of bone strength can be permanent. The great, sad irony is that weight-bearing exercise such as jumping is an ideal way to build bone mass, and that dancers who starve themselves actually undo the benefits of dancing.

Who Is at Risk for Eating Disorders?

Why are dancers so often afflicted? Ballet, like modeling and gymnastics, makes no secret of its preference for a lean body. Line is everything. Unlike models and gymnasts, however, dancers spend hours on end scrutinizing themselves in the mirror, wearing only tights and leotards that reveal every contour and magnify any perceived flaws. Furthermore, its atmosphere of courtesy and grace notwithstanding, ballet class can be tremendously competitive, a microcosm of the ballet world in general. There is pressure to be no heavier than the girl next to you, and to stay light enough to be partnered easily.

A study published in the *International Journal of Eating Disorders* found that in some ballet schools and modeling agencies, where thinness is necessary for professional success, the rate of anorexia nervosa is about ten times as great as in the general population. Equally disturbing were the results of a study from *Medicine and Science in Sports and Exercise*, which examined disordered eating in professional ballet companies across North America and Western Europe. The results showed that 15 percent of the Americans and 23 percent of the Europeans questioned had anorexia nervosa, while 19 percent of the Americans and 29 percent of the Europeans reported having bulimia. Most of the anorectic dancers were members of extremely competitive national dance companies.

Imbalances in the brain chemistry that regulates appetite and digestion may play a part in eating disorders. This is not yet fully understood; what we do know is that emotional problems, intensified by social and cultural pressures, contribute greatly to these illnesses. Depression, loneliness, anger, anxiety, low self-esteem, a sense that one lacks control over one's life, or an inability to express one's feelings—these psychological maladies are made worse if there are troubled family or romantic relationships, if there has been ridicule because of weight in the past, or if there has been abuse. A culture that equates beauty and desirability with thinness only makes matters worse.

Feeling a lack of control over your life can set the stage for an eating disorder, and a ballet class may easily trigger such feelings. It is so easy to be dissatisfied with oneself in class—with one's body and one's abilities—and to lose self-esteem over it. Adolescence is an especially vulnerable time because puberty affects both your body and your technique. Some dancers, in an effort to regain control of their lives or even to reverse the changes of puberty, try to seize control of their bodies with disordered eating. That's when things can get out of control.

In the long term, an eating disorder can destroy a successful dance career. Short term, it will interrupt your thinking, and steal hours, chances, and opportunities. If you recognize any of the symptoms of an eating disorder in your own life, take action now. You need to shift priorities from dance training to regaining your health. If you don't break the cycle of abuse you're inflicting on your body, you may even lose your life. The first step is to talk about it—with a parent, a teacher, a trusted friend. Sharing your concern out loud lifts the veil of shame and secrecy that is almost always associated with disordered eating. The next step is to find professional help.

Puberty and Dancing

Navigating the enormous transition from childhood to adulthood affects every aspect of a young person's life. If you happen to be a dancer, puberty may occur just as you begin a serious commitment to training. The combination of sudden growth, hormone fluctuations, changing proportions, and shifting moods can be overwhelming. The body you've trained so diligently is being replaced with a strange new one that feels, moves and responds differently in class. It's important to understand what's going on.

Physical Changes

Puberty often starts subtly and then quickly gains momentum in a dramatic growth spurt. In both boys and girls, height can increase as much as one centimeter a month. In girls it usually begins between ages eleven and fourteen, when the ovaries start to release estrogen and progesterone. Testosterone from the testes catalyzes the growth spurt in boys, who, on average, start puberty a year or so later than girls.

Not everything grows at the same rate; the arms and legs lengthen before the torso does. This change of proportion moves your center of gravity, which can throw off your balance and coordination. You may have to rediscover correct alignment. Adolescents may feel as if all their hard-earned technique has flown out the window when pirouettes or pointe-work suddenly become a struggle.

As the bones lengthen, the adjoining muscles can become overly taut, resulting in less flexibility and a feeling of tightness. Leg extensions may be lower and pliés more difficult. It can be harder to hold those long arms up in second position. Boys may experience greater power in their trunk and shoulder muscles but still lose flexibility if those muscles become out of proportion with growing bones. Muscles and tendons usually have to play catch up with bones. Strength and coordination may feel diminished while they do.

To prepare for childbirth, the whole reason for puberty, the hips widen in girls. Wider hips change the angle of the upper leg bone (the femur) to the knee. The new leg angle may slow down your batterie temporarily. Wider hips also affect your retiré position, which in turn affects pirouettes. In the absence of the fully developed muscle strength that protects adult knees, the knees of adolescent girls become more prone to injury.

Psychological Changes

If you are going through puberty and you feel more emotional, less confident, and altogether down on yourself, you're not alone. The hormones that are coursing through your body do affect your mental state. All teenagers go through this, but as a dancer you may feel especially discouraged because your ability to do what you love seems diminished. Perhaps you don't like your body at the moment. You may feel betrayed by its shifting size and shape—girls can gain up to 125 percent more body fat. It may seem that everyone else in class is either behind or ahead of you developmentally. Try to accept that your talent has not disappeared; you're just having temporary "technical difficulties."

This disequilibrium will pass. Once the bones stop growing, flexibility returns. As the muscles catch up, the body regroups and is in proportion once again. Of course, to the vulnerable young dancer the concept of "temporary" is a challenge. Try to maintain perspective—it goes a long way toward keeping you healthy and happy during this time.

Ballet's Folk Dance Tradition

The court of King Louis XIV in France was not the sole source of ballet's character and form. Story ballets, in particular, have often borrowed from folk-dancing traditions. Folk-dancing steps and styles enrich the drama and add to the authenticity of such story ballets as *Don Quixote, Raymonda,* and *Paquita.* Elements of folk dancing appear frequently in divertissements—the stylized finger pointing of the Chinese variation in *The Nutcracker,* or the squat thrusts often seen in Russian variations.

Folk traditions can also inform an entire ballet, as in Léonide Massine's celebration of Spain, *Le Tricorne* (*The Three-Cornered Hat*). Massine researched Spanish—especially Andalusian—music and dance meticulously, mastering its heel-work and castanets, traveling throughout Spain with Diaghilev, even hiring a gypsy to tutor him in flamenco dances. The Ballets Russes presented *Le Tricorne* in 1919, with music by Manuel de Falla and sets by Picasso.

Scottish dance also inspired Massine. He studied it extensively, had a Scottish dance coach oversee the rehearsals, and was careful to remain as true to the form as possible for his *Donald of the Burthens.* Other choreographers are concerned less with exact re-creations than with capturing the flavor and character of a place. Balanchine referred to Scottish dance in *Scotch Symphony,* set to music of Mendelssohn, and choreographed a huge pageant of kilted "regiments" for *Union Jack.* Choreographer Christopher Wheeldon drew on Scottish motifs for darker themes in *Shambards.*

Sometimes stately, often athletic, the folk dancing of Russia and Eastern Europe turns up frequently, as do sizzling gypsy dances. The line between folk and ballet is usually clear but not always: Jerome Robbins playfully alluded to the homeland of Baryshnikov and Makarova by sprinkling a few arm movements and steps from Russian folk dance in the short ballet he made for them, *Other Dances.*

Folk dance steps have found their way into ballet vocabulary, sometimes turned out and balleticized. Pas de bourreé appears in many folk dances; pas de basque is based on Basque dancing. Ballet students often study character dance in conjunction with technique classes; you may well find yourself dancing the mazurka, the polka, or the czardas. Folk dancing is vibrantly alive today; if you have the chance to see one of the great national troupes perform, don't miss it.

223

The Georgian State Dance Company.

Tour de Force

A TALE OF TWO CITIES: THE KIROV AND THE BOLSHOI

Moscow and St. Petersburg have been friendly rivals for three centuries. Both cities have magnificent theaters and world-class ballet companies; their differences mirror the differences in style between St. Petersburg, the seat of the tsars, and Moscow, the bustling and vibrant metropolis.

St. Petersburg's company, the Maryinsky, has, like its city, always been influenced by the refinement and elegance of France. Moscow's Bolshoi, like its name, which means "big," dances with passion, conviction, and drama. Its men are famous for their power. While the Bolshoi might occasionally sacrifice academic form for greater dramatic effect, the Maryinsky maintains technical purity and precision. As befits Petipa's company, the Maryinsky has an unparalleled corps that not only does the steps together but does them with one mind.

The aftermath of the Russian Revolution was the best and worst of times for Petrograd, as St. Petersburg was then called. There were shortages, hard times, and political crackdowns along with an extraordinary creative energy in both traditional and experimental ballet. Fyodor Lopukhov directed the former Imperial company, preserved the Petipa repertory, and produced his own innovative, music-driven work. He along with Kasian Goleizovsky, was among the first to choreograph the daring acrobatic lifts that, though shocking at the time, later became a hallmark of the Soviet style. The young George Balanchine presented his Evenings of the Young Ballet, one of which included a dance to a spoken poem. But the rigidity of the Soviet government drove many of its artists out of power or out of the country.

In the 1930s, with the city now called Leningrad, the company was renamed Kirov after an assassinated Communist party official. The *drambalet* trend of the time put plot and story above design and vocabulary. Leonid Lavrovsky's *Romeo and Juliet* was one of the best known, and it forms the basis for many Western productions. Agrippina Vaganova took over the company and continued her standard-bearing work at the school. Her protegées include the legendary ballerinas Marina Semyonova, Alla Osipenko, Galina

Ulanova, Natalia Dudinskaya, and
Irina Kolpakova.

Subsequent directors Konstantin Sergeyev
and Oleg Vinogradov continued to present
classics while overseeing the development
of star talent like Yuri Soloviev, Altynai
Asylmuratova, and Faruk Ruzimatov in addition to the famous defectors. The repertory
eventually expanded to include works by its
lost sons Fokine and Balanchine. It continues
to produce sumptuous versions of the Petipa
classics, including a historic restaging of
the epic original *The Sleeping Beauty*. Today,
Leningrad is once again St. Petersburg,
and the Kirov is once again the Maryinsky.
Makharbek Vaziev directs the company,
still often called the Kirov on tour for
familiarity's sake.

The roots of ballet in Moscow, as in St.
Petersburg, lie in the eighteenth century.
The Bolshoi Theater was founded in 1776;
Catherine the Great supported ballet training
for orphans. Petipa's student Alexander
Gorsky was the first important director of the
twentieth century. Ballet grew more intensely
dramatic as the Stanislavsky method of acting
gained wide acceptance; Gorsky sought
greater naturalism, realism, and characterization. He restaged several of Petipa's ballets;
the version of *Don Quixote* familiar today
derives much from his revisions.

During the Soviet era, government censors
made it difficult for choreographers to explore
dance that deviated from accepted norms
of the narrative mode, and the narrative had
to be politically correct. Not even Petipa was
safe: for a time *Swan Lake* had to have a happy
ending. Midcentury experimenters like Leonid
Yakobson and his muse Osipenko had to struggle to have their works produced.

Yuri Grigorovich, director of the Bolshoi
for thirty years starting in 1964, managed to
innovate within the system, eliminating tedious
pantomime in favor of dance. His signature
work, *Spartacus* (1968), the story of a heroic
slave, is ballet on a huge scale and features a
massive, leaping male corps. Alexei Ratmansky,
a choreographer and former dancer, became
artistic director of the Bolshoi in 2004.

The Bolshoi first visited the United States
in 1959; the Kirov soon followed. Bolshoi
stars Ulanova and Maya Plisetskaya thrilled
American audiences. Americans appreciated
not only the Russians' technique and style
but also their willingness to repeat—in its
entirety—a crowd pleaser. If an excerpted
pas de deux or solo drew great applause, they
just did it again. When Plisetskaya repeated
The Dying Swan, she would even die
differently the second time around.

Alexander Godunov and
Ludmilla Semenyaka in the
Bolshoi's *Spartacus*.

Anatomy Illustrated

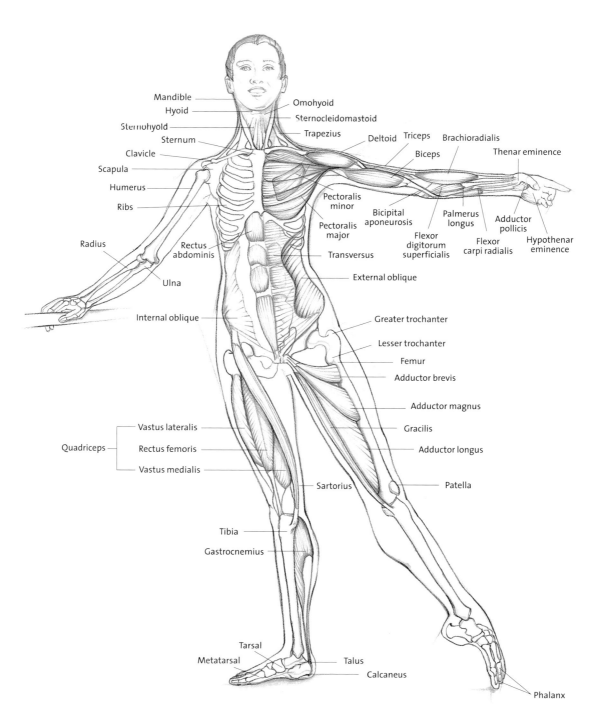

Mandible
Hyoid
Sternohyold
Sternum
Clavicle
Scapula
Humerus
Ribs
Radius
Rectus abdominis
Ulna
Internal oblique
Quadriceps
Vastus lateralis
Rectus femoris
Vastus medialis
Tibia
Gastrocnemius
Tarsal
Metatarsal

Omohyoid
Sternocleidomastoid
Trapezius
Deltoid
Triceps
Brachioradialis
Biceps
Thenar eminence
Pectoralis minor
Bicipital aponeurosis
Palmerus longus
Adductor pollicis
Pectoralis major
Flexor digitorum superficialis
Flexor carpi radialis
Hypothenar eminence
Transversus
External oblique
Greater trochanter
Lesser trochanter
Femur
Adductor brevis
Adductor magnus
Gracilis
Adductor longus
Sartorius
Patella
Talus
Calcaneus
Phalanx

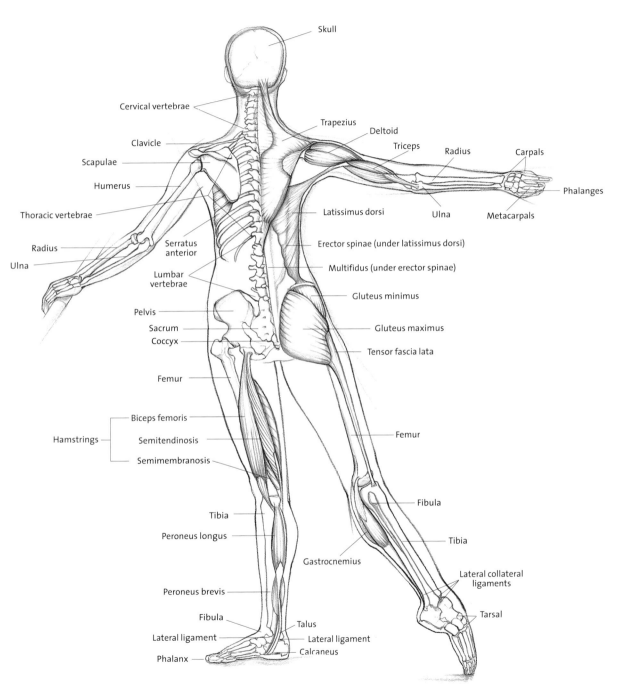

Skull

Cervical vertebrae

Trapezius

Clavicle

Deltoid

Scapulae

Triceps

Radius

Humerus

Carpals

Thoracic vertebrae

Phalanges

Radius

Latissimus dorsi

Ulna

Metacarpals

Ulna

Serratus anterior

Erector spinae (under latissimus dorsi)

Lumbar vertebrae

Multifidus (under erector spinae)

Pelvis

Gluteus minimus

Sacrum

Gluteus maximus

Coccyx

Tensor fascia lata

Femur

Biceps femoris

Hamstrings

Semitendinosis

Femur

Semimembranosis

Tibia

Fibula

Peroneus longus

Tibia

Gastrocnemius

Peroneus brevis

Lateral collateral ligaments

Fibula

Talus

Tarsal

Lateral ligament

Lateral ligament

Phalanx

Calcaneus

227

Tour de Force

BALANCHINE, KIRSTEIN, AND NEW YORK CITY BALLET

George Balanchine, the undisputed choreographic genius of the twentieth century, created more than one hundred ballets, cofounded a major company and school, and devised a technique and training method that produced the fastest dancers ever seen. While retaining the classical vocabulary, he developed a neoclassical aesthetic that, along with his fleet, bold style and his unparalleled musicality, influences choreographers to this day. That he did all this in America is because of Lincoln Kirstein.

Balanchine was born in St. Petersburg in 1904 and graduated from the Imperial Theater School. He left Russia to become a ballet master at Diaghilev's Ballets Russes in Monte Carlo, where he choreographed his first masterpiece, *Apollon Musagète*, now *Apollo*, and began his lifelong collaboration with Stravinsky.

Lincoln Kirstein (1907–1996) was an intellectual, a talented writer, and a poet. Smitten with dance, he resolved that America should have

Suzanne Farrell and Peter Martins in *Apollo*.

a ballet of its own and invited Balanchine to come to America to start a company. Balanchine famously said yes, "but first a school," and that school became the School of American Ballet. Balanchine created another early masterpiece, *Serenade*, for its first students.

Balanchine and Kirstein's first companies, American Ballet Company and Ballet Caravan, struggled. But Balanchine was an adaptable man: when jobs in ballet were scarce, he worked on Broadway or in Hollywood. In 1946 Kirstein and Balanchine formed Ballet Society. Two years later the New York City Ballet was born when the company became resident at City Center. It moved to its present home at Lincoln Center in 1964.

Balanchine's ingenuity and versatility was such that a "Balanchine ballet" can be many things. He made lovely tutu ballets, like *Symphony in C*, with ingenious and complex patterns for the corps. He made angular and strikingly sculptural "leotard" ballets like *Agon* with spare costumes and no set. He made big, lavishly costumed "theme" ballets with crowd-pleasing finales like *Stars and Stripes*. He made

still others that resist categorization. His *Nutcracker* became the gold standard.

New York City Ballet has never been a company of stars; the star is the company's inimitable repertory of ballets by Balanchine, Jerome Robbins, and others. Casting is not announced far in advance; the orchestra does not stop to allow bows before the end of a piece. But even if the company had no stars, the audience did. Allegra Kent, Diana Adams, Melissa Hayden, Jacques d'Amboise, Jillana, Violette Verdy, Edward Villella, Karin von Aroldingen, and Patricia McBride were loved by a generation; subsequent generations have always had their favorites, too. Balanchine tended to marry his muses, including Maria Tallchief and Tanaquil Le Clercq. His creative relationship with Suzanne Farrell was legendary.

Balanchine died in 1983. Since the mid-1980s Peter Martins, one of the company's leading dancers of the 1970s, has been ballet master in chief. Balanchine's ballets are performed throughout the world including, finally, in his native Russia.

229

Melissa Hayden in *Serenade*, a signature work of New York City Ballet.

Injury Prevention

A generation ago the field of dance medicine barely existed; now we have orthopedists, podiatrists, physical therapists, chiropractors, psychologists, and massage therapists who specialize in treating dancers, as well as volumes of research on athletes in general and dancers in particular. The medical profession's understanding of ballet technique in combination with its up-to-date expertise means that today's dancers are much better off in terms of prevention and treatment of injury. Teachers, too, are generally more cognizant of the importance of a safe, careful training regime and a healthy weight. It's a good time to be a dancer.

Avoiding Burnout

In a recent study published in the *Journal of Dance Medicine and Science*, 90 percent of professional dancers surveyed reported having felt tired at the time an injury occurred. Eighty percent reported that it had happened during high-intensity work; and 79 percent reported that they had danced at least five hours on the days of their injuries. Common sense suggests that even the amateur dancer can learn from these results. Pay attention to your body in ballet class; if after your fifteenth full-out tour jeté you feel that you are straining and that you need a break, then don't go across the floor that sixteenth time.

Maintain a realistic schedule of classes with time enough in between for adequate rest: if several ballet classes a week, a pileup of schoolwork, and an upcoming audition for the year-end performance start to take a toll, adjust your schedule. Be especially careful during periods of intense dancing, such as a week of late-night rehearsals before a recital or the first heady days of a summer intensive. Get enough rest. Eat well. Don't shortchange your warm-ups and stretching. Listen to your body. Pace yourself, and don't over do it; you—and your dancing—will be better for it.

The body can withstand hours of rigorous physical activity, but only if it also gets enough sleep. Athletes require more sleep than nonathletes, and teenagers require more sleep than adults. Why adolescents need more sleep is not fully understood, but it is known that the quality of their sleep is different; they spend more time in the deeper stages than adults do. Busy teenagers with hectic schedules are often the ones who deny themselves sleep, when they are the very ones who need it most.

Ballet Injury "Hot Spots"

Injury, especially for the amateur dancer, is by no means inevitable. Just be aware of certain areas of vulnerability, or "hot spots," and of what you can do to protect them. In addition, follow these general, common-sense safety measures:

▶ If something feels strained or overused, modify your activity level.

▶ Always warm up and stretch.

▶ Dance on a smooth, resilient floor. The best is a "sprung" floor, made of wood, with air space underneath and a protective nonslip surface on top. Never dance on concrete.

▶ Wear shoes that fit properly and are in good condition.

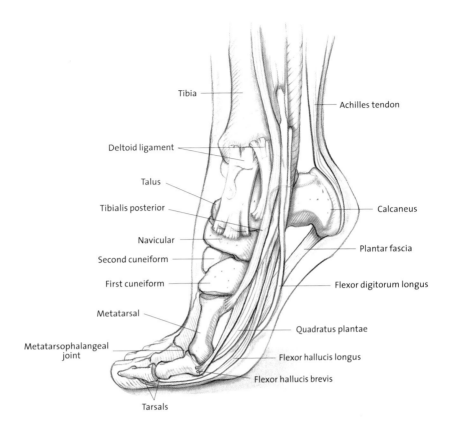

Tibia

Achilles tendon

Deltoid ligament

Talus

Tibialis posterior

Calcaneus

Navicular

Plantar fascia

Second cuneiform

First cuneiform

Flexor digitorum longus

Metatarsal

Quadratus plantae

Metatarsophalangeal joint

Flexor hallucis longus

Flexor hallucis brevis

Tarsals

Feet and Ankles

Flexor Hallucis Longus Tendinitis

Your calf muscles provide the power to point your foot. One of these muscles is the flexor hallucis longus, which specifically points the big toe and also helps to stabilize your ankle on pointe. Its tendon runs through a sheath on the underside of the inner ankle bone and continues along the bottom of the foot. If you feel pain on the inner side of the ankle, behind the bone and in front of the Achilles tendon in a tendu or on pointe, you may be suffering from flexor hallucis longus tendinitis—an injury almost unique to dancers. It may feel tender when touched, and you may notice a catching sensation in the region of the sheath if the tendon has become thickened as a result of prolonged inflammation.

Prevention. This can't be stressed enough: always warm up and stretch before dancing. Stretching and warming up are two different things.

Stretch gently before class and more vigorously once warmed up (see Warm Up and Stretch, pages 108–9). Avoid excessive rolling in of the feet, pointing the toes too forcefully, and overuse of the flexor hallucis longus from intensive rehearsals or classes. See a doctor if you feel catching or clicking in the sheath; this is a sign of chronic inflammation.

Treatment. The sooner you treat tendinitis, the easier it is to reverse. Chronic inflammation, left untreated, can result in weakening, thickening and even tearing of the tendon. Modify your activities, avoiding forceful pointing of the foot, pointework, and jumping until symptoms abate. Ice massage is one method of decreasing inflammation. Doctors will sometimes prescribe anti-inflammatory medications, but because they can mask your symptoms, it is important to rest when taking them. When you are free of pain, analyze and adapt your dance technique to eliminate the cause of the irritation: make sure you're not forcing turnout or rolling in, for example. Then gradually increase your activity level. A physical therapist may suggest taping to support the big toe joint and keep it aligned with the first metatarsal. Massage to release the muscles and joint mobilization to align the ankle are also helpful.

Sprained Ankle

This vulnerable joint is prone to sprains, often caused by a slip or a fall in which the foot is forcefully twisted or turned inward. That twisting may overstretch or even tear ligaments. The outer ankle's lateral collateral ligaments are the ones most often hurt. Although nearly all dancers know when they have sprained an ankle, for those in doubt, the symptoms are swelling and pain when twisting the foot or bearing weight. Other injuries such as a fracture or joint subluxation (partial dislocation of bones) can occur concurrently with a sprain. Sprains range from minor to severe, so it is important to consult a medical professional for proper diagnosis and treatment.

Prevention. Strengthening and conditioning the muscles supporting the ankle helps both to prevent and to treat sprains. Be vigilant, too, about checking the floor you are dancing on; it should be clear of debris, smooth, resilient, and flat.

Treatment. Start treatment with rest, ice, compression, and elevation (the RICE formula, explained below) and avoid putting weight on the ankle at first. A weak or lax ankle is prone to reinjury; therefore, strengthening the outer ankle muscles (called the peroneals) and retraining kinesthetic awareness with balancing exercises are essential to rehabilitation. Minor sprains can heal in as little as ten days; bad ones can take three months. Depending on the severity, a wrap, an air splint, or a cast may be necessary. Often ankle sprains are more bothersome and difficult to rehabilitate than fractures, so don't just wait for symptoms to go away.

Achilles Tendinitis

The strongest and thickest of the body's tendons, connecting the calf muscles to the heel bone, the Achilles tendon pulls the heel up so you can point your foot and relevé. It also dissipates the impact of landing from jumps. If you feel pain above the heel, if it hurts to flex and point, or if you hear a creaking sound, this tendon may be inflamed. Anatomically, some people are just more vulnerable to Achilles tendinitis, especially those with thin tendons or very pronated feet (feet that disproportionately bear more weight on the inside of the foot).

Prevention. Stretch your calf muscles regularly and strengthen the muscles that control your landings: lower back, deep abdominals, pelvis, legs, and feet. Avoid dancing on very hard floors; be sure to have adequate shock absorption in your shoes. Take care to not roll at the ankle in demi-plié and in landing jumps. Be sure to get your heels down on the floor when you land from jumps.

Pointe shoe ribbons tied too tightly may also create friction and compression of the mid-Achilles. Some dancers try to prevent tendinitis by "elasticizing" their pointe shoe ribbons; they remove a section of the satin ribbon and splice a two- to three-inch length of elastic in its place. Elasticized ribbons for this purpose are also commercially available.

Treatment. Left untreated, Achilles tendinitis can be a painful, recurrent long-term problem. At the first sign of discomfort, modify your activity level and apply ice twice a day until the pain has lessened. Be sure to stretch and avoid prolonged standing, running, jumping and making any other movements that pull on the tendon.

Pain above the heel is not automatically Achilles tendinitis. You may, for example, have a posterior impingement of the ankle joint, a separate condition caused by a prominent bone pressing on soft tissue when the foot points. It creates pain in the same general area that Achilles tendinitis does, hence the confusion in diagnosis. An X ray can help tell the difference.

Painful Bunions (Hallux Abducto Valgus)

A prominence of the metatarsophalangeal joint at the base of your big toe, a.k.a. a bunion, is not necessarily a problem. If the bunion rubs against your shoe, however, the little sacs of fluid under the skin called bursa may become inflamed and result in bursitis. Blisters and infection are other potential bunion complications. Besides faulty footwear and improper technique, the main cause of bunions is simply genetics. In the same way you inherited your grandmother's beautiful high arches, you may have inherited her bunions.

Prevention. First, be exacting about the fit of your shoes, both dance shoes and other footwear. The big-toe joint should always be lined up straight with its metatarsal. Avoid winging the foot (see page 81), angling the big toe in tendu, or otherwise putting sideways pressure on the big toe. Take care not to pull your toes forcefully back and toward the little toe when closing in fifth position. Soft toe spacers made of gel or foam work well, but be sure they are not too big or bulky. A physical therapist can show you how to tape the big- toe joint to keep it properly supported and aligned.

Treatment. If the bunion is inflamed, ice it for ten to fifteen minutes twice a day. Thin padding with a product like 2nd Skin can reduce irritation. You can also try a night splint to hold the big toe aligned while you sleep. Proper weight distribution when standing flat, on demi-pointe, and on full pointe is essential so that pressure is not unduly skewed toward the inner side of the foot and the big toe. Prevention is the best "treatment" for bunions because once you have them they don't go away.

Stone Bruise

Metatarsals are the long bones in the foot that connect with the toes. Metatarsalgia is an injury of the underside of one or more metatarsal heads, usually the second metatarsal. The condition can feel as if there is a stone in the shoe pressing painfully on the ball of the foot, hence the term "stone bruise." The undersides of the metatarsophalangeal joints bear the weight of your body when you rise onto demi-pointe, stand on demi-pointe, come down from jumps, and even when you push off in normal walking. The joints can become bruised from overuse, from faulty weight distribution across the ball of the foot, or from dancing on hard surfaces. The metatarsals may "drop" downward, shift farther apart, or move closer together as a result of the dynamic forces of bearing weight. Other metatarsal conditions such as stress fracture, fracture, and osteonecrosis can produce similar pain, so seek an accurate diagnosis and guidance from a medical professional.

Prevention. Do toe-strengthening exercises to develop the muscles that keep your toes long, not curled. When jumping, control your landings and absorb impact by using the whole foot—toe, ball, instep, heel. Avoid repetitive stomping movements or too much dancing that passes through demi-pointe or remains on demi-pointe (pirouettes, chaîné turns). Maintain even distribution of weight across the ball of the foot. Wear shoes that fit—not too narrow, tapered, short, wide, or unsupportive. Avoid prolonged dancing in high heels or character shoes that put excessive pressure on the ball of the foot.

Treatment. When a stone bruise develops, reduce the pressure on it. A stiff-soled flat shoe that does not bend at the metatarsal joint line, such as a clog, can be helpful. Avoid a lot of walking, stair climbing, and jumping; stay off demi-pointe. If the condition is mild, you can still do barre, omitting relevés, grand plies, and other movements in which the heels leave the floor. Ice applied for ten minutes to the area under the metatarsals may reduce pain and inflammation. Padding with thin felt, foam, or gel strips on both sides of the stone bruise so that it "floats" above the floor relieves pressure on the sore spot.

Metatarsal Stress Fracture

Stress fractures are overuse injuries. They can occur in any bone of the foot, ankle, shin, knee, hip, or spine. The second metatarsal base is the most common site of stress fractures in a dancer's foot. Symptoms include pain, tenderness, and aching in the middle of the foot. Stress fractures often don't show up on an X ray, so other tests such as a bone scan or MRI (magnetic resonance imaging) may be needed. Dancers with rigid, high-arched feet, long second metatarsals, or hormonal or metabolic deficiency due to amenorrhea and poor eating habits are more prone to stress fractures.

Prevention. Avoid sudden, intense increases in your dancing schedule. Don't "work through" foot pain. Be sure your floor and your shoes offer impact absorption.

Treatment. Full recovery (dancing in performance) after stress fractures is very slow, and it can take as long as four months after treatment begins. At first, complete rest from dancing is necessary, but as symptoms subside, you can resume partial weight-bearing exercises and then gentle ballet barre movements. Work from first position within your comfortable range of turnout, and avoid relevés, turns, pointework, and jumps until you are free of pain.

Plantar Fascitis

Plantar fascitis is an inflammation of the plantar fascia, the firm, fibrous tissue on the underside of the foot that connects from the front inner aspect of the heel to the base of the toes. The plantar fascia supports the arch of the foot. On demi-pointe the plantar fascia is pulled taut, which helps raise and stabilize the instep. A typical symptom of plantar fascitis is pain on the bottom of the foot when getting out of bed in the morning and first putting weight on it. The sharpest pain is usually at the heel.

Prevention. Do toe-strengthening exercises and calf stretches. Avoid rolling in at the ankle. Your doctor may recommend orthotics for your street shoes. Avoid walking barefoot whenever possible; cushioned footwear with a slight (one-to-two inch) heel is best.

Treatment. First, rest. Alternate warm and cold foot baths, and try to stay off your feet. Stretching and bodywork that includes calf massage with plantar fascia release may help. Gradually increase your activity level and ice the bottom of your foot after dancing. You may want to wrap the arch of your foot with supportive elastic tape. Physical therapy that includes ultrasound, massage, exercise, and taping can be helpful. Wear sturdy lace-up shoes with stiff soles. Don't jump until your feet are completely better.

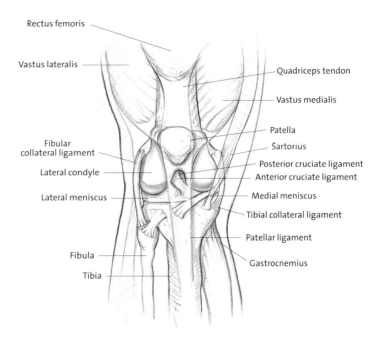

Rectus femoris

Vastus lateralis

Quadriceps tendon

Vastus medialis

Fibular collateral ligament

Patella

Lateral condyle

Sartorius

Lateral meniscus

Posterior cruciate ligament

Anterior cruciate ligament

Medial meniscus

Tibial collateral ligament

Patellar ligament

Fibula

Gastrocnemius

Tibia

Knees

Knees are hot spots for almost all athletes. The turnout required in ballet poses an extra challenge for this complex confluence of ligaments, tendons, cartilage, bones, and muscles. Professional dancers can suffer from numerous knee conditions, ranging from minor muscle strain to serious ligament and tendon injuries. Amateurs also endure knee injuries, but with common sense and prevention, you and your knees can dance as boldly as you like.

The quadriceps and hamstring muscles control knee function, and along with the ligaments give support and stability to the joint. Alignment of the pelvis and strength in the pelvic girdle muscles also directly affect knee function. That's one reason why pulling up through your entire leg is so important in ballet. Patellar tracking problems and patellar tendinitis ("jumper's knee"), common ailments for the dancer, typically result from a combination of muscle imbalance, weak inner quadriceps, alignment faults, and overuse.

It is tempting to try to compensate for lack of turnout at the hip by over-rotating at the knee and ankle. When turnout is forced, however, the lower leg bones (tibia and fibula) are torqued outward against the upper leg bone (the femur). The knee joint in between bears the brunt of this unnatural and dangerous twisting. Soft tissues like ligaments, capsule, and cartilage can be injured, especially if the effort occurs while the knee is flexing or locking out into a straightened position. Jumping in misaligned positions can also cause trauma to the knee.

Prevention. Respect the natural boundaries of your own anatomy, such as restricted turnout or limited mobility at the hip or ankle. You can work to improve your flexibility and turnout, but you should never force it. Knees are particularly vulnerable to injury from incorrect technique. Pay careful attention to your alignment in plié and relevé. In addition, the pace of class should be neither overzealous nor erratic, and you should follow a sensible dance schedule that doesn't overtax your mind and body. Avoid a sudden increase in training or dancing.

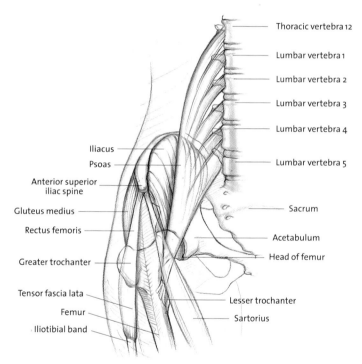

Thoracic vertebra 12
Lumbar vertebra 1
Lumbar vertebra 2
Lumbar vertebra 3
Lumbar vertebra 4
Iliacus
Psoas
Lumbar vertebra 5
Anterior superior iliac spine
Gluteus medius
Sacrum
Rectus femoris
Acetabulum
Head of femur
Greater trochanter
Tensor fascia lata
Lesser trochanter
Femur
Sartorius
Iliotibial band

Hip

Snapping Hip Syndrome

From an engineering perspective, the hip is one of the most elegant parts of the body. Its ball-and-socket joint, together with an intricate set of ligaments, affords a tremendous range of motion and at the same time withstands great weight. The occasional price for all that lovely motion is strain on the hip ligaments or, more frequently, the muscles associated with the hip. Ballet movements, from turnout to grand rond de jambe, often create imbalances among the various hip muscles. These differences in muscular elasticity and strength may lead to the most common hip conditions among dancers: impingement, hip flexor tendinitis, and snapping hip syndrome. Tightness of the muscles that cross the front or side of the hip cause the tendon to snap over the hip joint and often make a clicking sound. Weakness of the deep abdominal muscles and poor trunk and pelvis control may contribute to hip problems. Besides feeling a snapping sensation, you may notice tenderness across the front of the hip and a pinching pain in the knees-to-chest flexed position. Développé front and side, as well as grand rond de jambe, may be painful.

Prevention. Gradual stretching and strengthening hip flexors and abductors (gluteus medius, gluteus minimus, tensor fascia lata) helps prevent this condition. Correct torso alignment—no tucking or overarching—is important. Common technique mistakes that contribute to the condition include sinking into the hip of the standing leg (see page 79), hiking up the hip of the working leg, twisting the pelvis, and forcing positions.

Back

Spondylolysis

Ballet demands a lot of the lower back. Spondylolysis is the term for a type of stress fracture that occurs in the spine, caused by repetitive bending of bones. Bones are alive, constantly remodeling, with cells making protein in order to strengthen the structure. If too much bending stress is placed on a bone, the body may not be able to strengthen it sufficiently and a stress fracture may occur. Women dancers whose menstrual periods are absent (amenorrhea) and all dancers with poor nutrition (especially eating disorders such as anorexia or bulimia) are at a much higher risk for stress fractures.

Spondylolysis occurs in the lumbar spine (lower back) in young dancers, gymnasts, and other athletes. It is usually caused by increased hyperextension or back bending of the spine, associated with a swayback posture.

Prevention. Always work in proper alignment, with your spine in a neutral position, not tucked under, or with a swayback (see Alignment, page 78).

Lucia Chase in Antony
Tudor's *Pillar of Fire,*
circa 1942.

Tour de Force

AMERICAN BALLET THEATRE

242

From the outset, American Ballet Theatre was intended to be a "gallery of the dance" rather than the vision of a single choreographer. In the words of Richard Pleasant, its first general manager, it was for, "the collection and display of masterpieces of all times, places, and creators."

A.B.T. was born out of a small dance troupe started in 1937 by Mikhail Mordkin, one of Anna Pavlova's partners. Financial support came largely from his student Lucia Chase. In 1939 Chase and Pleasant expanded the company and renamed it Ballet Theatre. ("American" was added in 1957.)

The new company immodestly promised the longest season New York had ever seen, the most choreographers, and the largest cast. Its newspaper advertisement made so many impressive claims that *The New York Times* refused to run it until its dance critic could

confirm them. The inaugural season, in 1940, was a smash: the company presented eighteen ballets. Opening night's bill featured works by Mordkin and Eugene Loring, along with Fokine's own restaging of his *Les Sylphides,* which remained a company staple for forty years and was recently restored.

They danced *Giselle* the next night, but full-length story ballets weren't originally the mainstay of A.B.T.'s repertory; great one-act works have always played a fundamental part. Balanchine, Antony Tudor (who was associate director for a time), Agnes de Mille, Jerome Robbins, and later Eliot Feld all created important one-acts for the company.

A.B.T.'s great strengths were and continue to be its unparalleled repertory and the star power of its dancers. The choreographers are a ballet who's who: Frederick Ashton, John Cranko, William Forsythe, Jiří Kylián, Lar

Lubovitch, Léonide Massine, Kenneth MacMillan, Mark Morris, Kirk Peterson, Roland Petit, Twyla Tharp, Christopher Wheeldon, along with the ones above and numerous others.

From the oldest ballet still alive, *La Fille Mal Gardée*, the repertory ranges to the Romantic era's *La Sylphide*, to Petipa classics like *Swan Lake*, *Don Quixote*, *The Sleeping Beauty*, *Raymonda*, *La Bayadère*, to masterpieces of the twentieth century and new works of the twenty-first. Its breadth is not only chronological: A.B.T. has presented the work of decidedly modern dance choreographers like Graham, Taylor, Cunningham, and Limón.

A.B.T. has always mixed major international stars with stellar homegrown talent. In the early years notable imports were Alicia Alonso, Igor Youskevitch, Anton Dolin, Alicia Markova, André Eglevsky, Tamara Toumanova, Lupe Serrano, and Erik Bruhn; natives included Robbins, Nana Gollner, Nora Kaye, John Kriza, and Royes Fernandez.

In the 1970s A.B.T. fueled the dance boom with another superb roster: Mikhail Baryshnikov, Fernando Bujones, Eleanor D'Antuono, Carla Fracci, Cynthia Gregory, Gelsey Kirkland, Ted Kivitt, Toni Lander, Natalia Makarova, Kevin McKenzie, Kirk Peterson, Marianna Tcherkassky, and Martine van Hamel. Makarova's restaging of *La Bayadère* was a triumph for A.B.T.'s corps and a revelation to many American audiences.

Lucia Chase and scenic designer Oliver Smith ran A.B.T. for nearly forty years. Baryshnikov was artistic director for nine years in the 1980s, and McKenzie took over in 1992. Based in New York, A.B.T. reaches an enormous audience with extensive touring.

Kevin McKenzie and Martine van Hamel in *Swan Lake*, 1980.

243

ABT's huge repertory spans centuries and styles. Gillian Murphy, above, in a contemporary mode.

Pilates or similar exercises develop core strength in the deep abdominals and flexibility of the back and hips. If you experience back pain that is especially noticeable during arabesque or cambré back, see a physician.

Treatment. An accurate and timely diagnosis is essential. So if your doctor suspects spondylolysis, she may order an X ray or bone scan to confirm it. If spondylolysis is present, then an extended period of rest is prescribed, sometimes along with a brace to immobilize the back. After this, a regimen of strengthening exercises is necessary before you return to dance.

Muscles—Pulls and Tears

A "pulled" or strained muscle occurs when an overworked, fatigued muscle is given a sudden extreme stretch or load.

The muscles of the inner thigh, known as groin or adductor muscles, attach to the pubic bone. They may become pulled when forcefully overstretched in a side split or a side kick. Pulled groin muscles may also be precipitated by sacroiliac dysfunction, when the pelvis is not level or one hip is functionally higher than the other. Other common sites of muscle pulls in dancers include the calf (gastrocnemius), hamstrings, hip flexors, and low- back muscles.

Prevention. Avoid overuse, fatigue, and sudden, extreme stretches. Always warm up before stretching.

Treatment. Pulled muscles need rest. Apply ice, then alternate cold and warm compresses. Support with an elastic wrap. Liniments relieve symptoms but are not curative.

Anatomical Terms

Bursa: a sac or vesicle containing lubricating fluid and located between a tendon and a bone.

Capsule: a membrane or sac enclosing a body part; the knee joint is surrounded by a capsule.

Cartilage: the firm, flexible, and fibrous tissue found in joints and other body parts such as the ear, knee, nose, and throat; forms most of the skeleton in infancy and is converted to bone with growth.

Fascia: a band of fibrous tissue that binds together or encloses muscles, organs, or other soft structures of the body.

Ligament: a band of tough, fibrous tissue that connects bones at a joint or holds a body part in place. Ligaments help stabilize joints; they both guide and restrict motion. Ligaments often affected in dancers are those of the big toes, ankles, knees and shoulders (in men from partnering).

Muscle: a tissue made of specialized fibers that contract and relax to produce movement of body parts.

Soft Tissue: body tissue in the musculoskeletal system that is not made of bone or cartilage, including blood vessels, fat, fibrous tissue, ligaments, tendons, and muscles.

Tendon: A band of tough, fibrous tissue that connects a muscle to a bone or other part; also called sinew.

Daily Care for Dancing Feet

While most dancers must resign themselves to forgoing a second career as a foot model, dancers' feet need not become ugly, damaged, or deformed. Treat your feet with tenderness, and they will keep working for you forever. Ignore them or put them in shoes that don't fit, and you can expect any number of problems. A few basic habits should be as much a part of your daily hygiene as brushing your teeth.

Cleaning

Clean your feet thoroughly every day. Be sure to get in between the toes. Rinse soap off completely. Drying well is as important as washing. Soaking your feet after a hard day in the studio might feel delicious, but don't luxuriate *too* long or you may overly soften the calluses you need to protect your feet.

Toenails

Keep your nails trimmed. Cut them fairly straight across, on the short side, but not to any extreme. Try to conform roughly to the contour of your toe. Don't cut the corners or sides as this can cause ingrown toenails. You can relieve ingrown nails by soaking them in warm water for short periods or by placing a bit of cotton under the edge of the nail. If the problem persists, see a doctor.

Bruised toenails happen when the toe, usually the big toe, strikes or presses against the front of your pointe shoe. The nail can turn bluish-black, and sometimes it falls off. Runners and skiers get this when their footwear doesn't fit properly. Protect the tips of your toes, especially the vulnerable outer corner of the big-toe nail. (See Fitting Step by Step, page 193.)

Soft Corns

Corns can develop anywhere on the foot where prominent bones rub against a shoe or each other. Soft corns are particularly common between the toes. Wearing pointe shoes that are too tight, or not wearing tights or socks inside shoes, can aggravate the problem. Residual weakness in the foot or ankle from previous injuries may leave the foot in a more "collapsed" position, increasing pressure on the toes. Padding the pressure sites with lamb's wool, foam, or gel cushions can provide relief. If corns persist and are painful, consult a podiatrist.

Blisters

Almost a badge of courage for any dancer, blisters, which are caused by friction, can be a serious nuisance. You can try to prevent them by taping the areas that you know will rub against your shoe. A product called 2nd Skin has become popular among dancers who have recurring blisters in the same spot. You can also surround the blister with a doughnut made of foam or gel, taped in place, which prevents the shoe from touching the sore spot.

In addition to fitting your dance shoes perfectly, wear street shoes that don't rub your feet the wrong way.

Calluses

Like blisters, hardened skin goes with the territory of using your feet so relentlessly, and, again like blisters, calluses are exacerbated by ill-fitting shoes. Problems arise when a thick callus cracks open, leaving a painful, raw area prone to infection. Once you have calluses, do not try to treat yourself by trimming them with a razor or other cutting tool. Just rub them gently with pumice stone. Professional care, preferably by a podiatrist who knows about dancers, is safer.

Everyday Maintenance

Always wear clean socks or tights that fit properly, neither too snug, too short, or too loose. Never put on sweaty dance shoes; let them dry out completely before putting them on again.

If You Are Injured

It does happen. Even the most careful dancers get injured. See a doctor if something really hurts, if it's very swollen, if you suspect a fracture or other serious damage. Fortunately, we have a remarkable capacity to heal.

As you recover you can't always rely on instinct to know when to sit it out, when to work through it, or how much you can safely attempt—so ask your doctor or physical therapist. Sometimes you simply have to rest. At other times it is better just to modify your routine rather than abandon activity completely. In any case it is important to avoid aggravating an injury, even if it's only a minor one. If you have Achilles tendinitis, for example, skip those big jumps across the floor for a while. Your nondance activities contribute, too; for example, substituting low-heeled street shoes for sneakers will alleviate tension on your Achilles tendon when you are walking around town.

Many sports medicine experts recommend immediate RICE (rest, ice, compression, elevation) to minimize pain and swelling.

Rest

The body is quite good at mending itself but only if it's given a chance to rest thoroughly. Try to rest the moment you feel an injury coming on, not after you've been to a doctor. The sooner you rest, the less likely you are to further stress the damaged tissue. Resist the temptation to try using the injured part periodically just to see if it still hurts. A health care professional will be able to advise you whether to continue resting it, do isometric exercises, or resume your regular activities.

Ice

When it's applied immediately, ice is effective in reducing the pain and swelling of a soft tissue injury. You can make your own ice pack by putting crushed ice or ice cubes in a dish towel or a plastic bag. In a pinch, you can even use a bag of frozen peas. Commercial cold packs work, too, and it's a good idea for dance studios to keep them handy. The trick is to keep the ice on the injury long enough to be effective without causing discomfort or even frostbite. In the hours just after the injury occurs follow an on-again off-again routine of about twenty minutes each. Be sure to cover the *entire* area. For example, wrap the pack around the whole ankle rather than applying it only to the protruding anklebone. Always protect your skin with a layer of damp cloth. Dancers can ice frequently for the first three to five days after an injury (several times per day) and then decrease to one to two times a day, usually after activity or exercise.

Compression

Another way to reduce swelling is by gentle compression with an elastic wrap. Be sure that pressure is applied evenly. It should feel comfortable and supportive but not overly tight. Check your skin color at the edges of the compression material: if it's even the least bit red or white, reduce the compression. Use the wrap until the swelling dissipates, or until it seems to be more nuisance than help.

Elevation

Elevation also reduces swelling. Try to keep the injured part raised, ideally above the level of the heart, as much as possible. The afflicted area should be supported with pillows or a sling. Don't forget that elevation is equally important, albeit more challenging, while you sleep. Continue elevation as long as there is swelling, especially for foot and ankle injuries. This may be as long as seven to ten days.

P Is for Protection

Some physical therapists add *protection* in front of the RICE mnemonic (forming PRICE) to refer to crutches, slings, braces, splints, or taping—all of which help prevent further injury or reinjury.

Using Downtime While Staying Upbeat

In her autobiography, former New York City Ballet star Allegra Kent wrote: "As a child, I knew I had one great possession: my body... All we actually have is our body and its muscles that allow us to be under our own power, to glide in the water, to roll down a hill, and to jump into someone's arms." Her statement is a reminder that if, temporarily, you can't dance, you don't have to stop moving altogether. Resting the injured part of your body is essential; abandoning the rest of your body is a mistake.

Think creatively about how to keep up your mobility, strength, and endurance. Chances are you have some extra time free from rehearsals, performances, or classes. Use that time to exercise uninjured areas. If your foot is hurt, perhaps try to strengthen your back or arms. Check with a physical therapist for specific suggestions.

Non-weight-bearing movement such as swimming is almost always good for general conditioning. Pilates, floor barre, yoga, and strength training may provide viable ways of staying fit while your injury heals. (See Cross Training, page 253.)

Although your first reaction to an injury is naturally frustration, resentment, or discouragement, remaining gloomy does not help you or your body to recover. Practice stress relief techniques like yoga or meditation; positive coping strategies take your mind off your injury and may make a difference in how well and how fast you recover.

Try to focus on what you *can* do rather than on what you have to sit out. Besides cross training, take advantage of this opportunity to observe in luxurious detail a rehearsal or class. It's actually possible to improve your technique simply by observing and internalizing outside information. Watch ballet performance videos or any of several backstage dramas. (*The Red Shoes*, *The Turning Point*, *White Nights*, and anything with Fred Astaire are old favorites. *Center Stage*, with Ethan Stiefel, features students from the School of American Ballet as well as dancers from American Ballet Theatre and New York City Ballet; while Robert Altman's *The Company* showcases the Joffrey Ballet.) Think of your body as patiently waiting to put into practice tomorrow what your mind can be learning today. The act of thinking about something is surprisingly close to doing it.

Or expand your horizons and explore something altogether different. American Ballet Theatre's Rosalie O'Connor suffered a serious foot injury, and while it was mending she took up photography, snapping pictures of her colleagues. She even became adept at shooting while on crutches. O'Connor's trained eye and her insider's knowledge enabled her to produce exquisite photographic studies of dancers, both onstage and off. Although she was able to resume the roles she danced at American Ballet Theatre before she was injured, she stopped dancing in 2002, and photography is now her second highly successful career.

Other dancers have explored painting, playing a musical instrument, or reading those books one never seems to have time for.

Keep your perspective. Whether it's a three-day or three-week recuperation period, in a year or two you will remember it as a tiny fraction of your dancing life, if you remember it at all. Suzanne Farrell summed this attitude up in an interview: "You have the choice of looking at the doughnut, or the hole in the doughnut, and I chose to devour the doughnut. It's how you look at things. Yes, there are injuries, but there are injuries in everything. Yes, I got depressed, but you work yourself out of that. I have to really put my mind to work to think about what was painful, because I don't really remember…when I got on stage, I had no pain."

Ballet on Broadway

New York dance companies used to present their seasons in Broadway theaters; prohibitive economics put an end to that. Still, the Great White Way has welcomed great choreographers and has been generously repaid. Many of its biggest hits owe at least part of their success to the dances.

George Balanchine did several musicals in the 1930s and '40s, including *Cabin in the Sky*, one of the first musicals with an all-black cast, and *On Your Toes*. The plot of *On Your Toes* involves cross-pollination: an American hoofer, originally Ray Bolger, dances with a Russian ballet company. Another innovation was Balanchine's credit in the program: instead of "Dances by . . . ," the credit read "Choreography by George Balanchine."

Agnes de Mille's success with *Rodeo* led to her being asked by Rodgers and Hammerstein to do the dances for *Oklahoma!* She later choreographed *Carousel*, *Brigadoon*, and *Paint Your Wagon*, among others. Jerome Robbins has a string of Broadway classics to his credit: *West Side Story*, *Fiddler on the Roof*, *Gypsy*, and *The King and I*, the latter three he directed as well as choreographed. He made *Fancy Free* for Ballet Theatre in 1944; a few months later an expanded version moved to Broadway as *On the Town*. Balanchine went in the opposite direction and revived "Slaughter on Tenth Avenue" from *On Your Toes* for New York City Ballet.

The dancers in Bob Fosse's "Steam Heat" number from *The Pajama Game* moved in a way Broadway had never seen. The show was a hit, as were Fosse's next ones: *Sweet Charity*, *Pippin*, and *Chicago*. From dance-driven to just dance: Fosse dispensed with the plot entirely in *Dancin'*, a musical of nothing but dance numbers. Pure dance may be here to stay; recently Susan Stroman created *Contact* and Twyla Tharp took the songs of the pop star Billy Joel and fashioned them into *Movin' Out*.

But the monster hit of 1975 that broke the box office records, won the prizes, and seemed to run forever was a show about . . . dancers, Michael Bennett's *A Chorus Line*. And perhaps its most unforgettable song: "At the Ballet."

251

Oklahoma! on Broadway, 1943, starring my first ballet teacher, Bambi Linn (far right).

Mime

In story ballets, mime enables the audience to understand the plot. Without it you wouldn't know that Odette swims in a lake filled with her mother's tears, or that Giselle has a weak heart, or that Kitri's father wants her to marry Gamache against her wishes. Learning the gestures of mime and perfecting their delivery is an important part of dance education. As Bournonville wrote, "This chain of poses and movements is in itself a dance, but one that does not use turned-out feet."

252

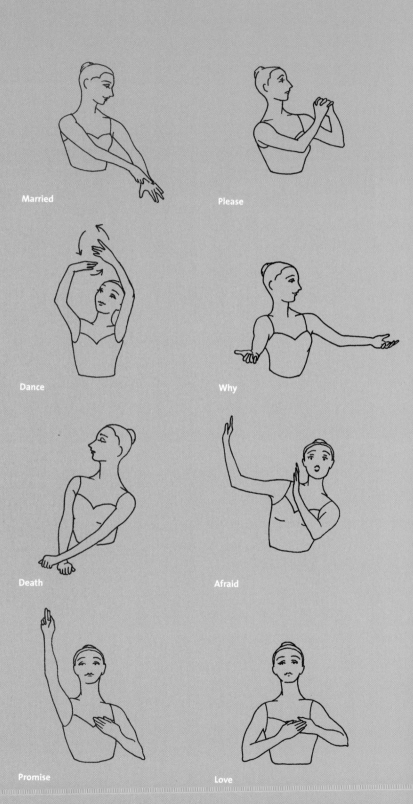

Married

Please

Dance

Why

Death

Afraid

Promise

Love

Cross Training

It may be that all you want to do is dance, but the well-rounded dancer can benefit from a variety of training tools. Pilates, resistance training, the ancient practice of yoga, along with thoroughly modern forms of exercise such as Gyrotonic and Floor-Barre can improve overall strength and stamina, help overcome specific weaknesses, and generally complement a dancer's regime. You can become a better, stronger, more capable dancer by doing more than just dancing.

Pilates *teaser*.

Pilates

Teasers, mermaids, elephants, boomerangs—these intriguingly named exercises are from the Pilates Method. Its recent surge in popularity makes Pilates look like just another fitness fad; in fact, it has been around for more than eighty years. Martha Graham and George Balanchine were among the first in the dance world to recognize Pilates (pronounced puh-lah-tes), as being especially beneficial for dancers.

Joseph Pilates, a German-born health and fitness innovator, turned his knowledge of yoga, boxing, martial arts, and gymnastics, along with his experience rehabilitating patients in World War I hospital wards, into a unique system of exercises meant to increase a person's core strength and overall flexibility. The precise, deliberate movements of Pilates, its prescribed breathing, and its emphasis on alignment increase strength and flexibility without creating bulky muscles. They build a dancer's "powerhouse"—her abdomen and lower back—creating a super-strong core that supports all other movement. For example, a long-legged dancer, or a teenager who just had a growth spurt, may have trouble holding her lower back still during grand battement front. By targeting those abdominal and back muscles, Pilates can develop the strength and control needed to perform the ballet exercise correctly.

Although Pilates excels as a torso toner, its exercises require contributions from various muscle groups, so comprehensive, all-over strength and agility are the result. Pilates works deep, finding those hard-to-target muscles so essential to ballet technique.

Pilates discovers and corrects imbalances and misalignments that can hinder a dancer's progress. Many dancers have one leg that is longer than the other, and/or one side that is stronger than the other. Pilates exercises are designed to ensure that both sides work equally; they won't let the strong side compensate for the weaker one.

Your first few Pilates lessons will be one on one with your instructor, who will help you establish your alignment, your breathing, your gaze, and especially your "powerhouse." You will do only a few of each exercise, but that's plenty because you will do each one perfectly, and there is much to think about and remember. As you become more advanced you work out in groups, and eventually on your own. You will also learn new exercises over time, as well as more challenging variations on original exercises.

Some exercises, called mat work, are done on a simple padded mat on the floor. Certain Pilates studios offer mat work-only classes, which prepare you to practice on your own after you've mastered the exercises. Other exercises are done on special pieces of equipment that Joseph Pilates himself designed, including the Guillotine, the Chair, the Barrel, the

Cadillac and the Reformer, the latter a bedlike contraption with footstraps and handles, which slides against the resistance of adjustable springs.

Not all studios have every piece of equipment; smaller studios often have only one or two and combine their use with instruction in mat work. That is one of the elegant (and convenient) things about the Pilates system: using the machines is great, if it's possible, but with the right concentration and control you can draw on the five hundred or so refined mat exercises that make up the Pilates Method to accomplish the same ends as the machine work. This makes Pilates utterly portable: you can do it anytime, anywhere.

Yoga shoulder stand, *Sarvangasana.*

Yoga

The word yoga means "union," as in a union of body and mind. For devotees, this ancient Indian practice is meant to be a lifelong discipline, training body and mind toward this union. For the dancer, the special benefits of yoga are the development of focus, mindfulness regarding breathing, easing tense muscles, and increased flexibility. Yoga is also a renowned stress buster and can be a soothing balance to a dancer's often intense training regimen.

Yoga *asanas*, or poses, are performed slowly, with particular concentration on fluid movement and purposeful breathing. The asanas can be performed individually or in flowing sequences, and for every stretch or movement there is an opposing effort. So a stretch to the left is followed by a stretch to the right; a forward bend is followed by a backward bend; a contraction is followed by an expansion.

Most yoga practices include basic breathing techniques, or pranas, such as the Cleansing Breath, the Breath of Fire, or the Victorious Breath. A prana is sometimes practiced alone, almost as an exercise in itself, often in a kneeling or cross-legged, seated position. You also engage in prana during yoga postures. Breathing is at the heart of yoga; it has the effect of bringing heat to the parts of your body that are being engaged, making possible a deeper stretch. When you consider that the average person uses only one-tenth of his lung capacity, you understand why yogic breathing, which fully utilizes the lungs, can energize the body and focus the mind.

Unlike poses in ballet, which strive to create beauty for an appreciative beholder, yoga asanas are performed not for their outward appearance but for their internal, therapeutic benefits. You start by learning an assortment of basic asanas, such as the Downward Dog, the Triangle, the Cobra. There are standing poses, balancing poses, seated poses, twisting poses, backward-bending poses, forward-bending poses, inverted (upside-down) poses, and restorative poses, each with its own benefits. Eventually you are led through more challenging variations and particular sequences of poses such as Sun Salutations or Moon Salutations. You build on a mastery of basic asanas to explore and expand your own breath control, strength, and flexibility.

Yoga has become popular just about everywhere, and there are a variety of styles from which to choose. Some include chanting and meditation. Some are more athletic, springing from posture to posture; others are slower. Some use props such as pillows, blocks, or straps. Some repeat movements over and over, others hold postures for as long as possible. Some always perform the same sequence of exercises in every class so you know exactly what to expect. Some offer a different class every time, to focus on different areas. Bikram, or "hot yoga," is for those who like to sweat; its sequence of twenty-six poses is performed in a particular order in a room heated to 100°F or higher. Ashtanga, Vinyasa, Iyengar, and Hatha yoga are all well-established styles; there is also a multitude of hybrids. It comes down to finding the yoga studio and instructor that suit you. B. K. S. Iyengar, or Guruji, as his followers know him, once said, "There is no distinction between one yoga and another. Yoga, like God, is one. But people call him by different names."

Although many instructors wear white (and one of mine wears a turban), you may wear whatever allows you to move comfortably and freely. It's not jazz class; modesty is expected. A T-shirt and loose cotton drawstring pants are preferable to highly elasticized tights and leotards that can bind your skin. You can bring your own mat, though most studios provide mats, blankets, and other props as necessary. Like mat-oriented Pilates, yoga can easily be practiced at home once you've mastered the basics. All you need is time, space, and quiet.

Both yoga and ballet class progress though a series of exercises led by an instructor, and both include a physical display of respect for the teacher like a bow or curtsy. But that is where the similarities end. Ballet students may be surprised to find that there is no mirror to encourage or rebuke you; there is an explicitly stated philosophy of noncompetition, either with your classmates or with yourself. Sometimes your ballet training will help yoga asanas come easily; sometimes you'll be surprised at the flexibility you lack. It can feel strange to work turned-in or parallel. Balancing is a completely different story; instead of looking inward to adjust your alignment and muscle engagement, you direct your focus out of your body and just allow the balance to happen without your controlling it. You will even learn to balance upside down. Just be sure that when you are ready to try headstands and handstands, your instructor is right there to guide and spot you. And when you master the headstand, be wise: resist the temptation to show it off at a party.

Frederick Ashton
(right) and Robert
Helpmann as
Cinderella's ugly
stepsisters, 1972.

Tour de Force

ASHTON, DE VALOIS, AND THE ROYAL BALLET

More perhaps than any other nation, England owes its ballet greatness
to women: two of them: Marie Rambert and Ninette de Valois.

Rambert (1888–1982)— born Cyvia Rambam in Poland, but in those
days dancers felt that only a French or Russian name would do—
originally trained in Eurythmy and joined Diaghilev's Ballets Russes
to assist Nijinsky with *The Rite of Spring*. In the early 1920s she
founded the Rambert Ballet School as well as an elegant boutique
of a ballet company where both Frederick Ashton and Antony Tudor
got their start. Called the Ballet Club, then Ballet Rambert, it is now
known as Rambert Dance and is a major contemporary troupe.

De Valois (1898–2001), born in Ireland as Edris Stannus, also danced
for Diaghilev and formed a company and school; her troupe evolved
from the Vic-Wells Opera Ballet into the Sadler's Wells Ballet, and
finally into the Royal Ballet (actually two: there is a second Royal
in Birmingham). De Valois, a choreographer herself, commissioned
scrupulous revivals of the nineteenth-century classics.

She believed that a good repertory should be a balance of traditional classical and Romantic works, enduring modern works, current works of topical interest, and nationalistic works using England's folk traditions. Ashton was her perfect ally. They forged a company style that melded rigorous schooling and corps work, gentle lyricism, and strong narrative instincts. Starting in 1935 Ashton created ballets for the company, most notably on a talented young dancer named Peggy Hookham, soon to be called Margot Fonteyn. Fonteyn succeeded Alicia Markova, née Lilian Alicia Marks, as the leading ballerina.

During World War II the troupe coped with blackouts, air raids, and the loss of their men, including Ashton, to the draft. But they performed throughout, sometimes doing three shows on Saturdays. The company moved to the newly reopened Royal Opera House at Covent Garden in 1946 with a landmark production of *The Sleeping Beauty*. This same production, with Fonteyn as a luminous Aurora, took New York by storm in 1949. Mayor Fiorello LaGuardia remarked to de

Massimo Murro and Tamara Rojo in Kenneth MacMillan's *Romeo and Juliet*.

Valois after an opening night of thunderous applause, "Lady, you're in!"

All the while, with Fonteyn as his muse, Ashton produced ballets that celebrated English style and sensibility, including *Symphonic Variations* and *Scènes de Ballet*. *Cinderella* (1948), Ashton's first full-length original work, was made on Moira Shearer of *The Red Shoes* fame (Fonteyn was sidelined by an injury), and Ashton himself was perhaps the most hilarious Ugly Stepsister ever. *Ondine*, 1958, showed Fonteyn's playful qualities in the role of a water sprite.

Ashton took over from de Valois in 1963 and presided over the company for seven years. The Royal Ballet has had only a few directors since, including Kenneth MacMillan and Anthony Dowell. A superb dancer, Dowell was an exemplar of the company's style: pure, elegant, modest. With Antoinette Sibley he formed another of the Royal Ballet's great partnerships. MacMillan's dark and psychological ballets, especially *Romeo and Juliet*, strongly influenced the company.

Today the Royal Ballet is directed by one of its former ballerinas, Monica Mason. Exciting stars include Darcey Bussell with her perfect line, Zenaida Yanowsky, Johan Kobborg, and the delicately brilliant Alina Cojocaru.

259

Ninette de Valois, 1949.

Resistance Training

Resistance training isn't just for bodybuilders; it's for anyone who wants to improve strength and stamina. It doesn't necessarily mean hoisting heavy barbells overhead or coming to terms with intimidating gym equipment. It's any kind of focused resistance training—that is, any exercise that involves resisting a force. The force can come from dumbbells or other freeweights, as in classical weight lifting, or from machines, resistance bands, or even from the weight of your own body, as with push-ups, sit-ups, or leg lifts.

The goal of resistance training for a dancer isn't to "bulk up" with overdeveloped muscles; in fact, women can't do so to the same degree that men can: you need a whole lot of testosterone to become Mr. Universe. The purpose is to enhance your strength the better to perform leaps, beats, sustained poses, and, if you're a male dancer, lifts. Strong muscles also help dancers avoid injury. Developing a strong, limber back now, for instance, may be the single best way to prevent back injury later on. Fortifying your bones with weight-bearing exercise builds and maintains bone mass; it's a safe, nonpharmaceutical way to prevent osteoporosis, the loss of bone density that makes fractures more likely.

To establish a strength-training program, it is best to work with a professional personal trainer, preferably one who is familiar with ballet's particular requirements. A trainer will assess your strength level in all areas of the body (arms, shoulders, chest, abdominals, back, and legs) and prescribe a comprehensive series of exercises. He will determine how many repetitions of each exercise you should do, as well as how much and what kind of weight you should use. He may also spot you, or assist in the preparation for or performance of certain exercises. As your strength and ability increase he will modify your routine accordingly.

The American College of Sports Medicine and the National Strength and Conditioning Association agree that resistance training is safe for young athletes, with a few important guidelines. First, you should be mature enough to take instruction and to perform the exercises correctly. Heavy, maximum, or power lifting is never to be undertaken, because it can put too much strain on young muscles and growing bones. In general, a young person's regime should emphasize correct technique and smooth movements. There should be more repetitions with lighter weights rather than fewer reps against heavy resistance. And supervision by a trainer or a coach helps ensure a safe, effective workout.

Once you have adopted a resistance-training program it's easy to keep up wherever there's a gym or even at home, if you have a little bit of room. Resistabands, for example, are the perfect portable weight-training tool. These long, wide rubber bands come in different tensions, and some resistaband exercises simulate the effort of traditional weight training. Other exercises can develop dancer-specific strengths that traditional forms of strength training cannot.

As with every step you take as a dancer, perform resistance-training exercises purposefully and correctly; form is everything to the safety and effectiveness of any strength-training program. A standard training schedule is thirty to sixty minutes, three days a week. You can work on different areas of the body on different days—for example, arms, shoulders, chest, and back on one day, abs and legs on the next. Or you can do a full-body workout each time you exercise, as long as you take a day off between sessions so your muscles can recover.

Floor-Barre

The Floor-Barre® Technique is all about alignment. Developed in the 1960s by Zena Rommett, a former dancer, this innovative method is based on the belief that dancers can achieve correct alignment and refine their movements if removed from the pull of gravity. In other words, you're not on your feet doing pliés and tendus; you're lying on the floor, carefully working through basic positions and movements. These floor exercises help dancers improve their technique; increase strength, extension, and turnout; and lengthen their bodies.

Rommett believes that on the floor a dancer's body can relearn correct alignment, which can dramatically improve the foundation on which to develop and improve technique. Floor-Barre classes are tough; they require control, focus, and careful attention to detail. But many dancers, athletes, and nonathletes take up Floor-Barre for the rewards: a strong center, lean muscles, and a refined mastery of the details of technique, all of which can improve performance and help to prevent injury.

Where to take an authentic Floor-Barre class? You can find out if there's a certified instructor near you and also order Floor-Barre videos by contacting the Zena Rommett Dance Foundation through the Floor-Barre Web site (see Resources).

Gyrotonic

Like the Pilates system, Gyrotonic® has its own superspecialized equipment to stretch and tone your body. There's no mat work in Gyrotonic; it's just you, an instructor, and a rather odd-looking machine.

Most people feel longer, lighter and looser after a Gyrotonic workout. It's great for freeing up hip, shoulder, and neck joints. Your head, for example, may turn more easily after Gyrotonic work, improving your spotting and therefore your pirouettes.

In the 1980s, Juliu Horvath, a principal dancer with the renowned Romanian State Opera, developed the Gyrotonic Expansion System (GXS) in New York City after injuring himself dancing. His first concept was Gyrokinesis, which was a series of side-bending and circular movements done while sitting on a low stool. Each exercise flowed into the next and was accompanied by yogalike rhythmic breathing. The principles of Gyrokinesis, along with a lot of workshop tinkering and trial and error, developed into the Gyrotonic equipment that defines the method used by many dancers today. "Gyrotonic" comes from the Greek, meaning "a circling (gyro) stretch (tonic)." And that's what this method is all about.

The emphasis of Gyrotonic is on flexibility and range of motion. An instructor carefully leads you through a variety of deep stretching and toning exercises, each movement with a countermovement for a balanced stretch and tone. The exercises consist of circular and spiraling movements done on a machine with weighted pulleys that create a controlled and variable resistance. One exercise resembles stirring an enormous caldron from a seated position, with the whole upper body in motion. The main machine is the Combination Pulley Tower Unit, and there are a few specialized side machines as well.

Seek out an instructor who has been properly trained through official Gyrotonic certification courses and, ideally, who has a dance background as well.

Swimming

Of all possible cross-training activities, swimming may be the best whole-body workout. It builds stamina without strain. A basic mixed-stroke workout strengthens both the large- and small-muscle groups of your legs, buttocks, abdominals, and upper body, especially the shoulders. Swimming is a great supplemental activity for a dancer because it engages the muscles without impact or stress, providing a break from the high-impact rigors of dance. That's why swimming is so often the preferred therapy after injury or surgery.

Like yoga, swimming requires that you pay careful attention to your breathing, a discipline of great value to the dancer when endurance is required. Best of all, swimming can be done wherever you are, that is, wherever you can find a pool. Once you have command of the basic strokes, no classes, teachers, trainers, or equipment are necessary—just you and the water.

You can swim for endurance (distance) or for strength (short bursts of concentrated effort)—or a combination of the two. Different swimming styles work different muscle groups; for instance, freestyle strengthens the back, while the backstroke works the hamstrings. The butterfly and breaststroke are powerful upper-body strengtheners. Create a workout that includes a variety of strokes for all-over conditioning.

The goal is to swim with a constant effort, keeping your arms and legs moving at all times. Be mindful of your technique and your breathing for an efficient, effective workout. Most important, though, is to enjoy the sensation of weightlessness and the soothing, meditative benefit of swimming. As any successful dancer will tell you, a calm, focused mind is as important as a strong, finely tuned body.

Mikhail Baryshnikov in New York City Ballet's production of *The Prodigal Son.*

Tour de Force

THE DANCE BOOM OF THE '60S AND '70S

Balletomania—extraordinary enthusiasm for dance—resurges from time to time. During the 1960s and '70s a lucky confluence of talent, creativity, vision, politics, and money created what is affectionately remembered as the dance boom.

Ballet, usually relegated to the back of the arts section, was on the front page. Outstanding dancers in highly charged defections from the Soviet Union seized the world's attention. The most prominent—Rudolf Nureyev, Natalia Makarova, and Mikhail Baryshnikov—sparked a renaissance in classicism, both classical ballet dancing and full-length classical ballets. Nonclassical ballets were revivified, too, and half-forgotten masterpieces presented. First-rate new ballets appeared. Ballet tackled political and social issues. Ballet was hip.

And there was money for it. Ballet enjoyed the embrace of the middle class. During the 1960s and '70s the federal government established the National Endowment for the Arts, individual states created their own arts councils, and private organizations like the Ford Foundation gave generously to dance and dance education.

Today a Russian dancer can move to New York without too much difficulty. Before the fall of communism it was unthinkable. Soviet Russia simply did not allow people, especially prized ballet dancers, to emigrate. On their few tours to Western countries Soviet dancers were under constant surveillance; they were not permitted to go on tour at all if the government harbored suspicions about them. Dancers lived in fear that the government would retaliate against families left behind; they had to assume that if they did defect they might never see their loved ones or their homeland again. Artistic freedom came at an enormous price, and it entailed a huge risk.

Natalia Makarova as Odette in *Swan Lake*.

Nureyev dominated the stage with his magnetism and put male dancing in the spotlight. Makarova possessed exquisite line and expressive phrasing on top of a formidable technique. Baryshnikov will rightly be remembered for his astounding leaps and turns, and how they seemed to come out of nowhere. They just happened, with no obvious preparation and no "ta-dah" at the end. He metamorphosed into his roles, whether in the classics or in other works made especially for him.

Dance had not been so very lackluster; on the contrary there was a great deal of talent both foreign—Carla Fracci and Erik Bruhn for example—and native. Many excellent dancers of the time were overshadowed by the defectors and the frisson provided by cold war politics. But in their dancing and their restagings of the classics, these exiles brought new excitement and drama to ballet.

Nineteenth-century ballets got a boost, and future classics were in full production. In Europe, Cranko, MacMillan, and Ashton choreographed important and enduring ballets. In New York, Arthur Mitchell founded the Dance Theater of Harlem. At New York City Ballet Balanchine and Robbins created some of their finest work for the company's distinctive dancers. With N.Y.C.B.'s move to Lincoln Center in 1964, the advent of dance on television, and the staging of his ballets by other companies, Balanchine's earlier works finally reached a more widespread audience. And just as his critics said he had run out of inspiration, there was an outpouring of creativity. The 1972 Stravinsky Festival offered twenty-two premieres in one week, ten by Balanchine.

265

Robert Joffrey demonstrated how ballet could rouse an audience to political protest. The Joffrey Ballet revived important but rarely seen ballets from the distant and not-so-distant past. (It also presented new work by then unknown choreographers like Tharp, Dean, Forsythe, Morris, and Gerald Arpino.) In 1967 Joffrey revived Kurt Jooss's 1932 harrowing antiwar ballet, *The Green Table*. Two years later when the Vietnam War was at its height, Joffrey, in a last-minute substitution on the evening of an antiwar demonstration, put *The Green Table* on the program. During that performance each dancer donned a black armband when his or her character was taken by Death; their final group appearance at the end creating an eloquent silent protest. Audience members were moved to follow the dancers, led by Rebecca Wright and Christian Holder, out onto the streets of New York to join the demonstration.

Part Five

Ballet Literacy

Must-See Ballet

The following is a highly subjective list of recommended choreographers and works. You may not agree with all my choices; it's an eclectic, idiosyncratic group. But I hope you will get to know at least some of them and decide for yourself. Debating the merits of a choreographer (or a dancer, or a restaging, or a costume) is part of the experience—and the fun—of going to the ballet. Seeing dance should stimulate discussion while it sharpens your eye. Go as often as you can. I also recommend that you supplement this opinionated overview with a comprehensive guide to ballet (see Further Reading), one that describes all the important works, summarizes plots, names original casts, and chronicles the works' histories through various restagings.

The ballets are listed by their creators because in most cases it's really the choreographer that I hope you will discover. Most of these choreographers are important enough that if you see a work other than the personal favorites I have listed, you will be rewarded, or at least provoked.

With some of the older ballets, however, the work of the original choreographer may be hard to discern today. Many works have been revised and restaged so often, sometimes with changes to the story and with different music, that they are quite transformed.

With more recent works, even when the ballets are well documented, the choreographer may have made changes over time, perhaps to accommodate a new dancer or because he rethought it. Choreography is often impermanent. And, of course, it looks different on each interpreter as well. No matter how many times you see a particular ballet, you never see the same thing twice.

The alphabetized list of titles (see Must-See Ballet at a Glance, page 290) is for quick reference. You can read more about each by looking under the choreographer's name. If the name of a ballet was originally in

Shoulder sit.

French, and the French is still more widely used today, then I have kept it. For the purposes of this list, "ballet" includes modern dance as well.

Pre-Nineteenth Century

Jean Dauberval

The earliest production of *La Fille Mal Gardée,* dates back to the French Revolution. Lise, the only daughter of the Widow Simone, loves Colas, a farmer, but Simone has her eye on a richer suitor. No matter that her candidate is a wee bit . . . strange. Simone tries to keep Lise out of trouble by locking her in the bedroom, not realizing who else might be locked in there as well. Frederick Ashton's much-loved version—with his own choreography—is one of his most humane works, a gem of characterization and pastoral choreography. Ashton, incidentally, had an unusual specialty: charming, witty dances for animal characters. No doubt the dancers in the barnyard scene swelter under their large chicken heads, but the effect is delightful.

Nineteenth Century

Jules Perrot

Pas de Quatre is the picture perfect lithograph of Romantic ballet, a cluster of four graceful women in tulle, flowers, and pearls; Anton Dolin's 1941 reconstruction of Perrot's original is the version most often seen today.

Jules Perrot and Jean Coralli

Giselle is the epitome of Romanticism, and Giselle perhaps the ultimate ballerina role. Giselle, an innocent peasant girl, dies of madness and despair when she discovers that Albrecht, who swore his love, is really a nobleman in disguise and betrothed to another. In Act II, transformed into a wili, or ghost, she forgives him and saves him from death. The choreography for the corps of wilis, with its interchanging rows and striking formations, is ballet blanc at its most frightening. The ballerina's dramatic challenge is to show her sweetness and vitality in the first act, her spirituality in the second. Coralli and Perrot choreographed the

original to a scenario by the poet Théophile Gautier. Petipa, Fokine,
and Lifar, among others, staged subsequent versions.

Joseph Mazilier

Le Corsaire features kidnapping, shipwreck, pirates, pashas, and beautiful
odalisques—an action/adventure ballet. It offers marvelous spectacle and
virtuosic variations. Many a great male dancer has made his mark as the
bare-chested slave, Ali, in the famous pas de deux, one of ballet's most
thrilling. Byron's great poem inspired a ballet by Giovanni Galzerani as
early as 1826, but what we see today is based on Mazilier's 1856 version,
albeit reinvented several times over, notably by Perrot in 1858 and Petipa
in 1868 and 1899. Today's productions reflect the work of many hands
and generally include Petipa's addition of music by Cesare Pugni, Léo
Délibes, and Riccardo Drigo.

Arthur Saint-Léon

If *Giselle* is ballet's great tragedy, *Coppélia* is its great comedy, though
it's not without a dark streak. Franz loves Swanilda, the prettiest, spunki-
est girl in town. But he can't keep his eyes off Dr. Coppelius's daughter,
Coppélia, who sits in the window and reads. Swanilda takes matters
into her own hands, breaks into the doctor's workroom, discovers that
Coppélia is a mechanical doll, and saves Franz from the doctor's sinister
plan to rob him of his life force. The original choreography of 1870

has undergone many restagings, among them a charming version by Balanchine and Alexandra Danilova.

Bournonville

La Sylphide, originally choreographed by Filipo Taglioni for his daughter, Marie, lives on today mainly in Bournonville's version. The teasing, dainty, flirtatious, winged sylph—a magical, woodland sprite—enchants a Scotsman, James, and leads him to the same, sad fate that awaits most nineteenth-century ballet heroes who get mixed up with supernatural women.

More typical of Bournonville's hallmark cheerful charm are the pas de deux from *Flower Festival at Genzano,* a young couple's virtuosic flirtation, and the full-length *Napoli,* a tale of a fisherman who rescues his lost love from the depths of the Blue Grotto—a real place near Naples. The third act with its famous tarantella is often presented by itself.

If you have a chance to see Bournonville performed by dancers trained at the Royal Danish Ballet School, drop everything and go. Even if the style is no longer as pure as it once was, seeing Bournonville danced by Danes is one of life's great pleasures.

Susan Jaffe in American Ballet Theatre's production of *Don Quixote.*

Petipa

The Don tilts at a windmill, but the real hero and heroine of most ballet versions of *Don Quixote* are Basilio and Kitri, yet another young couple in a match that lacks parental approval. Love conquers all, with the help of several burn-the-floor virtuoso variations for the leads and some sizzling character dances. The final pas de deux, with flirting fan, fouettés, leaps that draw gasps, is often performed on its own.

Swan Lake has it all: purest classicism, tragic drama, ballet blanc, colorful divertissements, magnificent Tchaikovsky music, and a tremendous ballerina role that challenges both technique and expressive range. Prince Siegfried pledges his love to Odette, a princess transformed into a swan by the wicked sorcerer Rothbart. But Siegfried is tricked by Odette's evil look-alike, Odile, and the lovers are doomed. Odette's tender and lyrical adagio must win the audience's hearts; Odile's bravura turns and allegro must wow them—and both must be danced by the same person.

There are as many versions of *The Nutcracker* as there are companies. This holiday classic tells the story of a young girl, her magical Christmas present, and her incredible journey to the Kingdom of Sweets. For millions of children, it is their introduction to ballet.

Tutus and Minkus's music for a ballet set in India was just the sort of incongruity Fokine rebelled against, but *La Bayadère*'s Kingdom of the Shades act is perhaps the greatest of the ballets blancs. Petipa's genius makes the repetition of simple steps en masse transcendent in this stand-alone choreographic jewel.

Whether it's the lavish restoration of the original Kirov version, which takes all afternoon, or the lovely streamlined one at New York City Ballet, *The Sleeping Beauty* embodies what is enchanting and enduring about Petipa's choreography. Based on the familiar fairy tale, set to Tchaikovsky's glorious score, the ballet includes some frequently excerpted "greatest hits": the Fairies' Variations; the children's Garland Dance; the "Rose Adagio" with its four consecutive, killer "look Ma, no hands" balances en attitude; and the bravura "Bluebird Pas de Deux," originally danced by Cecchetti himself.

Early Twentieth Century—Ballets Russes Legacy

Fokine

Who would have guessed that a few minutes of bourrées and fluttering arms would have such impact? By dancing *The Dying Swan* all over the world, Pavlova sowed a global passion for ballet, inspired future great choreographers, and fashioned her own legend. It's a ballet about dying, and it needs an extraordinary performer: one who can overcome the corniness to elicit the pathos.

When Fokine first choreographed *Chopiniana* in Russia, it was quite a different ballet from its later incarnation as *Les Sylphides*. The first had settings and stories which Fokine removed in favor of the ballet blanc of sylphs and their poet that we see today. Stripped down to the essential dance, *Les Sylphides* paid tribute to Romanticism while paving the way for neoclassicism. Not all dancers "get it": the Romantic port de bras, the achingly slow legato, the awkward-feeling forward bend at the hips that works only in a long tutu. But when they do, *Les Sylphides* is a window on ballet of a long-gone era and an explanation for the balletomania it inspired.

Schéhérazade, with stunning scenery and costumes by Léon Bakst and an equally opulent score by Rimsky-Korsakov, is set in a harem. Nijinsky enjoyed huge success as the favorite slave, and Bakst inspired the redecoration of many a Parisian living room.

Jerome Robbins in the title role of *Petroushka.*

Stravinsky incorporated charming folk melodies into his richly orchestrated score, and Fokine himself played Prince Ivan in *The Firebird*, based on a Russian fairy tale. Balanchine created his own version of *The Firebird* in 1949 using magnificent décor by Marc Chagall.

His leap out the window, his androgeny, his stamina—*Le Spectre de la Rose* was so identified with Nijinsky that for years it was said no one else could dance it. Diaghilev even knelt to kiss Nijinsky's leg after a performance. Fokine reverses traditional roles, in this case the elusive romantic supernatural creature is a man, not a woman, the spirit of the rose that a young girl has brought home from a ball. Maintaining the stylized, nonclassical, Art-Nouveau arm positions is almost as exhausting for the specter as the jumps, but it is vital to his characterization as the essence of a rose.

Petroushka juxtaposes folk elements in the setting and the music with modern themes of alienation and authority. This story of a puppet with a soul who longs for love has a timeless poignancy.

Massine

Léonide Massine, another Diaghilev protégé, was a master of character ballets like *The Three-Cornered Hat* that used folk motifs and other theatrical touches. He was also a proponent of the symphonic ballet, an important trend of the 1930s, a form that used large orchestral scores to tackle weighty themes. For Diaghilev, he choreographed *Parade* in 1917 with brilliant collaborators: cubist décor and costumes by Pablo Picasso, libretto by Jean Cocteau, score by Erik Satie. It features a street circus with a dancing horse, a Chinese conjurer, and throughout it all a Little American Girl. Picasso's horse alone is worth the price of admission.

Pablo Picasso's costumes for *Parade*.

Nijinska

Bronislava Nijinska may be less famous than her brother Vaslav Nijinsky, but as a choreographer she was no less talented. **Les Noces** (*The Marriage Rites*), made for the Ballets Russes to jangling Stravinsky music for four pianos, percussion, and chorus, shows preparations for an arranged peasant marriage in rural Russia. The two-dimensional formations of the tableaux are taken straight from Russian religious icons, but the unison dancing of the corps resembles an awesome but faceless machine. Also by Nijinska are **Les Biches** and **Le Train Bleu**, both about fashionable society, the latter with costumes by Coco Chanel.

Nijinsky

The original choreography for **Le Sacre du Printemps** (*The Rite of Spring*) is lost, but you can get a sense of what incited that famous riot in 1913 by seeing the Joffrey Ballet's reconstruction. At the very least listen to the music that would later be nicknamed "The Riot of Spring."

L' Après-midi d'un Faune (**The Afternoon of a Faun**) scandalized audiences, too, for its eroticism as well as its nonballetic, "primitive" movements. A faun, Nijinsky's own role, encounters seven nymphs on a lazy summer afternoon. He is intrigued and aroused, but they run in fear. The characters appear to have danced off a Greek vase, with heads and legs kept in profile and angular movements suggesting a two-dimensional plane.

Expressionism

Kurt Jooss

Kurt Jooss's *The Green Table* opens and closes with a group of grotesque old men, those who profit from war, fruitlessly arguing around a green table. Their scenes bracket the depiction of the tragedy and futility of war: massing soldiers, battle, refugees, a brothel. Throughout, the character of Death looms and takes his victims. The movement is stylized and dramatic rather than realistic or balletic. Death's dance is simple, steady, heavy-footed, relentlessly repetitive—and powerfully disturbing.

The Joffrey Ballet in Kurt Jooss's *The Green Table*, 1997.

Mid-Century Masters

Frederick Ashton

Frederick Ashton defined lyrical English classicism just as Balanchine pioneered the open American style. *Les Patineurs* (*The Skaters*) translates the ice rink to the ballet stage. With skating ladies, a whirling young boy in blue, and a romantic couple all dancing to Meyerbeer's thumping tunes, the ballet has remained an audience favorite since its premiere in 1937.

Danced against a backdrop of gently curving black lines on a cloth the color of the earliest leaves in spring, *Symphonic Variations* is an ode to beauty. Made after the close of World War II, it has all the quiet joy of a world that once again knows peace. At that time the trend was toward highly dramatic, theatrical ballets; Ashton wanted to return dance to top

Ethan Stiefel in American Ballet Theatre's production of *Les Patineurs*.

billing. *Symphonic Variations* pares ballet down to its simplest elements in a plotless work for three men and three women in Grecian costumes.

Monotones I and **Monotones II** were made a year apart in the mid-1960s, just before man walked on the moon. It took the serene purity of form of *Symphonic Variations* and moved it from the classical to the space age. The long, cool, pure lines of the ballet are part academic, part exotic fantasy, and part *2001: A Space Odyssey*.

Ashton started ballet late and did not train at a great national academy, but he was almost instinctively classical; he would sneak up to the balcony to watch *The Sleeping Beauty* again and again, saying he was getting a "private lesson" from Petipa. He was also a master of the narrative ballet. Works like *La Fille Mal Gardée* and **The Dream**—Shakespeare's *Midsummer Night's Dream* compressed into a Victorian valentine—show the results of those lessons: a superb balance of plot against classical dancing. (For a different but equally beautiful look at the same story, see Balanchine's *A Midsummer Night's Dream*.)

George Balanchine

George Balanchine defined American classicism. *Apollo*, made for the Ballets Russes in 1928, shows his pure, linear take on ballet as it tells the story of the young god's growth to maturity and his education by the muses. Writing about *Apollo* later, Balanchine said, "I could, for the first time, dare not use all my ideas."

Balanchine's first work in America, *Serenade*, is considered by many his signature ballet. Women in long flowing skirts dance to Tchaikovsky's lush, rhapsodic music. In a lunar blue landscape, hints of love, loss, and finally transfiguration are played out. I can think of no other ballet in which the opening tableau and the closing image both take your breath away.

Concerto Barocco, to Bach's double violin concerto, is one of Balanchine's greatest music visualizations. This plotless work with two leads (one per violin) lets you, as Balanchine said, "see the music and hear the dance."

Balanchine celebrates Baroque music in an ambience of gaiety in *Square Dance*. Folk dance provides the underlying structure and the overall theme. Later Balanchine added a searching male solo as if in counterpoint to the general joy and exuberance. Originally a real square dance caller was on stage exhorting the dancers; the caller was restored by the Joffrey ballet in 2005.

Choreographed for Ballet Society, the predecessor of New York City Ballet, to a commissioned score by Paul Hindemith, Balanchine imbued classical steps with austere angularity in *The Four Temperaments*. The temperaments are based on the "humors" of medieval physiology: melancholic (melancholy), sanguinic (confident, optimistic), phlegmatic (sluggish, unemotional), and choleric (hot-tempered). You will never think of grands battements devants the same way once you see the melancholic entrance. They are reprised in the finale, which is perhaps my favorite of all finales: from amid the ensemble unexpected sailing leaps arise—like fireworks or frolicking dolphins.

Ballet Theatre asked Balanchine to produce a ballet that could substitute for divertissements from *The Sleeping Beauty*. *Theme and Variations*, to the final movement of Tchaikovsky's Suite No. 3, distills Petipa's classical designs to their essence and contains meaty roles for the soloists, including a series of double tours that has been the bane of many a danseur.

For *Agon*, Stravinsky produced a complex, partly atonal yet still jazzy score—an urban, urbane beat. *Agon* was hailed as a masterpiece from its premiere. The ballet is one of the "black and white" ballets, so called because of the basic costumes but also because Arthur Mitchell and Diana Adams, the interracial leads in the original cast, danced a coolly sensual pas de deux that was daring at the time.

Wendy Whelan of New York City Ballet and Donald Williams of Dance Theatre of Harlem, in *Agon*.

Ballet Literacy

John Cranko

John Cranko was artistic director of the Stuttgart Ballet until his untimely death in 1973. *Onegin* is based on *Eugene Onegin*, Pushkin's story of the impossible love between a starstruck teenage girl and a cold, vain man. *The Taming of the Shrew* is a rich comic ballet based on Shakespeare's play.

Agnes de Mille

One of the original choreographers for Ballet Theatre, Agnes de Mille specialized in narrative dances. She made her greatest, *Rodeo*, in 1942 for the Ballets Russes. To a score by Aaron Copland that evoked the American West, de Mille tells the story of a Cowgirl (originally danced by de Mille as well) who awkwardly finds love with the Champion Roper.

Hoofer alert: He uses a virtuoso tap solo to win her heart. Copland also provided the music for a less happy tale of the West, Eugene Loring's *Billy the Kid*.

Harald Lander

Harald Lander was a director of the Royal Danish Ballet from 1932 to 1951. *Études* belongs to the genre of classroom ballets that show the dancer at work. Set in a studio, it traces the development of steps and technique, with a detour to the land of the sylphs in the middle.

Kenneth MacMillan

Kenneth MacMillan made narrative dance dramas often suffused with emotional torment. He was a master of the rapturous pas de deux; there are many versions of *Romeo and Juliet;* MacMillan's is one of the best.

Jerome Robbins

Jerome Robbins choreographed great dances for both Broadway and ballet. After first working with Ballet Theatre, he had a long association with New York City Ballet. *Fancy Free* officially lists its setting as "the

Angel Corella in American Ballet Theatre's production of *Fancy Free.*

present," and although it was choreographed more than sixty years ago it remains fresh and funny. Three sailors on shore leave in Manhattan—two girls, a bar, a dancing contest. *Plus ça change...*

Dances at a Gathering and *In the Night*, both to Chopin, feature intricate and daring partnering. Other favorite Robbins pieces are *In G Major* to Ravel, the humorous *The Concert*, and *The Afternoon of a Faun* set in a ballet studio, a fresh take on the original's themes of narcissism and eroticism.

Antony Tudor

Antony Tudor began his career in England and immigrated to America in 1940 to work with Ballet Theatre. His dramatic ballets explore the human psyche. *Lilac Garden*, made early in his career for Ballet Rambert in London, is the story of a woman on the brink of an unwanted marriage. *Pillar of Fire*, created for Ballet Theatre, again looks at a woman trapped, but this time in spinsterhood by a smothering family. In a poignant late work, *The Leaves Are Fading*, Tudor only hinted at plot in a suite of dances that opened and closed with a woman in a long dress tracing her way across the stage as if to set the dances in motion from her own memories.

Present Day

Eliot Feld

Eliot Feld is fluent in ballet but not limited to it. He specializes in lovely, sometimes quirky, chamber pieces and has choreographed more than 120 works, mostly for his own companies. He followed his early success, *Harbinger*, to Prokofiev, with ballets based on a far-ranging catalog of composers and themes—klezmer to Baroque—and sometimes refers to his musical choices with playful titles for his works like *The Jig Is Up* and *Ah Scarlatti! Asia*, to Ravel, evokes an exotic languor and pays homage to the Ballets Russes's "orientalist" ballets.

William Forsythe

William Forsythe's "attack ballets," including *In the Middle, Somewhat
Elevated*, created in 1987 for the Paris Opera, shock and thrill audiences
with their churning electronic scores and sleek, aggressive choreography.
His own troupes, Ballett Frankfurt and later the Forsythe Company,
are known more for cerebral dance-theater works. My favorite is *The
Vertiginous Thrill of Exactitude*—imagine classical ballet on amphetamines.
It has tutus resembling foam rubber discs, and is danced to the music
of...Schubert.

Jiří Kylián

Jiří Kylián was the longtime director of Netherlands Dance Theater, a
company that —like him— combined ballet with contemporary sensibil-
ities. He achieved international acclaim for *Sinfonietta* to the music of
fellow Czech Leoš Janáček. Kylián also created a delightful comic ballet,
Symphony in D.

Peter Martins

Balanchine encouraged several of his dancers to choreograph. *Calcium Light Night,* an edgy pas de deux to the inscrutable music of Charles Ives, was Peter Martins's first work. Since taking the reins of New York City Ballet, Martins has choreographed many ballets and explored a wide range of music, including American composer John Adams's *Fearful Symmetries*. His deft condensation of *The Sleeping Beauty* preserves beloved set pieces and divertissements while propelling the story with modern stagecraft.

Mark Morris

Mark Morris's contemporary choreography shows balletic origins and employs formal groupings while at the same time breaking away from a strict ballet vocabulary and often—in his own company—a traditional ballet body type. *L'Allegro il Penseroso ed il Moderato* is one of his best-known works. Morris can also be hilariously satirical and campy; his spoof of *The Nutcracker, The Hard Nut,* provides comic relief at the holidays.

Kirk Peterson

Kirk Peterson's inventive choreography, in both traditional and contemporary modes, draws on classical ballet vocabulary. *Amazed in Burning Dreams* is stylish, hard-driving ballet to a propulsive score by Philip Glass; the ballet's slower, lyrical passages are all the more arresting in their contrast to the forceful music and the sleek, futuristic costumes. Peterson has created his own versions of Petipa's classics including an American *Nutcracker* set in California during the Gold Rush.

Twyla Tharp

Twyla Tharp danced in Paul Taylor's company before forming her own group, and was one of the pioneer crossover choreographers coming from modern dance to work with ballet companies. She made *Push Comes to Shove* for Mikhail Baryshnikov, which he danced to ragtime wearing a bowler hat. Tharp later worked a similar magic for Ethan Stiefel in a pas de deux from *Known by Heart*. She has an affinity for a new type of virtuoso: the regular guy who can do incredible things. *Surfer at the River Styx* is the darker sibling of *Known by Heart;* both are to the "junk music" of Donald Knaack.

Christopher Wheeldon

Christopher Wheeldon was trained at the Royal Ballet and danced most of his career at New York City Ballet, a mix that is evident in his broad range. Though still young, the prolific Wheeldon has created narrative, nonnarrative, comedic, full-length, and historically themed works. He can be really funny or disturbing or intriguingly abstract. His imaginative choreography is grounded in ballet, and musically erudite. *Scènes de Ballet*, *Mercurial Manoeuvres*, *Polyphonia*, and *Carnival of the Animals* all show different aspects of his impressive talent.

Modern Dance and Beyond

Alvin Ailey

"That's my perception of what dance should be—a popular form wrenched from the elite." Alvin Ailey's vision triumphs in *Revelations*. For over forty years, when his company dances to "Rocka My Soul," jubilant audiences have been standing up, clapping their hands in time to the music, and joyously singing along. Ailey not only popularized modern dance, he created a multiracial troupe of versatile and highly accomplished dancers at a time when concert dance was overwhelmingly white. His work taps universal themes of spirituality, despair, and exultation, and also themes particular to the black experience. *Cry,* a stirring solo of suffering, survival, and triumph, is dedicated to black women everywhere, "especially our mothers." It was created for the powerful and statuesque Judith Jamison, who became artistic director when Ailey died in 1989. The company continues to perform Ailey's works along with those of other contemporary choreographers.

Les Ballets Trockadero de Monte Carlo

The well-informed parodies presented by the all-male "Trocks" poke
fun at ballet traditions, choreography, dancers, Russianized names,
costumes—not even the playbills are safe from satire and groan-
inducing puns. Choreographers from Petipa to Balanchine to Martha
Graham are knowingly skewered. In their *Dying Swan* (complete with
bourrées on pointe) the costume actually molts.

Maurice Béjart

Béjart's theatrical ballets are generally better received in Europe than
in the United States. His steamy *Boléro* features a dancer on top of a table,
surrounded by onlookers. The lead can be male or female, and can be
danced demurely—or not. The corps is usually but not necessarily
of the opposite sex.

Martha Clarke

An original and highly influential member of Pilobolus, Martha Clarke has gone on to create powerfully vivid, theatrical works on her own such as *Vienna: Lusthaus*.

Merce Cunningham

Merce Cunningham often collaborated with the composer John Cage, and their ideas were influenced by Eastern philosophy. Cunningham uses "chance operation," the flipping of a coin to determine the structure of a dance. Perhaps the most uniquely Cunningham of all performances is an "Event," a performance created out of sections of existing dances, reshuffled by chance operation to make a new dance.

Boris Eifman

Very few are lukewarm about Boris Eifman's over-the-top dance dramas. Working with his company based in St. Petersburg, Eifman spins grand-scale theatrical stories about historical or literary figures. See *Red Giselle*, based on the life of the ballerina Olga Spessivtzeva, and decide for yourself.

Martha Graham

The most influential modern dancer and choreographer of the last century, Martha Graham galvanized audiences throughout her long career with dramatic portrayals of mythological and historical heroines. Her students and dancers, including Merce Cunningham and Paul Taylor, became leaders of the next generation of modern dancers. *Appalachian Spring* is a dance of life among pioneers in a young America, *Diversion of Angels* a meditation on love. *Night Journey* and *Errand into the Maze* explore the myths of Oedipus and the Minotaur respectively, and retell them from the points of view of the heroines, Jocasta and Ariadne.

José Limón

José Limón was born in Mexico and moved to New York in 1928. He performed with the modern-dance pioneers Doris Humphrey and Charles Weidman before founding his own company in 1945, with Humphrey as artistic director. Limón created several classics of lyrical modern dance; the best known is his reduction of Shakespeare's *Othello* into the powerful quartet *The Moor's Pavane*.

José Limón and Betty Jones in *The Moor's Pavane.*

Momix

Pilobolus cofounder Moses Pendleton formed his own troupe of dancer-illusionists. They make ingenious use of lighting, costumes, and props to create humorous or eerily beautiful tableaux in works like *Opus Cactus*, *Baseball*, and *Sunflower Moon*, later called *Lunar Sea*.

Pilobolus

In the early 1970s undergraduates at Dartmouth applied their athleticism and wit to dance. The troupe that emerged is Pilobolus, named for a fungus. Pilobolus replaced a conventional dance vocabulary with its own style, and replaced the conventional model of one artistic director or choreographer with a collaborative one. Of the troupe's early members, Michael Tracy, Jonathan Wolken, Robby Barnett, and Alison Chase are now *all* artistic directors. Pilobolus's original approach to dance has endured over thirty years. My favorite Pilobolus works are *Untitled*, in which serene giantesses in nineteenth-century costume give birth to enigmatic near-naked men, and *Day Two*, to music of Brian Eno, David Byrne, and the Talking Heads. *Day Two*, inspired by a rain storm, builds to an extraordinary conclusion: the dancers whoosh across the entire width of the stage, sliding, splashing, and frolicking on a thin sheet of water.

Paul Taylor

Paul Taylor has created scores of works for the troupe he founded in 1954. The Taylor style is weighted but has a more balletic quality than other "modern" techniques. Taylor can be fall-off-your-chair funny or nostalgic or scary or exuberant. His work ranges from joyful, even ecstatic pieces to Baroque music such as *Aureole* to dark, probing works of social criticism such as *Speaking in Tongues* to the romantic and poignant *Sunset*. He has been called the greatest living dancemaker, and with good reason.

Must-See Ballet at a Glance

The Afternoon of a Faun
1912 Vaslav Nijinsky/Claude Debussy
1953 Jerome Robbins/
Claude Debussy

Agon
1957 George Balanchine/
Igor Stravinsky

L'Allegro il Penseroso ed il Moderato
1988 Mark Morris/George Frederick
Handel

Amazed in Burning Dreams
1993 Kirk Peterson/
Philip Glass

Apollo
1928 George Balanchine/
Igor Stravinsky

Appalachian Spring
1944 Martha Graham/
Aaron Copland

Asia
1989 Eliot Feld/Maurice Ravel

Aureole
1962 Paul Taylor/
George Frederick Handel

Baseball
1994 Moses Pendleton/
various mixed media

La Bayadère
1877 Marius Petipa/Ludwig Minkus

Les Biches
1924 Bronislava Nijinska/
François Poulenc

Boléro
1961 Maurice Béjart/Maurice Ravel

Calcium Light Night
1978 Peter Martins/
Charles Ives

Carnival of the Animals
2003 Christopher Wheeldon/
Camille Saint-Saëns

The Concert
1956 Jerome Robbins/
Frédéric Chopin

Concerto Barocco
1941 George Balanchine/
Johann Sebastian Bach

Coppélia
1870 Arthur Saint-Léon/
Léo Délibes

Le Corsaire
1856 Joseph Mazilier/Adolphe Adam

Cry
1971 Alvin Ailey/Alice Coltrane, Laura
Nyro, the Voices of East Harlem

Dances at a Gathering
1969 Jerome Robbins/
Frédéric Chopin

Day Two
1981 Daniel Ezralow, Robert Faust,
Jamey Hampton, Carol Parker, Moses
Pendleton, Peter Pucci, Cynthia
Quinn, and Michael Tracy (for
Pilobolus)/ Brian Eno, David Byrne
and the Talking Heads

Diversion of Angels
1948 Martha Graham/
Norman Dello Joio

Don Quixote
1869 Marius Petipa/
Ludwig Minkus

The Dream
1964 Frederick Ashton/Felix
Mendelssohn, arr. John Lanchbery

The Dying Swan
1905 Michel Fokine/
Camille Saint-Saëns

Errand into the Maze
1947 Martha Graham/
Gian Carlo Menotti

Études
1948 Harald Lander/ Carl Czerny, arr.
Knudåge Riisager

Fancy Free
1944 Jerome Robbins/
Leonard Bernstein

Fearful Symmetries
1990 Peter Martins/John Adams

La Fille Mal Gardée
1789 Jean Dauberval/(Original composer unknown, Ferdinand Hérold's
score added 1828)
1960 Frederick Ashton/
Ferdinand Hérold, arr. Lanchbery

The Firebird
1910 Michel Fokine/Igor Stravinsky
1949 George Balanchine/
Igor Stravinsky

Flower Festival at Genzano
1858 Auguste Bournonville/
Holger Simon Paulli, Edvard Helsted,
and M. Strebinger

The Four Temperaments
1946 George Balanchine/
Paul Hindemith

Giselle
1841 Jean Coralli and Jules Perrot/
Adolphe Adam

The Green Table
1932 Kurt Jooss/Fritz Cohen

Harbinger
1967 Eliot Feld/Sergei Prokofiev

The Hard Nut
1991 Mark Morris/
Pyotr Ilyich Tchaikovsky

In G Major
1975 Jerome Robbins/Maurice Ravel

In the Middle, Somewhat Elevated
1987 William Forsythe/
Thom Willems

In the Night
1970 Jerome Robbins/
Frédéric Chopin

Known by Heart Duet
1998 Twyla Tharp/Donald Knaack

The Leaves Are Fading
1975 Antony Tudor/Anton Dvorak

Lilac Garden (Jardin aux Lilas)
1936 Antony Tudor/Ernest Chausson

Mercurial Manoeuvres
2000 Christopher Wheeldon/
Dmitri Shostakovich

Monotones I and Monotones II
1965 Frederick Ashton/Erik Satie

The Moor's Pavane
1949 José Limón/Henry Purcell

Napoli
1842 August Bournonville/
Niels Wilhelm Gade, Edvard Helsted,
Holger Simon Paulli,
Christian Lumbye

Night Journey
1947 Martha Graham/
William Schuman

Les Noces
1923 Bronislava Nijinska/
Igor Stravinsky

The Nutcracker
1892 Lev Ivanov/
Pyotr Ilyich Tchaikovsky

Onegin
1965 John Cranko/
Pyotr Ilyich Tchaikovsky

Opus Cactus
2001 Moses Pendleton/various

Parade
1917 Léonide Massine/Erik Satie

Pas de Quatre
1845 Jules Perrot/Cesare Pugni

Les Patineurs
1937 Frederick Ashton/Giacomo
Meyerbeer, arr. Constant Lambert

Petroushka
1911 Michel Fokine/Igor Stravinsky

Pillar of Fire
1942 Antony Tudor/
Arnold Schönberg

Polyphonia
2001 Christopher Wheeldon/
Gyorgy Ligeti

Push Comes to Shove
1976 Twyla Tharp/Franz Joseph
Haydn, Joseph Lamb

Red Giselle
1997 Boris Eifman/Pyotr Ilyich
Tchaikovsky, Alfred Schnittke,
Georges Bizet

Revelations
1960 Alvin Ailey/
traditional spirituals

Rodeo
1942 Agnes DeMille/Aaron Copland

Romeo and Juliet
1965 Kenneth MacMillan/
Serge Prokofiev

Le Sacre du Printemps
1913 Vaslav Nijinsky/Igor Stravinsky

Scènes de Ballet
1999 Christopher Wheeldon/
Igor Stravinsky

Schéhérazade
1910 Michel Fokine/
Nikolai Rimsky-Korsakov

Serenade
1934 George Balanchine/
Pyotr Ilyich Tchaikovsky

Sinfonietta
1978 Jiří Kylián /Leoš Janáček

The Sleeping Beauty
1890 Marius Petipa/
Pyotr Ilyich Tchaikovsky

Speaking in Tongues
1988 Paul Taylor/Matthew Patton

Le Spectre de la Rose
1911 Michel Fokine/
Carl Maria von Weber

Square Dance
1957 George Balanchine/Antonio
Vivaldi, Arcangelo Corelli

Sunflower Moon (Lunar Sea)
2004 Moses Pendleton/various

Sunset
1983 Paul Taylor/Edward Elgar

Surfer at the River Styx
2000 Twyla Tharp/Donald Knaack

Swan Lake
1895 Marius Petipa and Lev Ivanov/
Pyotr Ilyich Tchaikovsky

La Sylphide
1836 August Bournonville/
Herman Lovenskjøld

Les Sylphides
1909 Michel Fokine/Frédéric Chopin

Symphonic Variations
1946 Frederick Ashton/César Franck

Symphony in D
1976 Jiří Kylián/Joseph Haydn

The Taming of the Shrew
1969 John Cranko/Domenico
Scarlatti, arr. Kurt-Heinz Stolze

Theme and Variations
1947 George Balanchine/
Pyotr Ilyich Tchaikovsky

The Three-Cornered Hat
1919 Léonide Massine/
Manuel de Falla

Le Train Bleu
1924 Bronislava Nijinska/
Darius Milhaud

Untitled
1975 Robby Barnett, Alison Chase,
Martha Clarke, Moses Pendleton,
Michael Tracy, Jonathan Wolken
(for Pilobolus)/ Robert Dennis

The Vertiginous Thrill of Exactitude
1996 William Forsythe/
Franz Schubert

Vienna: Lusthaus
1986 Martha Clarke/Richard Peaslee

Historical Time Line

Early-mid 1400s Dancing, both as an entertainment and an activity, grows popular among the nobility of northern Italy. Elaborate pageants and extravaganzas feature dancing. Courtiers hire dancing masters for private instruction.

1463 Guglielmo Ebreo (William the Jew of Pesaro), disciple of dancing master Domenico da Piacenza, writes a treatise on dancing, exhorting courtiers to develop grace, rhythm, and memory. His contemporary Antonio Cornazano publishes a manual describing various dances.

1489 The Duke of Milan's marriage is celebrated with a lavish theatrical feast; the various courses are accompanied by danced entrées, each relating to the food being served.

Early-mid 1500s *Spectaculi* flourish in Italy. Held both indoors and outdoors, they feature a variety of entertainments, including dancing. Horse ballets are popular.

1533 Catherine de Medici marries the future King Henri II of France and introduces Italian dancing to the French court.

Mid-late 1500s Ballet de cour (court ballet), blossoms in France with help from imported Italian ballet masters. Dancers are elaborately masked and wigged.

1580 Florentine artists, aristocrats, scholars, and musicians, in an attempt to re-create ancient Greek tragedy, form the Camerata group and produce the forerunner of modern opera.

1581 *Ballet Comique de la Reine*, created by ballet master Balthazar de Beaujoyeulx, is presented at the court of France. The first major unification of mime, music, decoration, and dance for a narrative purpose, it is a spectacle for ten thousand guests lasting nearly six hours.

1588 Thoinot Arbeau (a.k.a. Jehan Tabourot) publishes *Orchésographie*, an influential treatise on dance steps, rhythms, and notation.

1594–1596 Shakespeare writes *Romeo and Juliet* and *A Midsummer Night's Dream*.

Early 1600s Poet/dramatist Ben Jonson and architect/set designer Inigo Jones collaborate to make the court dancing of England, the masque, as splendid as France's ballet de cour.

Early-mid 1600s Ballet de cour evolves, through the musically intensive ballet melodramatique and the spectacle-intensive ballet mascarade, into ballet à entrées, sets of danced divertissements. Men wear tights, women are concealed under enormous skirts up to six feet in diameter.

1653 Louis XIV of France, avid dancer and patron of ballet, becomes forever known as the Sun King (*le Roi du Soleil*) when he dances the role of Apollo, god of the sun, in the *Ballet de la Nuit*.

1661 Louis XIV establishes the Académie Royale de la Danse, and in 1669, the Académie Royale de Musique, forerunner of the Paris Opera Ballet School.

1661 Dramatist Molière creates *Les Facheux*, the first comédie-ballet, a play with danced segments throughout; in which the dancing relates directly to the story being told.

1670–1671 After its successful debut at court, Molière's *Le Bourgeois Gentilhomme*, with music by Jean-Baptiste Lully and dances by Pierre Beauchamps, is presented at the theater of the Palais Royale.

Mid-late 1600s Lully—violinist, composer, conductor, dancer and mime—is court composer to Louis XIV, collaborating with Molière on comédie-ballets and creating numerous musical court entertainments. Ballet master Beauchamps, virtuosic dancer and reputed inventor of the pirouette, creates dances for Louis XIV's court, codifies ballet technique with an emphasis on turnout, and defines the five basic positions of the feet. What will later be called danse d'école—formalized, academic dance—emerges. French terminology becomes the standard.

1681 The first performance by a professional female dancer at a public theater, Lully and Beauchamps's *Le Triomphe de L'Amour*, originally created for a court wedding, is produced at the theater of the Palais Royale. Mademoiselle Lafontaine dances the leading female role, originally performed by Beauchamps himself.

Late 1600s–early 1700s Opéra-ballet becomes popular. Singing introduces danced entrées relating to the action. Stage dancing becomes more distinct from ballroom dancing and requires real turnout. Women, though allowed to dance in public, are still encumbered by their wigs and heavy skirts, and have only a limited vocabulary of steps.

1687 Lully dies from a wound caused by stabbing his foot with his music stick.

1700 Building on the work of Beauchamps and his successor Pécour, Feuillet publishes *Choréographie*, a system of dance notation.

Early 1700s Louis Dupré, known as the god of the dance, Michel Blondi, and Claude Balon, are leading male dancers. Danse haute or danse d'élévation (high dancing) begins to supersede danse

basse or danse terre à terre (low dancing) as dancers take to the air with jumps and beats.

1725 Pierre Rameau publishes *The Dancing Master*. Although a manual for social dancing, it defines terms, emphasizes correct placement and elegant carriage, and describes the correct execution of steps, including the correct ways to bow, curtsy, and remove one's hat.

1730s A scandalous costume reform: Marie-Anne Cupis de Camargo shortens her skirts and takes the heels off her shoes the better to perform (and be seen performing) "mens' steps" such as cabriole and entrechat quatre.

1734 More scandalous costume reform: Marie Sallé literally lets her hair down to dance *Pygmalion*, and she wears a gown appropriate to her character—thin and loose, without the customary stiff bodice and oversized skirt.

1735 *Les Indes Gallantes*, an opera-ballet of record opulence, is a triumph for its composer, Jean-Philippe Rameau.

1740s La Barbarina (Barbara Campanini), exemplifying the speed, strength, and virtuosity of the Italian school, delights audiences with entrechat huit.

1760 Choreographer Jean Georges Noverre, reformer and champion of the ballet d'action, publishes *Lettres sur la Danse et le Ballet*.

1766 Anne Heinel of Stuttgart excels at turning and introduces pirouettes à la seconde.

Mid-late 1700s Gaetan Vestris, a leading male dancer and ballet

master at the Académie Royale de la Danse, exemplifies the danseur noble genre with his tall, elegant physique and stately manner. His son Auguste is acclaimed for his virtuosic turns and jumps.

1789 Jean Dauberval creates *Le Ballet de la Paille*, now known as *La Fille Mal Gardée*, the oldest ballet still performed today. Its lighthearted story about ordinary people is a noteworthy departure from ballet's previous mythological subjects.

1796 Charles-Louis Didelot achieves spectacular success with *Flore et Zéphyre*, in which the dancers soar over the stage suspended by wires.

Early-mid 1800s Female dancers rise onto the tips of their toes for brief, thrilling moments. Heavy skirts and headdresses are replaced by the "Romantic tutu," a simple white gown. Ballerinas' costumes are also influenced by the fashion for flowing dresses with a high, Empire waist.

1801–1834 Didelot is ballet master in chief to the tsar of Russia.

1812–1821 Salvatore Vigano, after a successful twenty-year performing career, becomes ballet master at La Scala in Milan and creates the *Choréodrame*, mimed performance hailed as theatrical genius. Beethoven composed his only ballet score for Vigano.

1830 Carlo Blasis publishes *The Code of Terpsichore*, a manual on technique and training. It emphasizes the importance of daily practice and, among other terms, it defines "attitude."

1830–1877 Auguste Bournonville is ballet master and choreographer at the Royal Theater in Denmark. Ballet flourishes in relative isolation.

1832 Marie Taglioni stars in *La Sylphide*, the first full-length ballet on pointe.

1834 Fanny Elssler's Paris debut marks the beginning of her success and her great rivalry with Taglioni.

1836 Bournonville produces his own version of *La Sylphide*—the one usually seen today—starring Lucile Grahn.

1839 American ballerina Augusta Maywood debuts in Europe.

1840–1842 "The Divine Fanny" Elssler enchants American audiences during her United States tour.

1841 Newcomer Carlotta Grisi becomes a star dancing the premiere of *Giselle*, by Jean Coralli and Jules Perrot, at the Paris Opera.

1841 Christian Johansson, Taglioni's partner, accompanies her to St. Petersburg and remains there as a leading dancer and influential ballet master.

1842 Bournonville's *Napoli* premieres.

1845 *Pas de Quatre*, the historic assembly of four of the greatest ballerinas of the day—Taglioni, Grisi, Grahn, and Fanny Cerrito (affectionately nicknamed Mademoiselle Cherry-toes)— with choreography by Perrot, is performed in London.

1846 Mazilier's *Paquita*, starring Grisi, premieres in Paris. Petipa's 1881 revision is most often seen today.

1848–1859 Perrot is ballet master in chief to the tsar of Russia.

1859 Jules Léotard, the French aerialist who inspired the song "The Daring Young Man on the Flying Trapeze," is the first to somersault from one trapeze to the next. He called the long-sleeved, tight-fitting garment he designed a maillot; it now bears his name.

1859–1869 Arthur Saint-Léon is ballet master in chief to the tsar of Russia.

1862 Teenage prodigy Emma Livry is mortally burned when her tutu catches fire from the open gas lamps that light the stage.

Late 1800s "La Décadence" in Paris, ballet declines; women dance male roles. In St. Petersburg, however, ballet enjoys a golden age under Petipa's artistic direction and the tsars' patronage.

1869 Marius Petipa creates his version of *Don Quixote* in Russia and becomes ballet master in chief to the tsar.

1870 Saint-Léon's *Coppélia* premieres in Paris.

1876 Mérante's *Sylvia* premieres in Paris. Délibes's lovely score inspires numerous restagings over the years.

1877 In Russia, the premiere of Petipa's *La Bayadère* in St. Petersburg is a success; the premiere of Reisinger's *Swan Lake* in Moscow a failure.

1880s–1890s Italian ballerinas like Pierina Legnani, Virginia Zucchi, Antonietta Dell'Era, and Carlotta Brianza dazzle Russian audiences with their virtuosic technique.

1890 Petipa's *The Sleeping Beauty* premieres with Carlotta Brianza as Aurora and Enrico Cecchetti as the Bluebird.

1892 Petipa's *The Nutcracker* premieres with Antonietta Dell'Era as the Sugar Plum Fairy.

1893 Pierina Legnani, wearing special reinforced Italian-made shoes, and able to spot her turns, performs thirty-two fouettés on full pointe in *Cinderella*. Audiences are thrilled.

1895 A new version of *Swan Lake*, with choreography by Petipa and Lev Ivanov, to music by Tchaikovsky and starring Legnani— who inserts thirty-two fouettés into the Black Swan pas de deux— is a tremendous success.

1897 The Danish ballerina Adeline Genée performs in London, where she remains to become England's leading dancer.

1898 Petipa's *Raymonda* premieres with Pierina Legnani as Raymonda.

1890s–1900s Legnani is declared *prima ballerina assoluta*, a title later bestowed on Russian ballerina Mathilda Kchessinska. Russian ballerinas try to imitate Legnani's prodigious multiple pirouettes and sustained balances on pointe, but find their soft shoes inadequate. Cobblers attempt to reinforce ballet slippers with the only materials available: burlap, leather, paper, and paste. The modern pointe shoe is born.

1905 Isadora Duncan, who calls herself the "enemy of ballet," performs in Russia. Her novel, nonacademic barefoot dances to the works of Chopin and other "serious" composers encourage Michel Fokine in his efforts to reform ballet.

1905 Fokine creates *The Dying Swan* for Anna Pavlova. It premieres at the Maryinsky in 1907.

1907 Fokine's *Chopiniana* premieres at the Maryinsky. A later version, *Les Sylphides*, dispenses with the story line.

1908–1912 Fokine works with Serge Diaghilev's Ballets Russes and creates *The Polovtsian Dances from Prince Igor* (1909), *Les Sylphides* (1909), *Schéhérazade* (1910), *Firebird* (1910), *Le Spectre de la Rose* (1911), *Petroushka* (1911) and others. Tamara Karsavina and Vaslav Nijinsky are the leading dancers.

1909 The Ballets Russes debuts in Paris. Until Diaghilev's death in 1929 the troupe enjoys immense success and produces innovative and influential works—collaborations among the greatest choreographers, dancers, composers, and artists of the time.

1910 Jaques-Dalcroze, a reformer of music education, builds a school in Switzerland for teaching Eurythmy, his method of bringing out innate musicality through movement.

1910 Anna Pavlova, after dancing with the Maryinsky and then briefly with Diaghilev, launches a relentless international touring career unsurpassed in ballet history.

1912 Nijinsky's choreographic foray for the Ballets Russes, *Afternoon of a Faun*, scandalizes Paris audiences with its primal and sexually suggestive depiction.

1913 The Paris audience riots at the premiere of Nijinksy's *Rite of Spring*.

1915 Ruth St. Denis, famous for her dances evoking exotic locales, and husband, Ted Shawn, form a dance troupe and open the first Denishawn school in Los Angeles, California.

1917 The Ballets Russes presents Léonide Massine's *Parade*, the first cubist ballet, with sets and costumes by Picasso and music by Satie.

1918 Enrico Cecchetti, renowned first for his virtuosity as a dancer and then for his brilliance as a teacher, having taught the greatest dancers of the day in St. Petersburg and then for Diaghilev, establishes a school in London. The Cecchetti Society is created in 1922 to further expand the "Cecchetti method."

1920 Philip Richardson establishes the Association of Teachers of Operatic Dancing, later to become the Royal Academy of Dancing.

1921 Diaghilev revives *The Sleeping Beauty* for the London season. Nicholas Sergeyev, former régisseur at the Maryinsky, recon-

structs Petipa's choreography from notebooks in Stepanov notation. Starring Olga Spessivtseva, with décor by Léon Bakst, it is an artistic triumph and a financial catastrophe.

1923 The Ballets Russes presents Bronislava Nijinska's *Les Noces*, to music of Stravinsky.

1924 Diaghilev hires Georgi Balanchivadze, soon to be known as George Balanchine, to choreograph for the Ballets Russes.

1926 Martha Graham, trained at Denishawn, founds her dance company and school in New York.

1928 The Ballets Russes presents the premiere of Balanchine's *Apollon Musagète*, later *Apollo*, to music by Stravinsky. Serge Lifar is Apollo. Balanchine later described it as a turning point in his creative life.

1929 The Ballets Russes presents the premiere of Balanchine's *Prodigal Son*, to Prokofiev's score, with Serge Lifar as the prodigal.

1929 Dorothy Alexander forms the Dorothy Alexander Concert Group, forerunner of the Atlanta Ballet.

1932 *The Green Table*, Kurt Jooss's expressionist, antiwar ballet, wins a choreography competition in Paris.

1931–1935 Ninette de Valois and Marie Rambert engage Frederick Ashton to choreograph ballets for their respective companies, the Camargo Society and the Ballet Club, in London.

1932 The Ballets Russes is resurrected as the Ballet Russe de Monte Carlo—the first of several successor troupes—under the leadership of Colonel de Basil and René Blum, with Balanchine and Massine as choreographers, Serge Grigoriev as régisseur, and Alexandra Danilova as leading dancer. "Baby ballerinas" Tatiana Riabouchinska, Irina Baronova, and Tamara Toumanova, are featured stars. Blum will later die at Auschwitz.

1933 Fred Astaire's film debut in *Dancing Lady*, with Joan Crawford. He soon stars in *The Gay Divorcée* with Ginger Rogers and the screen's most famous dancing couple is born.

1933 Lincoln Kirstein persuades Balanchine to come to the United States.

1933 San Francisco Opera Ballet is founded. In 1942 William Christensen, one of three brothers who influenced ballet in the American West, becomes artistic director of the now separate San Francisco Ballet and in 1944 stages the first complete *Nutcracker* in America. Lew Christensen, and later Helgi Tomasson, both leading Balanchine dancers in their time, are subsequent artistic directors.

1933 Ted Shawn and his Men Dancers present lecture demonstrations at Jacob's Pillow, Shawn's farm in western Massachusetts. The troupe tours over the next seven years, raising the status of male dancers in America.

1934 With Alicia Markova as her star, de Valois stages full-length classics, including *Giselle*, *Swan Lake*, and—for the first time in the West—*The Nutcracker*.

1934 Balanchine and Kirstein establish the School of American Ballet. Balanchine creates *Serenade*, with his students in the cast; it is first performed privately at an estate outside New York City.

1934 Russian teacher Agrippina Vaganova publishes *Basic Principles of Classical Ballet*, her precepts and codification of Soviet technique.

1936 Ballet Rambert presents the premiere of Antony Tudor's *Jardin aux Lilas* at its tiny Mercury Theater in London.

1938 Sergei Denham takes over the Ballet Russe de Monte Carlo with Massine as choreographer. Massine creates, among other works, *Gaîté Parisienne*, an instant and enduring hit. The company tours extensively for the next twenty-four years, greatly influencing American taste and perception of ballet. Alexandra Danilova and Frederic Franklin are its long-time stars.

1938 Ruth Page, dancer, prolific choreographer, and founder of the Ruth Page Ballets, creates *Frankie and Johnny*—a controversial use of public funds—and remains prominent in Chicago for over thirty years.

1939 Ninette de Valois revives *The Sleeping Princess* (*The Sleeping Beauty*) starring Margot Fonteyn for her Sadler's Wells Ballet with the help of Sergeyev and music

director Constant Lambert—a landmark production.

1939 Lucia Chase and Richard Pleasant found Ballet Theatre (later American Ballet Theatre) and present its first season, in New York, in 1940.

1939 The Winnipeg (later Royal Winnipeg) Ballet is founded by Betty Farrally and Gweneth Lloyd.

1940 Leonid Lavrovsky's *Romeo and Juliet* to Prokofiev's score premieres at the Kirov starring Galina Ulanova.

1942 The first theater in America designed just for dance, the Ted Shawn Theater, opens at Jacob's Pillow. Shawn directs Jacob's Pillow Dance Festival for the next thirty years.

1942 Antony Tudor creates *Pillar of Fire*, his first choreography for Ballet Theatre.

1942 Ringling Brothers and Barnum and Bailey Circus presents Balanchine's *Ballet of the Elephants* to commissioned music by Stravinsky at Madison Square Garden.

1943 Rodgers and Hammerstein's *Oklahoma!* opens on Broadway with choreography by Agnes de Mille.

1944 Ballet Theatre presents Jerome Robbins's *Fancy Free*, to music by Leonard Bernstein, with Robbins himself in the cast.

1944 Martha Graham's *Appalachian Spring* to Aaron Copland's score premieres.

1946 The Sadler's Wells Ballet presents a splendidly refurbished *Sleeping Beauty* and the premiere of Frederick Ashton's *Symphonic Variations* at its new home at Covent Garden.

1948 Balanchine and Kirstein's Ballet Society becomes the New York City Ballet and a resident of City Center. The company presents *Orpheus*, *Symphony in C*, and *Concerto Barocco* at its inaugural performance.

1948 *The Red Shoes*, a film starring Moira Shearer and featuring Léonide Massine and Robert Helpmann, is a surprise box office hit that draws a new audience to ballet.

1949 José Limón's *The Moor's Pavane* premieres.

1949 At the New York City Ballet Maria Tallchief offers an extraordinary performance in Balanchine's *Firebird*. Jerome Robbins joins the company.

1950 Harald Lander organizes the first Royal Danish Ballet Festival revitalizing the Royal Danish Ballet.

1951 Celia Franca founds the National Ballet of Canada in Toronto. Betty Oliphant founds its school. Karen Kain is leading ballerina for many years. James Kudelka, an acclaimed choreographer, becomes artistic director in 1996.

1952 Robert Joffrey and Gerald Arpino found The American Ballet Center—known as the Joffrey Ballet School—in New York's Greenwich Village.

1954 Paul Taylor presents his first work, *Jack and the Beanstalk*, a collaboration with artist Robert Rauschenberg.

1956 In London Ninette de Valois's Sadler's Wells Ballet becomes the Royal Ballet.

1956 Roman Jasinski and Moscelyne Larkin, former Ballet Russe dancers, found the Tulsa Ballet, later Tulsa Ballet Theatre.

1957 *West Side Story*, conceived, choreographed, and directed by Jerome Robbins, with music by Leonard Bernstein and lyrics by Stephen Sondheim, opens on Broadway—a hit that successfully integrates dance with storytelling.

1957 Balanchine and Stravinsky collaborate to create *Agon* for the New York City Ballet.

1957 Ludmilla Chiriaeff founds Les Grands Ballets Canadiens de Montréal.

1958 Alvin Ailey American Dance Theater debuts in New York.

1959 Despite cold war politics, Sol Hurok, the impresario responsible for introducing great ballet to many Americans, brings the Bolshoi, starring Maya Plisetskaya and Galina Ulanova, to New York. For many in the United States it is a first look at Soviet ballet.

1960 Alvin Ailey choreographs *Revelations* to traditional black gospel music.

1961–1974 Dramatic defections from the Soviet Union's Kirov Ballet: Rudolf Nureyev (1961), Natalia Makarova (1971), and Mikhail Baryshnikov (1974) all

seek political and artistic freedom in the West.

1962 Rudolf Nureyev dances *Giselle* with the Royal Ballet's Margot Fonteyn; a legendary partnership begins.

1963 The Ford Foundation creates a $7.5 million grant and scholarship program for ballet, supporting New York City Ballet, the School of American Ballet, and regional organizations.

1963 Barbara Weisberger founds the Pennsylvania Ballet.

1963 E. Virginia Williams's troupe becomes the Boston Ballet.

1964 The Cincinnati Ballet debuts.

1963–1970 Frederick Ashton directs the Royal Ballet; featured dancers include Fonteyn, Nureyev, Antoinette Sibley, Anthony Dowell, Merle Park, Monica Mason, Georgina Parkinson, Svetlana Beriosova, Leslie Collier, and the powerfully dramatic Lynn Seymour.

1965 President Lyndon B. Johnson signs into law the National Endowment for the Arts and Humanities; American Ballet Theatre receives the first federal grant to an arts organization.

1965 Ronn Guidi founds the Oakland Ballet. Karen Brown, the first African American woman to lead a ballet company, succeeds him in 2000.

1965 Kenneth MacMillan choreographs *Romeo and Juliet* for Royal Ballet.

1965 In Germany, John Cranko's *Eugene Onegin* premieres at the Stuttgart Ballet, starring Marcia Haydée.

1967 Robert Joffrey revives Kurt Jooss's *The Green Table* to great acclaim.

1968 William Christensen's Utah Civic Ballet becomes Ballet West.

1969–1971 Arthur Mitchell, the first African American principal at New York City Ballet, forms a classical ballet school for black dancers with Karel Shook as associate director. The Dance Theatre of Harlem debuts in 1971.

1970 Kenneth MacMillan becomes artistic director of the Royal Ballet on Ashton's retirement.

1970 Italian ballerina Carla Fracci is unforgettable as *Giselle* in guest appearances at American Ballet Theatre with Erik Bruhn of Denmark.

1971 Dartmouth undergraduates Robb (Moses) Pendleton, Steve Johnson, and Jonathan Walken present a work called *Pilobolus*, later the name of the immensely popular troupe.

1974 Eliot Feld forms the Eliot Feld Ballet, forerunner of Feld Ballets/NY and Ballet Tech.

1975 Paul Taylor premieres *Esplanade*.

1976 Ben Stevenson, a former dancer at the Royal Ballet and the English National Ballet, becomes artistic director of the Houston Ballet (founded in 1969).

1976 Mary Day founds the Washington Ballet; Choo San Goh is chief choreographer.

1977 Francia Russell and Kent Stowell, formerly of New York City Ballet, become artistic directors of Seattle's Pacific Northwest Ballet (founded in 1972). They are succeeded by fellow N.Y.C.B. alumnus Peter Boal in 2005.

1978 Eliot Feld creates a free dance program for public school students in New York and will eventually recruit almost exclusively from it for his company.

1977 The film *The Turning Point* starring Mikhail Baryshnikov, Alexandra Danilova, Shirley Maclaine, Anne Bancroft, and Leslie Browne, sparks popular interest in ballet.

1978 Baryshnikov joins the New York City Ballet.

1980 American Ballet Theatre presents Natalia Makarova's staging of the full-length *La Bayadère*, the first outside of Russia. The corps is an unqualified success in the demanding Kingdom of the Shades act.

1980–1989 Baryshnikov is artistic director of American Ballet Theatre.

1983–1989 Rudolf Nureyev is artistic director of the Paris Opéra Ballet.

1983 Peter Martins and Jerome Robbins become co-ballet masters in chief at New York City Ballet on the death of Balanchine. Robbins steps down in 1990.

1986 Miami City Ballet debuts under the leadership of former New York City Ballet star Edward Villella.

1987 The Balanchine Trust is established to maintain the integrity of Balanchine's work, setting a precedent in the dance world for preserving choreography.

1987 The Joffrey Ballet presents a vivid and powerful reconstruction of Nijinsky's *Sacre du Printemps*, by Millicent Hodson and Kenneth Archer.

1989–1999 William Forsythe's Frankfurt Ballet presents seasons in Paris to great acclaim.

1992 The Kirov again becomes the Maryinsky.

1995 The Joffrey Ballet moves from New York to Chicago. Gerald Arpino continues as artistic director.

1998 Artistic director Kevin McKenzie presents Petipa's full-length *Le Corsaire* at American Ballet Theatre, an artistic and box office success that showcases its virtuosic dancers.

2001 Peter Martins names Christopher Wheeldon resident choreographer at New York City Ballet, the first time anyone has held this title.

2002 Alvin Ailey American Dance Theatre breaks ground at the site of its new permanent home in New York, to open in 2004. The Joan Weill Center for Dance is the largest facility devoted exclusively to dance in the United States.

2003–2004 Balanchine's centennial is celebrated in a tribute season at New York City Ballet and elsewhere.

Glossaries

Ballet Terms

Note: All jumping steps are initiated with, and finish in, demi-plié unless otherwise stated.

Abstract ballet A ballet without a narrative, which may or may not directly respond to musical accompaniment. A dance that presents movement in a pure form.

Adage/adagio [ah-**dahzh** or ah-**dah**-jee'ō] Italian: *ad agio*, at leisure or at ease. 1. Slowly and fluidly. 2. An exercise in ballet class, at the barre and/or center floor, that includes slow, fluid movements such as développés; clear, linear positions such as arabesques and attitudes; and smooth, controlled pirouettes, all intended to build strength, poise, grace, and aplomb. 3. The section of a classical ballet pas de deux in which the female dancer executes most of the smooth, extended poses and movements with the support and assistance of her male partner.

Air, en l' [ahn **layr**] French: in the air. Indicates a movement's location off the ground. such as rond de jambe en l'air, or tour en l'air.

Allegro [ah-**leh**-grō] Italian: lively, quick, merry. Brisk, elevated steps such as jeté, brisé, assemblé, sauté. Allegros often follow adagio in classical ballet classes and are classified as "petit," "medium" or "grand," depending on whether the steps are small and fast or big and traveling.

Arabesque [ah-rah-**besk**] From the Italian *arabesco*, which means "in Arabian fashion" and refers to a style of intricate ornamentation. In ballet, a position in which the dancer stands on a straight or bent supporting leg with the other leg straight and extended directly behind (derrière), with the foot on the floor (à terre) or in the air (en l'air). See page 98.

Arrière, en [ahn ah-ree-**ayr**] French: backward. Indicates any movement that travels backward.

Arrondi [ah-rohn-**dee**] French: round or curved. Any movement or position with a round or curved shape. For example, battement or bras arrondi.

Artistic director One who leads and manages the creative operations of a dance company (also called ballet master or mistress in chief). Responsibilities include selecting artistic personnel, such as dancers, choreographers, and set, costume and lighting designers; determining and sometimes choreographing the repertory; and maintaining artistic standards.

Assemblé [ah-sohm-**blay**] French: assembled or gathered. A step in which, from a plié on both legs, the dancer brushes the working leg, pushes off with the supporting leg, springs into the air, and brings the legs together in the air before landing on both feet together in fifth position. Assemblé may be either petit or grand depending on the height of the brushed leg. The many variations of the basic assemblé include assemblés dessus, dessous, devant, derrière, en avant, en arrière and en tournant (see also assemblé, en tournant, grand).

Assemblé, en tournant, grand [grahnd ah-sohm-**blay** ahn tour-**nahn**] An assemblé that travels and turns, usually on the diagonal or in a circle. The dancer brushes the working leg 90 degrees à la seconde, pushes off with a strong plié of the supporting leg, and assembles the legs in the air while turning 180 degrees to end in fifth position.

Attitude [ah-tih-**tood**] From the Italian, *attitudine*, which refers to a way of holding the body. A pose developed by the Italian ballet master Carlo Blasis, based on Gian de Bologna's statue of Mercury. The working leg extends back or front and is bent. See page 100.

Avant, en [ahn ah-**vahn**] French: forward. Indicates any movement that travels forward.

B plus Colloquial term for a preparatory or waiting position in which the working leg is bent and the working foot is turned out, pointed, and resting on the floor behind the standing leg.

Balancé [bah-lahn-**say**] French: to sway or rock. Usually executed to a waltz (3/4 time), this step can travel or stay in place. On count one, the dancer brushes the working leg and lightly jumps onto it. On count two, she crosses the other leg behind or in front to press the ball of the foot onto the floor for a slight lift. On count three, she replaces the original working leg on the floor in plié with the other foot in sur le cou-de-pied.

Balançoire, en [ahn bah-lahn-**swahr**] French: seesaw or teeter-totter. A movement usually with grands battements or attitudes, in which a dancer swings her leg front (devant) and back (derrière) through first position. The upper body moves in opposition to the working leg, leaning slightly away from it.

Ballerina Derived from the Italian, *ballare*, which means to dance. A female principal dancer of a company. Commonly used to indicate any female dancer in a ballet company.

Ballet master, mistress The man or woman who oversees company rehearsals and sets and reviews pieces in the repertory, and/or regularly conducts company class.

Balletomane [bah-**leh**-toh-mayn] One who has great enthusiasm and excitement for ballet, not necessarily someone who practices ballet himself.

Ballon [bah-**lohn**] French: balloon. A buoyant quality in jumping, including springing lightly into the air, sustaining elevation, descending with control, and bouncing up again.

Ballonné, pas [pah bah-loh-**nay**] French: puffed out. Also called "ballonné simple." A jump in which the dancer springs off the supporting leg, extends the working leg front, back, or side, and lands with the extended leg in sur le cou-de-pied or retiré.

Ballotté [bah-loh-**tay**] French: tossed. A series of coupés dessous and dessus, performed with a forward and backward rocking of the upper body, usually in effacé.

Barre [bahr] A horizontal dowel or railing, either attached to the walls of a dance studio or freestanding with supports, which the dancer holds for balance during beginning exercises of a ballet class. The first part of ballet class is often referred to as "the barre."

Barrel turn A turning jump usually done as a series across the floor—often part of a jazz dance class. From a deep plié, the dancer steps across herself and presses off into the air with both legs in attitude, rotating 360 degrees to land and initiate the next one. The dancer's body mimics the shape of a barrel.

Bas, en [ahn **bah**] Indicates a low position of the arms. For example, fifth position en bas.

Battement [baht-**mahn**] French: beating. An action in which the dancer "beats" with a straight or bent working leg. Variations include battement tendu, battement dégagé, grand battement, grand battement en cloche, petit battement sur le cou-de-pied.

Battement dégagé [baht-**mahn** day-gah-**zhay**] Similar to battement glissé (French) and battement tendu jeté (Russian). Starting in the first or fifth position, the leg extends through battement tendu, front, side, or back, slightly off the floor, and returns to the starting position. See page 135.

Battement en cloche [baht-**mahn** ahn-**klohsh**] French: bell or bell tower; like the swinging of a bell. The movement of the working leg, either petit or grand, as it swings front and back through the first position.

Battement, grand [grahn baht-**mahn**] Also called grand battement jeté (Russian). The working leg is thrown away from the supporting leg, the dancer dynamically brushes her leg through the battement tendu and dégagé, up to 90 degrees or higher in all directions and controls its descent back to the starting position.

Battement serré [baht-**mahn** sayr-ay] Also known as battement battu. French: tightened or squeezed. Small, quick beats of the pointed working foot usually while en relevé. With the upper leg held firm, the working foot rapidly taps the supporting ankle and never extends farther than a few inches away from the supporting leg. See page 145.

Battement sur le cou-de-pied, petit [puh-**teet** baht-**mahn** soor leh koo-deh-pee-**ay**] The lower leg moves sur le cou-de-pied front to back and vice versa, en relevé or standing flat. See page 145.

Batterie [bah-**t'ree**] The entire vocabulary of beaten steps, or steps to which beats are added. Batterie can also refer to the portion of a dance class that includes all allegro exercises.

Battu [bah-**too**] French: beaten. To enhance a step by adding leg beats, e.g. pas battu, assemblé battu, changement battu, etc.

Bras [brah] Arm or arms.

Bras bas [brah **bah**] Arms in a low position. See page 88.

Brisé [bree-**zay**] French: broken or snapped. Like a traveling assemblé with a beat. The dancer brushes the working leg out from fifth position plié, springs off the supporting leg, and before landing beats the working leg against the supporting leg, which has moved out to meet it, devant or derrière. The movement is said to be *broken* by the battu of the legs. The dancer's upper body leans into the direction of the movement.

Cabriole [kah-bree-**ōl**] French: caper, a playful leap. Italian: *capriola*, literally a goat's leap. A large jump often included in grand allegro, in which the working leg forcefully brushes out while the supporting leg springs up to beat

against and slightly elevate the extended leg. Cabriole may be petite or grande, according to the height of the legs in the air (45 degrees or 90 degrees), and may be executed devant, derrière and à la seconde.

Cambré [cahm-**bray**] French: curved or arched. A backward, forward or sideways arch of the upper body, with the arms and head following the movement. Cambré devant requires a bend from the hips with a straight back; cambrés à côté and derrière bend from the waist. See page 132.

Canon See Musical Terms.

Catch step A syncopated step in which the dancer transfers her weight by bringing the ball of one foot just behind the other to push the supporting leg forward. Frequently used in jazz and tap.

Cavalier [kah-vuh-**leer**] French: escort. A ballerina's male partner.

Cecchetti method [cheh-**keh**-tee method] See page 68.

Chaîné [sheh-**nay**] French: chained. A shortened term for tour chaîné déboulé, literally "linked, rolling turns." A step in which the dancer executes a series of half turns on alternating feet. See page 178.

Changement [shahnzh-**manh**] A jump from fifth position that changes feet in the air to land with the opposite foot in fifth position front. Sometimes called changement de pieds, literally, "change of the feet."

Chassé [shah-**say**] French: chased. A sliding step in which the dancer

transfers her weight outward from either first or fifth position. From demi-plié, she slides into a second or fourth position, springs off both feet, joining them en l'air. The second foot appears to *chase* the first as it slides out again through the first or fifth position demi-plié. In the Cecchetti method, the dancer stays grounded and the transfer of weight through plié ends in a pointe tendu.

Choreographer [kore-ee-ah-gruh-fur] From the Greek words *choriea* (dance) and *graphos* (writer). One who creates dances.

Choreologist [kore-ee-ah-loh-jist] One who records and notates a piece of choreography, as outlined by the system of choreology (see Choreology).

Choreology [kore-ee-ah-loh-gee] A system devised by Rudolf Benesh for recording the movements, orientations, and entrances of dancers as well as their relationships to other dancers on the stage. All movements are recorded on a five-line staff with a series of frames corresponding to specific time frames or frames of musical accompaniment. Also included are notations of other production considerations, such as costumes, lighting, scenery, and so on.

Chug A step in which the dancer leans her weight onto one or two feet in plié and sharply and quickly slides along the floor, usually about six to twelve inches away from the starting position, without her feet leaving the floor.

Cinquième [sang-**kyem**] French: fifth. Refers to one of the five positions of the arms or feet. See pages 87 and 90.

Classique [klas-**eek**] One of the genres, or body types, sometimes used in classifying and casting dancers. Shorter, and slighter in build than the danseur noble, the classique excels at faster movement and elegant virtuosity.

Cloche, en [ahn **clohsh**] French: like a bell. The brushing of the working leg back and forth through first position with a strong swinging movement, often done as grands battements en cloche and grands battements en cloche en attitude.

Cobra A rippling arm movement from one extended arm through the shoulders to the other arm and back. A wavelike upper body movement.

Coda Like that of a musical composition, the final section of a ballet or pas de deux usually with the principal dancers reappearing for a concluding dance—the finale.

Contraction Used most often in modern dance, a tensing or shortening of the muscles. Usually the lower abdominals contract, causing the lower back to round. A contraction followed by its release can spring the dancer into the next step or position and create a strong, accented quality of movement.

Contretemps [kahn-tra-**tohn**] French: against time. A step that allows the dancer to switch weight and direction before the downbeat of the musical phrase. From pointe tendue croisée derrière, the dancer executes rond de jambe en dedans, with a change of direction to the other downstage corner. With a

small jump that begins with the rond de jambe or just after it, the legs exchange places in midair to land in effacé devant, and the dancer immediately tombés forward onto the extended leg.

Corps de ballet [kor duh bah-**lay**] The group of dancers that constitutes the main portion of a ballet company, excluding the principal dancers and soloists.

Coryphée [koh-ree-**fay**] One of the leading dancers in the corps de ballet, often a soloist.

Côté, de [duh koh-**tay**] French: sideways. The direction of movement sideways, either to the right or left.

Cou-de-pied, sur le [soor leh koo-duh-**pyay**] French: on or above the neck of the foot. The position in which the working foot is pointed and held just above the supporting ankle, devant or derrière, with the heel near midcalf and the toes touching the top of the ankle, or a position in which the working foot wraps around the supporting ankle. See page 94.

Coupé [koo-**pay**] French: cut. A changing of feet in which one foot *cuts* either in front of (dessus) or behind (dessous) the other, ending with the new working foot pointed by the ankle of the supporting leg. Coupé is commonly used as a connecting step to another jump or movement (see Coupé jeté); it can be performed sauté or en relevé.

Coupé jeté [koo-**pay** zheh-**tay**] Also called coupé brisé. A two-part step in which a coupé dessous is followed by jeté battu dessus.

Croisé [kwah-**zay**] French: crossed. One of the main orientations of the body. The dancer is angled to the audience with the legs in a crossed position; the downstage leg is the front leg. See pages 102–3.

Croix, en [ahn **kwah**] French: crosswise. Indicates that an exercise is to be done in each direction—devant, à la seconde, derrière—and then again à la seconde.

Danseur (or **danseuse**) **noble** [dahn-**soor**, dahn-**suhz** nō-bluh] One of the genres, or body types, sometimes used in classifying and casting dancers. Also called serieux/serieuse, the noble type is tall, long-limbed and aristocratic, and specializes in grave, slow movements and expressive mime.

Dedans, en [ahn duh-**dahn**] French: inward. In a circular direction in toward the supporting leg.

Dégagé, pas [pah day-gah-**zhay**] French: disengaged or released. The extension of a pointed, fully arched foot à terre or en l'air in any direction.

Dehors, en [ahn-duh-**or**] French: outward. In a circular direction out away from the supporting leg.

Demi-caractère [deh-**mee** kar-ak-**tayr**] One of the genres, or body types, sometimes used in classifying and casting dancers. Shorter and stockier than classique or noble types, the demi-caractère excels at jumps, turns, and other lively elements, many of which derive from folk dance rather than court ballet.

Demi-plié [deh-**mee** plee-**ay**] A half bend of the knee or knees. See page 128.

Demi-pointe, sur la [soor lah deh-**mee** pwahnt] Note: The French pronunciation is "pwahnt," but "poynt" is the accepted pronunciation in English. French: on the half pointe. Standing on the ball of the foot (or balls of the feet), with the heels high off the ground, as opposed to standing on the entire foot (as in standing flat) or on full pointe.

Derrière [duh-ree-**ayr**] French: behind. The direction of a movement or placement of the working foot or leg behind the body.

Dessous [duh-**soo**] French: underneath. Indicates that the working leg passes behind or under the supporting leg, as in coupé dessous.

Dessus [duh-**see'oo**] French: on top of or above. Indicates that the working leg passes in front of or above the supporting leg, as in coupé dessus.

Détourné [day-toor-**nay**] French: turned away. From fifth position, the dancer rises sur les pointes or demi-pointes and fully rotates toward the back leg so that the feet switch positions and finish either en pointe or flat in fifth.

Deuxième [duh-**zyem**] French: second. Refers to the second of the five positions of the arms or feet. See pages 86 and 89.

Devant [duh-**vahn**] French: in front of. The direction of a movement or placement of the working foot or leg in front of the body.

Développé [day-vloh-**pay**] French: spread or stretched. The commonly shortened term for temps développé, referring to the extension of the leg from the standing fifth position through sur le cou-de-pied, retiré, and attitude to a fully stretched leg devant, à la seconde, or derrière. Frequently incorporated in adagio at the barre or in the center.

Divertissement [dee-vayr-tees-**mahn**] French: amusement or recreation. A short but complete dance within a larger ballet that displays the technical abilities of one or more dancers. Also, a dance scene in an opera.

Écarté [ay-car-**tay**] French: separated, open or scattered. One of the main orientations of the body. The dancer is angled diagonally to the audience with the working leg open à la seconde (either à terre or en l'air) toward either the downstage or the upstage corner (devant or derrière). See pages 102–3.

Échappé [ay-shah-**pay**] French: escaped. An action in which both legs "escape" from first or fifth position to second or fourth position. Échappé sauté springs from demi-plié into the air, landing in demi-plié in the open position; échappé relevé shoots the legs out from demi-plié to the open position en pointe or demi-pointe.

Effacé [eh-fah-**say**] French: shaded. One of the main orientations of the body, sometimes referred to as en ouvert. The dancer is angled to the audience, with the legs in an open position; the upstage leg is the front leg. See pages 102–3.

Emboîté [ahm-bwah-**tay**] French: boxed or fitted together. In the Russian and Cecchetti schools, a step that springs without brushing from one foot to the other, with the front leg in sur le cou-de-pied or attitude position. Emboîté is often done turning across the floor (emboîté en tournant). In emboîté sur les pointes the back leg extends from fifth position to à la seconde, and sweeps around to close in fifth position front. The knees are straight and the dancer is on full or demi-pointe. The step is then repeated with the other leg working, and with continued alternations the dancer travels forward. It may also be done with the working leg moving from front to back so the dancer travels backward.

Enchaînement [ahn-shen-**mahn**] French: linking or chaining. A sequence of steps.

Entrechat [ahn-tra-**shah**] Italian, *intreccaire*, to interweave or braid. A jump from fifth position in which the legs cross and beat in the air a certain number of times and land in either fifth position or on one foot with the other foot in sur le cou-de-pied. The number of beats varies from two to ten (entrechat deux, trois, quatre, cinq, six, sept, huit, neuf, dix) with even numbers ending in fifth position and odd numbers ending on one foot in demi-plié. See pages 166–67.

Enveloppé [ahn-vloh-**pay**] French: enveloped or wrapped. A développé in reverse. Often part of an en dedans turn, the extended working leg pulls in to the supporting leg and down through retiré and sur le cou-de-pied to finish in fifth position relevé or plié.

Épaulé [ay-paw-**lay**] French: of the shoulder. One of the eight orientations of the body in the Cecchetti system, in which the dancer faces one of the downstage corners in second arabesque with épaulement, and the head tilted slightly toward the audience.

Épaulement [ay-pawl-**mahn**] Twisting the upper body and shoulders and inclining the head in order to extend the line of a position. See page 93.

Eurythmy Interpreting musical compositions, poetry, or the rhythm of spoken words with free-style body movement.

Extension The working leg in its highest position, devant, à la seconde, or derrière. A dancer is said to have excellent extension if she can maintain proper form while holding her extended leg straight, with the foot above shoulder level.

Face, en [ahn **fahss**] French: in front, facing. Any position directly facing the audience, with both hips square to the front.

Failli [fah-**yee**] French: coming near or to the point of. An elevated connecting step in which the dancer first lifts or springs from a croisé fifth position, squeezes her legs together as her body rotates a quarter turn, and lands on the front foot in effacé as her back leg extends to a low arabesque, then slides through first position plié, reaching the croisé fourth position front with her weight on the front foot.

Fermé, fermée [fehr-**may**] French: closed. A movement that ends with both feet in a closed position, such as fifth position, as in sissonne fermé.

Fish dive A spectacular step in partner work in which the ballerina jumps to her partner and ends with her head lower than her feet in a completely supported, arched position with one leg extended in arabesque and the other in retiré, arms crossed in front of her chest or extended. The pose suggests that of a fish with its flexible body.

Flic-flac [fleehk-**flahk**] A quick, sharp movement often included in the barre exercises. The dancer briskly brushes her working leg from an extended position à la seconde at 45 degrees through a fifth position front, then back (or the reverse), then extends it again à la seconde. In flic-flac en tournant en dehors, the working foot brushes in from the extended position to an overcrossed sur le cou-de-pied derrière; the dancer relevés and, while turning, opens the working foot to brush again and cross in front of the supporting leg and then finish à la seconde. For flic-flac en dedans, the movement reverses.

Fondu [fahn-**doo**] French: melted. Bending the knee of the supporting leg (the term plié is also used). In battement fondu, the working and supporting legs bend and straighten at the same time with the working leg finishing in an extended position front, side, or back. See page 138.

Fouetté [fooh-eh-**tay**] French: whipped. The whipping movement of the working foot or leg or a forceful whipping around of the body to change direction.

Fouetté, grand A turning of the body, en relevé or with a jump, toward or away from the working leg, in which the supporting leg remains in position but rotates in the hip socket, usually finishing with the working leg in its extended position. The many variations include grand fouetté effacé en face and grand fouetté battu en tournant.

Fouetté rond de jambe en tournant [fooh-eh-**tay** rohn duh **zhahm** ahn toor-**nahn**] Turning fouettés. See page 177.

Frappé [frah-**pay**] French: struck. Short for battement frappée. A sharp, forceful motion of the working leg to an extended position several inches off the floor. See page 140.

French school See page 64.

Gargouillade [gar-goo-**yahd**] French: gurgle or rumble. An embellished pas de chat. In gargouillade en dehors, the front leg executes a small rond de jambe en l'air en dehors as the back leg springs off the ground. Before landing, the back leg executes a rond de jambe en l'air en dedans in time to finish devant in fifth position. Gargouillade en dedans starts with the back leg and reverses the directions of the ronds de jambe en l'air.

Glissade [glee-**sahd**] French: glide. An essential connecting step, used often as a preparation for steps of elevation. From a fifth position plié, one leg brushes out to a few inches off the ground. With a small push from the supporting leg, the dancer transfers her weight onto the extended leg, lands in plié with the other leg now extended, and smoothly glides the extended leg into fifth position plié. Several variations of glissade (depending on starting and ending position): devant, derrière, dessous, dessus, en avant, en arrière, or sur les pointes.

Grand [grahnd] French: big, large, great.

Grotesque One of the genres, or body types, formerly used in classifying and casting dancers. An almost extinct genre (and a word that has a harsher meaning today than when originally applied), grotesques were like our modern character actors, playing the supporting roles, many of which—rustics, monsters—were, in fact, grotesque.

Isolation Focused movement of one particular part or area of the body, for example, shoulder or head roll, hip tilt, or rib thrust.

Italian school The Italian style of dancing and teaching, specifically as developed under ballet master Carlo Blasis, who became director of the Imperial Dance Academy in Milan in 1837. He codified all that was known of ballet technique up until that time and, with a more detailed understanding of human anatomy, introduced a degree of skill and mastery that differentiated the Italian school from the French. One of the Italian school's greatest students and subsequent teachers was Enrico Cecchetti.

Jazz hands A position of the hands in which the fingers are splayed wide apart. Sometimes the hands shimmy and shake for added effect.

Jeté [zheh-tay] French: thrown. A movement that transfers the dancer's weight from one leg to the other with a strong, thrown movement of the initiating leg. There are many types of jeté.

Jeté battu [zheh-tay bah-too] A jeté with beats. The dancer brushes the working leg to the side, springs off the supporting leg, beats it in front or in back of the brushed leg, and lands in sur le cou-de-pied devant or derrière.

Jeté entrelacé [zheh-tay ahn-truh-lah-say] A jeté interlaced. Specific term of the Russian school. See tour jeté.

Jeté, grand [grahnd zheh-tay] A large jeté, usually forward. The dancer brushes the working leg to hip level (as in grand battement), pushes forward off the supporting leg, momentarily suspends the legs in a horizontal position in the air, and lands in arabesque or attitude.

Jeté, petit [puh-tee zheh-tay] A small jeté, in which the dancer brushes the working leg to 45 degrees, springs off the supporting leg, stretches both legs in the air, and lands with the working leg extended or in a sur le cou-de-pied. Petit jeté is buoyant, sprightly, and an essential step in developing ballon.

Layout A jazz step in which the dancer reaches up or forward with her arms and vigorously pulls them down to arch backward, causing a ripple effect from the top of her body downward, often performed with one leg extended and the other in a deep plié.

Line The relationship of the various body parts to one another: head, neck, shoulders, hips, legs, arms, feet, hands. A graceful and fluid arrangement of the body parts is essential in all positions.

Manège [mah-nezh] French: ring. Indicates a combination of dance steps that travel in a circular path.

Ouvert, ouverte [ooh-vayr, ooh-vayrt] French: open. Indicates body, arm, or foot positions, or specific steps that are not crossed or closed. For example, second and fourth positions of the feet and sissonne ouverte. In the French school, indicates the effacé orientation.

Par terre [pahr tayr] French: on or along the ground. Rond de jambe par terre moves along the ground. À terre means on or to the ground. In arabesque à terre the working foot touches the ground.

Pas [pah] French: step or pace. A dance step that often involves a transfer of weight. Also indicates a dance that specifies the number of dancers, usually fewer than ten—for example, pas de deux means dance for two.

Pas de basque [pah duh bahsk] French: Basque step. A step based on folk dancing of the Basque region in northern Spain; in ballet, a three-part step either par terre or with sauté. The dancer begins in fifth position plié croisé, brushes the foot in front, then sweeps it across and open in a circular motion; the supporting leg pushes up to spring the dancer across and onto the open leg, thus transferring the weight; the former supporting leg sweeps through first position to slide croisé devant with the back leg extended in tendu. With sauté, a jump is added at the end to complete the movement.

Pas de bourrée [pah duh booh-**ray**] Bourrée step. The most common version is a three-part step in which the dancer steps onto demi-pointe or full pointe on one leg, then transfers her weight onto demi-pointe or full pointe on the second leg, then returns her weight to the first foot à terre. Often a linking step to other movement, pas de bourrée has numerous versions, including pas de bourrée dessous, dessus, devant, derrière and en tournant. Pas de bourrée couru is executed on pointe with the dancer in a tight fifth position relevé with the back foot initiating a brisk gliding movement across the floor. Commonly referred to as simply bourrée.

Pas de chat [pah duh **shah**] French: cat's step. A jump in which the working leg lifts through retiré and the supporting leg then does the same creating a moment of suspension with both legs in retiré in the air; the feet land one after the other in fifth position. See page 168–69.

Pas de chat, grand [grahnd pah duh **shah**] In grand pas de chat développé the first leg executes a quick développé from the retiré out to à la seconde and the second leg immediately bends at the knee to bring the foot in close to the body. The dancer travels in the air

in this position and lands on the extended leg. Russian school: the dancer brushes the back leg diagonally forward and springs off the supporting leg; then in the air, the extended leg pulls sharply into retiré, the feet land together in plié, and the back leg slides through first position to croisé front.

Pas de cheval [pah-duh shu **vahl**] French: horse's step. Like a horse's hoof pawing the ground, from point tendu the working foot is drawn along the floor in to the supporting leg, passes through fifth position and sur le cou-de-pied or retiré, and returns to an extended position with a small développé.

Pas de deux, trois, quatre, cinq, six [pah-duh-**duh**, twah, katr, sank, seess] A dance for two, three, four, five, or six people.

Passé [pah-**say**] French: passed. Movement in which the working leg passes from one position to another. For example, from fifth position, the working foot slides up the supporting leg with a pointed foot to pass by the supporting knee and back down the supporting leg to fifth on the opposite side. Or from an extended position front, the working leg can pass by the supporting knee into an arabesque. Can also take a simpler form as in tendu front passing through first position to tendu back. See page 97.

Penchée [pahn-**shay**] French: leaning. A movement in which the dancer's body leans or tilts away from an elevated working leg. It is important to maintain the same

angle or relationship between the working leg and the upper body, and from the stretched arm to the pointed toes during the movement. Most commonly, penchée is done with an arabesque.

Petit [puh-**tee**] French: small.

Piqué [pee-**kay**] French: pricked. Stepping directly onto the demi-pointe or pointe of the new, straight supporting leg with the other leg raised as in piqué arabesque or piqué retiré, sometimes with a turn. Also, a brisk lifting of pointed feet when on pointe, as in pas de bourré piqué. In the French school piqué à terre is the same as pointe tendu.

Pirouette [peer-oo-**wet**] The classic ballet turn in which the dancer completes a full revolution on one foot, either on demi-pointe or full pointe, en dedans or en dehors. See pages 176–77.

Pirouette à la seconde [peer-oo-**wet** ah-lah-seh-**gond**] A pirouette with the working leg held straight out to the side position. Often done with the supporting leg continuously lifting to relevé and pressing in plié to propel the turns.

Pirouette piqué [peer-oo-**wet** pee-**kay**] A French school term. Same as piqué tour en dedans.

Plié [plee-**ay**] French: bent. A bending of the knee or knees. Pliés are either demi or grand, according to the depth of the bend. In demi-plié the knees bend and press open over the toes, and the heels stay on the ground. In grand plié, the knees press open and as far down as possible, causing the heels to lift off the floor. Only in second position of the feet do the heels stay down in grand plié. See page 128.

Pointes, sur les [soor lay **pwahn**] Note: "Sur les pointes" should be pronounced the French way; otherwise say "on pointe" (on poynt). French: on the points. Steps executed while on the tips of the toes with the help of pointe shoes.

Port de bras [por duh **brah**] French: arm carriage. Refers to all movements of the arms in ballet, either the codified arm positions or as requested by a teacher or choreographer.

Posé [pô-**zay**] French: poised. A term of the Cecchetti method, similar to piqué, a transfer of weight from one foot to the other à terre, demi-pointe or pointe, often preceded by a dégagé or petit développé.

Première, en [ahn pruh-**mee'yayr**] French: first. Placement in or moving through a codified first position.

Prima ballerina [**pree**-mah bal-ler-**een**-a] A preeminent or exceptional female principal dancer. See page 69.

Prima ballerina assoluta [**pree**-mah bal-ler-**een**-a ah-soh-**loot**-a] The greatest or "absolute" ballerina. See page 69.

Principal dancer A male or female dancer in a ballet company who has reached a level of prominence and performs solo or leading roles in the company's repertory. See page 69.

Promenade [prah-meh-**nahd**] French: stroll. A pivoting movement while holding a specific position or shape, often arabesque. While maintaining her position, the dancer rotates on her supporting leg with slight and regular movements of the supporting heel. Also done en relevé with the help of a partner as a smooth rotation rather than as pivots with heel movements. Also refers to any stylized walk.

Quatrième [kah-tree-**yem**] French: fourth. Refers to the fourth of five positions of the feet and arms. À la quatrième devant and derrière are two of the major orientations of the body. See page 87, 90, and 102–3.

Raccourci [rah-koor-**see**] French: shortened. In the French school, synonymous with retiré (see definition below). Variations include battement raccourci, in which the working leg brushes to the side from fifth position and pulls swiftly in to touch the supporting leg at the knee with a pointed foot. Also, coupé fouetté raccourci, either with battu or sauté, when the dancer executes coupé dessous, then briskly extends the working leg out to the side and in again.

Régisseur [ray-zhee-**sir**] The person responsible for setting and/or maintaining choreography in a ballet company, often directing rehearsals and teaching company class. Can also mean a ballet master or production manager.

Relevé [ruh-leh-**vay**] French: raised or lifted. Any movement in which the dancer lifts one or both feet up to demi-pointe or full pointe.

Most schools define it as pressing up from a small plié.

Renversé [rahn-vayr-**say**] French: reversed or upset. A movement of the body during a turn in which the dancer's balance appears to be momentarily upset as the torso twists away from the extended working leg. In renversé en dehors, after a preparatory step such as coupé dessus or failli, the working leg is thrown out to croisé devant en l'air then sweeps through à la seconde in a grand rond de jambe to croisé derrière, either arabesque or attitude. The movement finishes with a turning pas de bourrée en dehors into fifth position. Renversé sauté includes a jump as the working leg passes through à la seconde.

Repertoire [reh-per-**twahr**] French: index list or catalogue. The complete inventory of dance pieces that a company has learned and is ready to perform. English version of the word is "repertory."

Répétiteur [re-peh-**ti-ter**] Generally a rehearsal director; may also mean the same as régisseur.

Resident choreographer A person who works regularly and sometimes exclusively with a dance company to create new ballets.

Retiré [ruh-teer-**ay**] French: withdrawn. A position in which the working leg is raised to hip level with the knee bent and pointed toes touching in front of, behind, or at the side of the supporting knee. Also, the action of lifting the working leg from fifth through the bent shape at the knee and back down to fifth. See page 97.

Révérence [ray-vayr-**ahnss**] French: bow or curtsy. The last exercise of a ballet class, in which the dancers acknowledge and pay respect to the teacher and pianist, often with curtsies, bows, and ports de bras.

Rond de jambe à terre, grand [grahnd rohn duh zhahm a **tayre**] The same movement as rond de jambe, with the supporting leg in demi-plié, thus creating a wider arc of the working leg.

Rond de jambe en l'air [rohn duh zhahm ahn **layr**] French: leg circle in the air. The foot of the working leg draws an oval or a letter "D" in the air by moving from an extended position à la seconde (90 degrees) to the inside of the supporting knee and out again. Can also be executed at 45 degrees with the working foot circling to the inside of the supporting calf. See page 146.

Rond de jambe, grand [grahnd rohn duh **zhahm**] The same movement as rond de jambe but with the working leg off the ground. See page 144.

Rond de jambe par terre [rahn duh **zhahm** par **tayr**], also called **rond de jambe à terre** French: leg circle on the ground. The working foot of a straight leg describes an arc on the floor, moving from front to back (en dehors) or back to front (en dedans). See page 137.

Rosin A powdery, sticky substance derived from the sap of pine trees that is applied to ballet shoes for friction. Dancers press the outer soles and tips of their slippers or pointe shoes in rosin before class

or performances as a safeguard against slippery floors.

Royale [roy-**yahl**] French: royal or regal. Also known as changement battu. From fifth position the dancer springs into the air and beats the thighs together before changing the feet to land in fifth position with the other foot in front. An embellished changement. See page 166.

Russian school See page 70.

Saut de basque [so duh **bahsk**] A Basque jump. A traveling, turning jump. The dancer steps out to second position plié, and does a half turn en dedans as the other leg forcefully brushes up and out to the side. The first leg pushes off the ground and moves to retiré as the turn is completed in the air.

Sauté [soh-**tay**] French: jumped or leaped. A step that is jumped such as grand fouetté sauté or échappé sauté.

Sautillé [soh-tee-**yay**] Hopping or with a hop.

Scissors jump A high, forceful jump in which the dancer brushes one leg forward and immediately swings it back as the other leg shoots forward in the air, creating the effect of a scissors. The dancer should reach a full split leg and horizontal position in the air at the height of the jump.

Seconde, à la [ah lah seh-**gond**] One of five arm and foot positions, meaning "to the second" position. See pages 86 and 89. Also refers to arm and leg movements to the side. For example, battement

à la seconde, tendu à la seconde, and so on.

Serré [seh-**ray**] French: closed or tight. Indicates compact movement such as petit battement serré.

Shimmy A shaking back and forth, usually of the shoulders.

Shorty George A low, comic walk with the knees bent and swinging from side to side. Named for Shorty George Snowden, a star Savoy Ballroom dancer in the late 1920s and early 1930s.

Sickling From "sickle," a curved farm implement. An incorrect, inwardly twisted position of the pointed foot. A correctly pointed foot should always have the heel forward and toes pointing downward in a straight line from the ankle. See page 81.

Sissonne [see-**sôn**] Derived from the name of the creator, the Count of Sissonne. In the basic form, a jump in which the dancer darts from two feet onto one foot in any direction, usually starting from fifth position and landing at least a hip distance away with one leg extended. See page 165.

Soubresaut [soo-bruh-**sô**] French: sudden jump. A jump that can travel across the floor or be done in place. Springing up from a fifth position plié, the dancer squeezes her thighs together in the air, points her feet and lands in the same foot position in fifth plié from which she started. The Russian school includes a slightly arched back in the air, with the feet also pushed slightly back to complete the line. See page 165.

Soubrette [soo-**bret**] A type of female role in which the character is coquettish and perky, or a type of body that is traditionally considered well suited to such a role, generally a petite dancer who excels at allegro.

Soussus [soo-**syoo**] French: under-over. A relevé from fifth position in which the legs pull closer together in a compact, crossed position. A dancer may assume the soussus position either in place or traveling.

Soutenu [soo-teh-**noo**] French: sustained or held up. Any step with sustained moments, such as assemblé soutenu en tournant.

Soutenu en tournant [soo-teh-**noo** ahn tor-**nahn**] Also known as assemblé soutenu en tournant, the turn executed by bringing the working leg in from tendu à la seconde. See page 178.

Spotting The action of the head that enables dancers to avoid becoming dizzy while turning. At the beginning of a turn, the dancer focuses on a stationary spot and continues to focus on it for as long as possible while turning, then quickly turns her head to refocus on it.

Stag leap A jump in jazz dance in which the front leg is bent and its toes touch the extended back leg mimicking the shape of a leaping deer.

Standing or supporting leg The leg on which the dancer stands while the working leg extends or moves.

Suspension 1. Sustaining and elongating a position of the arms or legs to enhance the dynamic of a movement, respond to a musical cue, or emphasize a character quality. 2. Pausing in a position while moving through it.

Taqueté [tah ke **tay**] French: wedged or pegged. Sharp, staccato pointework. Taqueterie is steps on pointe with a taqueté quality.

Teaser 1. A short, highlighted portion of a show that precedes the main performance and whets the audience's appetite for what's to come. 2. A Pilates exercise. See page 253.

Temps de cuisse [tahn duh **kweess**] French: thigh movement. A two-part movement starting in fifth position, in which one foot passes through dégagé or sur le cou-de-pied from back to front (or vice versa) on the preparatory beat. From there the working leg returns to fifth position plié and springs into sissonne front or back.

Temps de flèche [tahn duh **flehsh**] French: arrow movement. The action of the legs in which one acts as a bow and the other, a shooting arrow. There are several variations, all starting from fifth position plié:

The back leg brushes back and, as the supporting leg springs off the ground, bends and pulls in to retiré, as the front leg shoots forward in développé effacé and the dancer lands in plié on the other leg.

The front leg brushes forward in grand battement, pulls through retiré as the supporting leg springs off the ground to développé forward and the dancer lands in plié on the first leg.

The back leg brushes back, either straight or in attitude, while the supporting leg pushes off, then moves back to pass the first leg in the air. The dancer lands in plié on the first leg with the other leg either in attitude or stretched behind.

Temps de poisson [tahn duh pwah **sahn**] French: fish movement. Similar to a soubresaut, a jump that springs up from a fifth position plié, but with the back arched and the pointed feet crossed to resemble the tail of a fish. See page 164.

Temps levé [tahn luh-**vay**] French: lifted movement. A jump defined as pushing off from either one or both feet. See page 165.

Temps lié [tahn lee-**ay**] French: linked movement. A movement in which the dancer fluidly transfers her weight from one leg to the other. From fifth or first positions, the dancer pliés to slide open to fourth or second position, transfers the weight onto the sliding foot, and extends the pointed foot of the other leg either à terre or in an en l'air position such as à la seconde or arabesque. Temps lié is one of the oldest ballet steps, originating in French court dancing. More complex versions of the step involve jumping with the weight transfer.

Tendu [tahn-**doo**] French: stretched. Short for battement tendu. The sliding of the working foot, from first or fifth position, to the front, side, or back, with the working toes on the floor and the legs straight and stretched. See page 134.

Terre, à [ah **tayr**] French: on the ground. See par terre.

Time step A basic tap step that originated in vaudeville as a means of setting the tempo of a piece for the accompanying musicians. The most basic form uses a set rhythm of shuffle, step, hop, flap, step, then often repeats those moves on the opposite side.

Tire-bouchon [teer boo-**shahn**] French: corkscrew. A term of the Russian school. A turn toward the supporting leg in which the dancer brushes the working leg à la seconde and pulls it into retiré to execute a full turn on demi-pointe or pointe, finishing in plié. The movement simulates that of a corkscrew.

Tombée [tohm-**bay**] French: fallen. Movement in which the dancer "falls" or steps dynamically in any direction onto an extended and elevated working leg, ending in plié. Often used as a connecting step as in tombée pas de bourrée.

Tour de force [toor duh **forss**] French: feat of strength. A technically brilliant and virtuosic exhibition.

Tour en l'air [toor ahn **layr**] French: turn in the air. An important step in the male dancer's vocabulary, but not exclusive to men. From a fifth position plié the dancer jumps up, fully rotates with pointed feet crossed and extended downward, and ends in a fifth position plié with the opposite foot in front. More complex variations include two or three rotations in the air, or landings in arabesque, attitude, or on one knee.

Tour jeté [toor zheh-**tay**] Also known as jeté entrelacé and grand jeté dessus en tournant. A large jump in which the dancer brushes one leg in front, jumps straight up, and rotates 180 degrees in the air, landing on the first leg with the other leg extended in arabesque.

Tournant, en [ahn toor-**nahn**] French: turning. Any step done with a turn, as in pas de bourrée en tournant or assemblé en tournant.

Triplet A movement occurring on a musical count of three, as in balancé. In modern dance, a forward traveling movement that includes one step down in plié and two steps forward in relevé on the balls of the feet.

Troisième [twah-**zyem**] French: third. Refers to the third of the five positions of the arms and feet. See pages 87 and 90.

Turnout The rotation of the legs at the hip joints that governs the placement of the dancer's lower body in ballet.

Volé [vō-**lay**] French: flown. A buoyant, soaring quality as part of a step, such as brisé volé.

Working leg The leg that executes all the movement, either on the ground or in the air.

Music Terms

A tempo [ah **tehm**-pō] Indicates a return to the original speed of a musical composition after a temporary departure.

Adagio [ah-**dah**-jee'ō] Italian: at ease. A slow tempo.

Agitato [ah-gee-**tah**-tō] Italian: excited. In an exuberant and animated manner.

Allegro, Allegretto [ah-**leh**-grō, ah-leh-**greh**-tō] Italian: merry, cheerful. A fast tempo. Often the first or last movement of a sonata or symphony.

Andante [ahn-**dahn**-tay] At a walking speed. A moderate tempo that can be made slower or faster. For example molto andante indicates faster than a standard andante; meno andante means slower than a standard andante. Often the middle section of a sonata or symphony.

Andantino [ahn-dahn-**tee**-nō] Indicates a short andante musical piece or a variation of the andante within a composition; andantino is often, but not always, interpreted as meaning slightly faster than standard andante.

Canon From the Latin for "rule." Originated in the thirteenth century, the canon is the strictest form of contrapuntal imitation; one part imitates another exactly and entirely, at a specified moment. For example, "Row, row, row your boat," sung in a round, is a canon. (A canon in dance uses the same sort of imitation. Balanchine choreographed them often in imitation of the music. Stravinsky's music for the men's duet in *Agon* is a canon for two trumpets; the two men also dance in canon.)

Cantabile [kahn-**tah**-beeh-lay] Italian: singing. In a singing style.

Crescendo [creh-**shen**-dō] Italian: growing. A gradual increase in volume, indicated with a < sign or the abbreviation "cresc."

Decrescendo [deh-creh-**shen**-dō] A gradual decrease in volume, indicated with a > sign or the abbreviation "decresc." Also called diminuendo [deh-**meen**-yoo-ehn-doh].

Downbeat The first beat of a measure, so named because of the conductor's downward sweep of the arm when directing a musical ensemble to sing or play on the first note.

Fermata [fehr-**mah**-tah] A "hold" pertaining to a specific rest or note, indicating that it be sustained.

Flat A symbol, similar to a *b*, indicating that the note be lowered by one half tone.

Forte [**for**-tay] Italian: loud. Loudly, indicated with an *f*.

Fortissimo [for-**tee**-see-mō] Extremely loudly, indicated with an *ff*.

Grave [**grah**-veh] Italian: solemn. 1. Very slowly, in a weighty and austere manner. 2. One of the lowest possible musical pitches. 3. An extremely slow tempo.

Largo [**lahr**-gō] Italian: broad. Slowest tempo, demonstrative and poignant.

Legato [leh-**gah**-tō] Connected, flowing, and uninterrupted. Indicated with a curved line over the notes to be connected. Opposite of staccato.

Leggierro [leh-gee-**ehr**-rō] Italian: light. With a light touch in an agile and lively manner.

Lento [lehn-tō] Italian: slow. Very slow tempo.

Measure A unit of musical time containing a group of beats. The division of music into measures is determined by its pulse; often the accent, or downbeat, is on the first note.

Moderato [moh-deh-**rah**-tō] Moderate tempo, slightly faster than andante.

Molto [**mohl**-tō] Italian: much or very. Used to modify another term and increase it, as in *molto vivace* (very lively).

Non troppo [nohn **troh**-pō] Italian: not too much. With moderation. Also, a gauge of moderation in connection with another musical term, such as forte non troppo (not too loud).

Pianissimo [pee-yah-**nee**-see-mō] Extremely softly and quietly, indicated with a *pp*.

Piano [pee-yah-nō] Italian: quiet. Quietly, softly, indicated with a *p*.

Pizzicatto [pit-see-**kah**-tō] Italian: plucked. To pluck the strings of stringed instruments with the fingers instead of using the bow.

Poco [**poh**-kō] Italian: little. Used to modify another term and lessen it, as in ritard poco a poco (slow down little by little).

Prestissimo [prehs-**tee**-see-mō] The fastest possible tempo.

Presto [**prehs**-tō] Very fast tempo.

Ritard [ree-**tahrd**] Abbreviation for ritardando [ree-tahr-**dahn**-do]. A gradual decrease in tempo. Also

called rallentando [rah-lehn-**tahn**-do].

Scherzo [**shkayr**-tzō] Italian: joke. Commonly the third section of symphonies, quartets, and sonatas, often in 3/4 time, with brisk and lyrical rhythm and a playful manner.

Sharp A symbol, #, indicating that the note be raised by one half tone.

Sostenuto [soh-steh-**noo**-tō] Sustaining or prolonging the length of a note.

Staccato [stah-**cah**-tō] Sharp, separated, and distinct. A dot or wedge above or below a note in the music indicates staccato. Opposite of legato.

Staff An arrangement of five horizontal lines in, above, and below which the notes and other musical directives are drawn.

Syncopation [sihn-koh-**pay**-shun] An intentional disruption of the normal rhythm, pulse, beat, or meter of a musical phrase by shifting the accent away from the dominant beat.

Tempi [**tehm**-pee] Plural of tempo.

Tempo [**tehm**-pō] Italian: time. The speed of a musical composition or section within a composition, varying from very fast to very slow.

Time signature Indicates the specific meter of a musical composition, noted by two numbers at the beginning. For example, 3/4 indicates that each measure consists of the equivalent of three beats, and a quarter note equals one beat.

Vibrato [vee-**brah**-tō] A pulsing or vibration that enhances and adds a slight tremor to the tone. Singers waver the tone with their vocal cords; string instrumentalists shake their hands slightly to vibrate the strings.

Vivace [vee-**vah**-cheh] In a buoyant and sprightly manner.

Vlvacissimo [vee-vah-**chee**-see-mō] Even quicker and perkier than vivace.

Theater Terms

Apron The part of the stage extending in front of the curtain.

Bridge An elevated backstage walkway above the stage space that gives the backstage crew access to equipment.

Call The summoning of performers—the time they are expected to be at a particular place.

Call sheet A sheet posted backstage (or at a dance studio) that lists the dancers' names and at what times they are expected at the theater or rehearsal. Dancers must sign the sheet daily to indicate their presence and readiness for performances or rehearsals.

Catwalk An elevated walkway, not necessarily over an open area or stage space, that gives backstage crew access to equipment.

Crossover The area where performers cross behind the stage to make an entrance on the opposite side.

Curtain call The moment directly after the end of a performance when the entire cast comes on stage to bow or curtsy to the audience. The standard ending to a performance in response to applause.

Cyclorama A wall or curtain, often painted and often concave, placed at the back of the stage to give added dimension to the set, and to enhance the décor.

Downstage The front of the stage, closest to the audience. Originates from the early European stages that were raked, on a slant: thus, the performer's position would be literally *down*stage.

Dry tech A technical rehearsal in the performance venue but without actors; used to rehearse integration of lights, scenery, and sound.

Flyman A stage assistant responsible for operating the system of ropes, pulleys, and lines used to raise and lower scenery or to "fly" actors or dancers across the stage.

Footlights A set of lights inset at the front of the stage that temper the shadows often cast by overhead lights. Also used for special lighting effects.

Fresnel [freh-**nehl**] A lighting instrument invented by Augustin-Jean Fresnel (1788–1827). The lens is bumpy on one side and etched with concentric circles on the other, which produces a broad, soft light.

Gel The term for a color filter that slips onto a backstage light and consists of two clear pieces of plastic with a color adhesive in between. When light passes through, the filter absorbs all color except for that of the inner adhesive.

Green room The backstage room where performers wait and rest before going onstage. The origin of the name is unknown, but in deference to tradition most theaters still call it that. One explanation is that the color green is thought to be restful to the eyes and provides a relief from bright onstage lights.

Pit The area in front of or below the stage where the orchestra sits.

"Places" The backstage call from the stage manager or director of a company requesting that the dancers take their positions either on or offstage for the beginning of the ballet.

Scrim A coarsely woven cloth through which lights shine or action is viewed, creating specific lighting and staging effects. Usually unpainted, but when painted and lit from the front, the cloth appears opaque; when lit from behind it is transparent.

Shinbuster The lowest light on a vertical backstage lighting pole, so named because it illuminates the calves of the performer's legs.

Stage manager One who oversees all the backstage action during rehearsals and performances, including directing the stagehands and technical crew, calling out cues for lighting, curtains, and scene changes, and ensuring that the dancers are in their places for the start.

Upstage 1. Near the back of the stage, farthest from the audience. Originates from the early European stages that were raked, on a slant: thus the performer's position would be literally *up*stage. 2. A performer's moving toward the back of the stage in order to force another performer to turn his or her back to the audience, diverting attention away from the downstage performer. 3. To take the audience's attention away from another actor or dancer.

Wet tech A full technical rehearsal with dancers and all technical elements such as lighting, scenery, and sound.

Wings The sides of the stage, unseen by the audience, where the performers gather and prepare to enter the main stage.

Social Dances

Medieval, Renaissance, and Baroque Dances

Bourrée A lively Baroque era dance from France similar to, but faster than, the gavotte.

Chaconne A slow dance in 3/4 time.

Country dances Several cultures have dances for two, four or multiple couples, often involving rows, circles, or patterns. English country dancing originated in the seventeenth century or earlier and enjoyed a revival in the early twentieth century. In Europe, country dance became **contredanse**, to which the French **quadrille**, danced by four or more couples,

is also related. **Square dance** is popular in America and involves a caller who announces the steps.

Courante A French dance for couples popular in the sixteenth and seventeenth centuries in 3/2 or 6/4 time. According to a dancing master of the time, Louis XIV danced it with "unusual grace."

Galliard A vigorous dance in 6/8 time that originated in Italy in the sixteenth century. It was often paired with a pavane, a slower dance.

Gavotte A cheerful folk dance in 4/4 time that became a court dance under Marie Antoinette and later increased in complexity and difficulty to the point that only professional dancers could master the steps.

Gigue (also **Jig**) A lively folk dance in 6/8 time. Popular in Ireland and England, it migrated to the Continent and changed along the way from a folk to a court dance. Often the last dance in a suite.

Minuet (also **Menuet**) A slow, graceful dance in ¾ time, featuring much bowing and curtsying, it replaced the Courante in popularity when introduced at the court of Louis XIV and became the official court dance. Its floor pattern is an S or a Z.

Passepied "Pass the feet." Brittany's version of the bransle, a charming, spirited dance similar to a fast minuet but in 6/8 or 3/8 time.

Pavane From the Spanish word for peacock, a stately, dignified court dance usually in 2/4 or 4/4 time.

Polonais A celebratory dance from Poland in 3/4 time; later a favorite processional dance at the beginning of a ball or other festivity.

Rigaudon (also **Rigadoon**) A lively dance for couples. It originated in seventeenth-century Provence, and became a court dance.

Round dances One of the earliest forms of group dancing, in which dancers hold hands in a circle. In Germany, there is the **reigen**; in France, the **bransle** is a round dance that may also be danced in a line. Others include the **hora**, the Catalonian **sardana**, and the Russian **khorovod**. The Princess's dance in *The Firebird* is a khorovod.

Sarabande A dance of Spanish origin from the seventeenth and eighteenth centuries in 3/3 time. There were both slow and fast versions; in time slow became favored. It was often done at court in a group as an entrée. The male solos in Balanchine's *Square Dance* and *Agon* are variations of contrasting sarabandes by Corelli and Stravinsky.

Tarantella A lively, celebratory Italian folk dance in 6/8 time. Tarantella means tarantula, and according to legend only a frenzied dance could prevent those who were bitten from falling into a fatal trance.

La Volta A fast dance of the Renaissance in 3/4 or 6/8 time with jumps, quick aerial turns, and ladies lifted by their partners. A favorite of Queen Elizabeth I.

Eighteenth- and Nineteenth-Century Dances

Cancan A spirited, sometimes bawdy dance of Parisian origin, featuring high kicks; immortalized in Henri de Toulouse-Lautrec's paintings of dancers at the Moulin Rouge and featured in Massine's *Gaîté Parisienne*.

Czardas A Hungarian folk dance and later a ballroom dance in two parts: the slow **lassu** and the fast **friska**, which has many jumps. Czardases are in 2/4 or 4/4 time and feature many en dedans steps. They appear as divertissements in *Swan Lake* and *Raymonda*.

Fandango A brisk Spanish dance in 3/4 or 3/8 time, usually danced to guitar, castanet, or tambourine accompaniment.

Mazurka A lively Polish folk dance for couples in 3/4 time originating in the sixteenth century and becoming a ballroom dance throughout Europe in the nineteenth century. The accent is on the second beat, not the first as in the waltz. It features stamping, heel clicking, and turning.

Merengue A Caribbean dance that originated in the mid-nineteenth century, characterized by a stiff-legged, shuffling step. Over time, the merengue became slower and acquired more hip movements.

Polka A fast dance for couples, usually with a pattern of step-step-step-hop, in a quick 2/4 time with origins in Bohemia in the early nineteenth century. It quickly became popular throughout Europe.

Tango A dance developed in Central and South America in the late nineteenth century and associated particularly with Argentina and specifically Buenos Aires. Usually a sensual dance for couples that incorporates slides and sudden pauses in 2/4 time.

Waltz A sweeping ballroom dance for couples in 3/4 time, featuring much turning. The Viennese waltz was faster and couples turned in circles in only one direction; the American version, the Boston waltz, was slower and couples turned in circles in various directions. Waltzes appear in well-known ballets like *The Nutcracker*, *The Sleeping Beauty*, and *Swan Lake* among others.

Twentieth-Century Dances

Bossanova A lively Brazilian ballroom dance, a variation of the samba.

Charleston Named for the city in South Carolina, the Charleston was a craze in the 1920s. It can be done solo, in couples, or in groups; its rhythms are derived from African ones.

Fox-trot An American ballroom dance, circa 1915, on which many dance steps in 2/4 time are based.

Hustle Made famous by *Saturday Night Fever* and the disco craze of the 1970s, the hustle is both a couples and a line dance.

Rumba A fast Afro-Cuban dance for couples, with distinctive hip and shoulder movements, usually in 2/4 time and often incorporated into jazz music.

Samba A Brazilian folk dance with syncopated rhythms in 2/4 or 4/4 time, often danced in large circles or groups of couples.

Swing dance An entire family of dance including the **Lindy hop** and **jitterbug**. Swing is an American social dance style that grew out of jazz clubs in Harlem. The Lindy hop, often shortened to the Lindy, was named in honor of Charles Lindbergh's transatlantic flight in the late 1920s. The dance, usually for couples, is a fusion of several social dances of the time, including the Charleston.

Twist The Twist existed before the song recorded by Chubby Checker in the late 1950s, but Checker created the craze that found its way onto dance floors everywhere. Dancers twist the hips—also feet and shoulders—back and forth and add variations like changing the angle of the body or sinking in a plié.

Dancer Slang

Every generation of dancers has its slang; here's some of the current lingo.

À la sebesque An academically incorrect arabesque position with very open hips, in between à la seconde and arabesque.

Banana feet Very high arches; very flexible feet that resemble bananas when pointed.

Bunhead A dancer who dances ballet exclusively and so often that her hair is always in a tight dancer's bun.

Dolly Dinkle A name for a fictitious, unknowledgeable, and poorly trained teacher. Also applied to a school.

Full out To perform at full energy in class or rehearsal, as if there were an audience present.

Ginch To distort a position by collapsing or bending.

Give class To teach a class.

Gumby Very flexible, but without the strength to hold proper alignment.

Mark To dance with less energy, indicating steps rather than executing them full out, in order to learn a combination or to conserve energy during a long rehearsal.

Merde A French obscenity (it means excrement), used to wish good luck before a performance. Dancers do not use the expression "break a leg" as actors do. Be careful saying this outside a theater.

Mirror To perform the same steps as your counterpart on the other side of the stage, but with the opposite side of the body. If she steps to the left, you step to the right.

Puff (or **puffy**) Choreography so strenuous that dancers become winded.

Run through To perform a ballet, or a section of a ballet, from start to finish in rehearsal.

Set To stage or restage a ballet, i.e., "*Agon* was set on Dance Theatre of Harlem in 1971." Also means to establish the bows at the end of the ballet. Not to be confused with the stage "set," short for setting, meaning scenery or décor.

Take class To be a student in a dance class. Can be confusing, in Britain, a teacher "takes" class rather than "gives" it.

Walk through Like a run through but walking rather than dancing, to positions, which are usually marked; used during spacing or technical rehearsals when actual dancing is not called for.

Whack To do a grand battement or développé without control or proper form.

Further Reading

The following is by no means a comprehensive dance book list—there are ballet histories old and new, compendia of ballet descriptions, volumes about individual choreographers and dancers, technique manuals, classic picture books, and collections of critics' opinions—too many to name here. I offer this not only to acknowledge the works that were so helpful to me in writing this book—several became my constant and indispensable companions—but also as a starting point for further reading by curious dancers. These book listings refer to the editions I used personally; some older books may have been reissued, while others may actually be out of print. Most can still be found via the Internet and in libraries as well as bookstores.

Asterisk indicates especially good reference books for descriptions of important ballets.

Alpers, Amy Taylor, and Rachel Taylor Segel with Lorna Gentry. *The Everything Pilates Book*. Avon, MA: Adams Media Corp, 2002.

*Balanchine, George, and Francis Mason. *101 Stories of the Great Ballets*. New York: Anchor Books, 1975, 1989.

Barringer, Janice, and Sarah Schlesinger. *The Pointe Book: Shoes, Training & Technique*. Hightstown, NJ: Princeton Book Company, 1998, 2004.

*Beaumont, Cyril W. *Complete Book of Ballets*. Garden City, New York: Garden City Publishing Co., Inc., 1941.

Bland, Alexander. *The Royal Ballet: The First Fifty Years*. Garden City, New York: Doubleday and Company, Inc., 1981.

Brumberg, Joan Jacobs. *The Body Project: An Intimate History of American Girls*. New York: Vintage, 1998.

"The Challenge of the Adolescent Dancer," IADMS Education Committee (Kathryn Daniels, Chair). International Association for Dance Medicine and Science, 2000.

Chujoy, Anatole, and P. W. Manchester. *The Dance Encyclopedia*. New York: Simon & Schuster, 1967.

Clarke, Mary, and Clement Crisp. *Ballet: An Illustrated History*. New York: Universe Books, 1978.

*———. *The Ballet Goer's Guide*. New York: Alfred A. Knopf, Inc., 1981.

Clarke, Mary, and David Vaughn. *The Encyclopedia of Dance & Ballet*. New York: G. P. Putnam's Sons, 1977.

Clarkson, Priscilla. "Fueling the Dancer," IADMS Education Committee. International Association for Dance Medicine and Science, 2003.

De Mille, Agnes. *The Book of the Dance*. New York: Golden Press, 1963.

Fitt, Sally Sevey. *Dance Kinesiology*, second edition. Belmont, CA: Wadsworth, 1997.

Friedman, Philip, and Gail Eisen. *The Pilates Method of Physical and Mental Conditioning*. New York: Warner Books, Inc. 1981.

Garafola, Lynn. *Diaghilev's Ballets Russes*. New York: Oxford University Press, 1989.

Grant, Gail. *Technical Manual and Dictionary of Classical Ballet*, third edition. New York: Dover Publications, 1967, 1982.

Greskovic, Robert. *Ballet 101: A Complete Guide to Learning and Loving the Ballet*. New York: Hyperion, 1998.

Grieg, Valerie. *Inside Ballet Technique: Separating Anatomical Fact from Fiction in the Ballet Class*. Princeton, NJ: Princeton Book Company, 1994.

Hamilton, L. H., J. Brooks-Gunn, M. P. Warren, and W. G. Hamilton. "The Role of Selectivity in the Pathogenesis of Eating Problems in Ballet Dancers." *Medicine and Science in Sports and Exercise*, 20 (1988): 560-565

Hamilton, L. H., J. Brooks-Gunn, and M. P. Warren. "Sociocultural Influences on Eating Disorders in Professional Female Dancers." *International Journal of Eating Disorders*, 4 (1986): 465–587.

Howse, Justin. *Dance Technique and Injury Prevention*. New York: Routledge, 2000.

Iyengar, B. K. S. *Light on Yoga*. New York, NY: Schocken Books, 1979.

Kirstein, Lincoln. *Dance: A Short History of Classic Theatrical Dancing*. Brooklyn: Dance Horizons, 1969.

———. *Four Centuries of Ballet: Fifty Masterworks*. New York: Dover Publications, 1984. (Previously published as *Movement and Metaphor: Four Centuries of Ballet*, Praeger, 1970.)

Koegler, Horst. *The Concise Oxford Dictionary of Ballet*. Oxford: Oxford University Press, 1987.

Kostrovitskaya, V., and A. Pisarer. Translated by John Barker. *School of Classical Dance*. Moscow: Progress Publishers, 1979.

Lawson, Joan. *Mime: The Theory and Practice of Expressive Gesture*. New York: Dance Horizons, 1957, 1973.

Lawson, Joan. *Teaching Young Dancers: Muscular Coordination in Classical Ballet*. New York: Theatre Arts Books, 1975.

Liederbach, Marijeanne. "General Considerations for Guiding Dance Injury Rehabilitation," *Journal of Dance Medicine & Science*, 4, no. 2 (2000): 54–65.

Liederbach, Marijeanne, and Julietta M. Campagno, "Psychological Aspects of Fatigue-Related Injuries in Dancers," *Journal of Dance Medicine & Science*, 5, no. 4 (2001): 116–120.

Maine, Margo. *Body Wars: Making Peace with Women's Bodies*. Carlsbad, CA: Gurze Books, 2000.

Mara, Thalia. *The Language of Ballet: A Dictionary*. Hightstown, NJ: Princeton Book Company, 1987.

Migel, Parmenia. *The Ballerinas*. New York: The Macmillan Company, 1972.

Molnar, Marika, and Katy Keller. *The Dancer's Dozen: Resistabands & Exercises*. New York: Gaynor Minden, 1998.

Pilates, Joseph Hubertus. *Your Health: A Corrective System of Exercising that Revolutionizes the Entire Field of Physical Education*. Ashland, OR: Presentation Dynamics, 1998.

Pipher, Mary. *Hunger Pains: From Fad Diets to Eating Disorders*. New York: Ballantine Books, 1997.

Prudhommeau, Germaine, and Geneviève Guillot. *Danse Classique*. Paris: Hachette, 1969.

"Report on the Sixth International Congress on Obesity in Kobe, Japan." *Eating Disorders Review* 2, no. 5, (1991).

Reynolds, Nancy, and Malcolm McCormick. *No Fixed Points: Dance in the Twentieth Century*. New Haven, CT: Yale University Press, 2003.

Ryman, Rhonda. *Dictionary of Classical Ballet Terminology*, Royal Academy of Dancing. London: Royal Academy of Dancing, 1995.

Scott, John. *Ashtanga Yoga: The Definitive Step-by-Step Guide to Dynamic Yoga*. New York: Three Rivers, 2001.

The Simon & Schuster Book of the Ballet. New York: Simon & Schuster, 1979.

Smakov, Gennady. *The Great Russian Dancers*. New York, Alfred A. Knopf, 1984.

Sorell, Walter. *The Dance Through the Ages*. New York: Grosset & Dunlap, 1967.

*Terry, Walter. *Ballet Guide*. New York: Dodd, Mead and Company, 1976.

Ungaro, Alycea. *Pilates: Body in Motion*. New York, NY: Dorling Kindersley, 2002.

Vaganova, Agrippina. *Basic Principles of Classical Ballet*. New York: Dover, 1946, 1953, 1969.

Warren, Gretchen Ward. *Classical Ballet Technique*. Gainesville, FL: University Press of Florida, 1989.

Watkins, Andrea, and Priscilla M. Clarkson. *Dancing Longer, Dancing Stronger: A Dancer's Guide to Improving Technique and Preventing Injury*. Hightstown, NJ: Princeton Book Company, 1990.

Whitehill, Angela, and William Noble. *The Parents Book of Ballet*. Hightstown, NJ: Princeton Book Company, 2003.

317

Resources

Videos

Performance

Below is a brief list of some recommended performance videos. Robert Greskovic has compiled an excellent and far more extensive list in his book, *Ballet 101*.

Balanchine: Dance in America
The Balanchine Celebration, Parts I and II, 1993
Wea/Atlantic/Nonesuch, 1996

La Bayadere
(Royal Ballet, 1992)
Music: Minkus
Choreography: Makarova
(after Petipa)
Dancers: Altynai Asylmuratova (guesting from the Kirov), Irek Mukhamedov, Darcey Bussell
Kultur, 1992

Le Corsaire
(American Ballet Theatre, 1999)
Music: Adam, et. al.
Choreography: Petipa
Dancers: Julie Kent, Angel Corella, Joaquin de Luz, Paloma Herrera, Vladimir Malakhov, Ethan Stiefel
Kultur, 1999

Don Quixote
(American Ballet Theatre, 1984)
Music: Minkus
Choreography: Baryshnikov
(after Petipa, Gorsky)

Dancers: Richard Schafer, Mikhail Baryshnikov, Cynthia Harvey, Victor Barbee, Susan Jaffe
Kultur, 1999

The Dream
(American Ballet Theatre, 2004)
Music: Mendelssohn
Choreography: Ashton
Dancers: Ethan Stiefel, Alessandra Ferri, Herman Cornejo
Kultur, 2004

La Fille Mal Gardee
(Royal Ballet, 1981)
Music: Herold, Lanchbery
Choreography: Ashton
Dancers: Leslie Collier, Michael Coleman, Brian Shaw, Garry Grant, Leslie Edwards
PGD/Philips, 1990

The Nutcracker
(New York City Ballet, 1993)
Music: Tchaikovsky
Choreography: Balanchine
Dancers: Darci Kistler, Damian Woetzel
Warner, 2003

Romeo and Juliet
(Royal Ballet, 1966)
Music: Prokofiev
Choreography: MacMillan
Dancers: Rudolf Nureyev and Margot Fonteyn
Kultur, 1988

The Sleeping Beauty
(Royal Ballet, 1994)
Music: Tchaikovsky
Choreography: Petipa
Dancers: Viviana Durante, Zoltan Solymosi, Anthony Dowell
Kultur, 1997

Swan Lake
(Kirov Ballet, 1990)
Music: Tchaikovsky
Choreography: Ivanov
(after Petipa)
Dancers: Yulia Makhalina, Igor Zelensky, Eidar Aliev
Wea/Atlantic/Nonesuch, 1992

Many videos are readily available from Internet DVD and video retailers. There are also a number of distributors that specialize in dance videos and DVDs, including:

Active Videos
10 First Avenue East
Mobridge, SD 57601
(800) 342-4320

Dance Horizons Book Club
Princeton Book Company
614 Route 130
Hightstown, NJ 08520
(800) 220-7149

Hoctor Dance Enterprises
P.O. Box 38
Waldwick, NJ 07463
(201) 652-7767

Kultur
195 Highway 36
West Long Branch, NJ 07764
(908) 229-1199

Video Artists International, Inc.
158 Linwood Plaza, Suite 301
Fort Lee, NJ 07024
(201) 944-0099

V.I.E.W., Inc.
34 East 23rd Street
New York, NY 10010
(800) 843-9843

Instruction

Recommended instruction videos
are available from the distributors
above as well as from various
Internet retail sources:

*Basic Principles of Pointe with
Patricia Dickinson*, Dance
Horizons.

*Take a Master Class with David
Howard*, Volumes I & II, Dance
Horizons.
www.dancer.com

*Cathy Roe's Basic Anatomy and
Kinesiology for Dancers*, Dance
Horizons.

*"On Your Toes" with Kathryn
Sullivan*, Hoctor Dance
Enterprises.

Other

*Introduction to Dance Medicine:
Keeping Dancers Dancing*, featuring
William Hamilton, M.D., along
with Marika Molnar and Katy
Keller. Dance Medicine Education
Fund (718) 426-8606

New York City Ballet Workout, with
Peter Martins and the New York City
Ballet, Ryko Video, 2001.

*Zena Rommett: Floor-Barre
Technique II*. Zena Rommett
Dance Foundation
(877) FL-BARRE

Organizations

American Alliance for Health,
Physical Education, Recreation,
and Dance
1900 Association Drive
Reston, VA 20191
(703) 476-3400
www.aahperd.org

The Benesh Institute
36 Battersea Square
London SW11 3RA
United Kingdom
44-0-20 7326 8031
www.benesh.org

The Cecchetti Council of America
23392 Meadows Avenue
Flat Rock, MI 48134
(734) 379-6710
www.cecchetti.org

Cecchetti Society, Inc., USA
619 Ashland
Huntington Beach, CA 92648
(714) 960-4361
www.cecchettiusa.org

Classical Dance Alliance
331 West 57th Street
New York, NY 10019
(212) 397-1400
www.classicaldancealliance.org

Dance Notation Bureau
151 West 30th Street
Suite 202
New York, NY 10001
(212) 564-0985
www.dancenotation.org

Harkness Center for Dance Injuries
Hospital for Joint Diseases
301 East 17th Street
New York, NY 10003
(212) 598-6022
harkness@med.nyu.edu

International Association of
Dance Medicine and Science
c/o Department of Dance
1214 University of Oregon
Eugene, OR 97403-1763
(541) 465-1763
www.iadms.org

National Eating Disorders
Association
603 Stewart Street, Ste. 803
Seattle, WA 98101
(206) 382-3587
(800) 931-2237 (Referral Hotline)
www.edap.org

Royal Academy of Dance
36 Battersea Square
London SW11 3RA
United Kingdom
44-0-20 7326 8000
www.radacadabra.org
www.rad.org.uk
www.radusa.org

Magazines and Publications

Ballet Review
46 Morton Street
New York, NY 10014
(212) 924-5183

Dance
333 7th Avenue, 11th floor
New York, NY 10001
(212) 979-4803
www.dancemagazine.com

Dancer
2829 Bird Avenue, Suite 5PMB 231
Miami, Fl 33133
(305) 460-3225
www.danceronline.com

Dance Spirit
Lifestyle Media, Inc.
110 William Street, 23rd floor
New York, NY 10038
(646) 459-4800
www.dancespirit.com

Dance Teacher
Lifestyle Media, Inc.
110 William Street, 23rd floor
New York, NY 10038
(646) 459-4800
www.danceteacher.com

Pointe
Lifestyle Media, Inc.
110 William Street, 23rd floor
New York, NY 10038
(646) 459-4800
www.pointemagazine.com

Index

Schnittke, Alfred, 291
Schönberg, Arnold, 291
School of American Ballet, 71, 229, 296
Schubert, Franz, 291
Schuman, William, 291
Scotch Symphony (Balanchine), 223
self-esteem, 214–15
Semenyaka, Ludmilla, *225*
Semyonova, Marina, 224
Serenade (Balanchine), 175, 229, *229*, 279, 291, 296
Sergeyev, Konstantin, 225
Sergeyev, Nicholas, 127, 295
Serrano, Lupe, 243
Shambards (Wheeldon), 223
Shawn, Ted, xiv, 151, 295, 296
   Men Dancers, *151*
Shearer, Moira, 175, 259, 297
Shostakovich, Dmitri, 291
shoulder sit, *268*
shoulder stretch, 117, *117*
Sibley, Antoinette, 52, 297
Siegenfeld, Billy, 24
Simone, Kirsten, 83
Sinfonietta (Kylián), 283, 291
sissonne, 165
Skaters (Les Patineurs) (Ashton), 174, 277, *278*, 291
slang, dancers', 314–15
Slaughter on Tenth Avenue (Balanchine), 251
Sleeping Beauty, The, 51, *58*, 68, 119, 136, *224*, 259
   adagio in, 154
   (Ashton), 259
   (Martins), 284
   (Petipa), 67, 127, 158, 225, 243, 273, 291, 294, 295
   petit allegro in, 158
   turns in, 174
Smith, Oliver, 243
smoking, 214
snapping hip syndrome, 240–41
social dancing, 25
socks, clean, 247
soft corns, 246
soft tissue, 245
Soloviev, Yuri, 225
soubresaut, 165
Sousa, John Philip, 185
soutenu en tournant, 178
spacing rehearsals, 35

Spartacus (Grigorovich), 225, *225*
Speaking in Tongues (Taylor), 289, 291
Spectre de la Rose, Le (Fokine), 205, 275, 291, 295
Spessivtseva, Olga, 68, 204, 295
spondylolysis, 241, 244
spotting, 175, 178–79
sprained ankle, 234–35
Square Dance (Balanchine), 279, 291
stage fright, 38
stage makeup, *35*, 37
stage manager, 34
Stanislavsky method of acting, 225
Stars and Stripes (Balanchine), 229
Stiefel, Ethan, 179, 249, *278*, 284
stone bruise, 236–37
story ballets, 223
Stowell, Kent, 71, 298
Stravinsky, Igor, 182, 184, 185, 204, 205, 228, 275, 280, 290, 291, 295, 296, 297
Strebinger, M., 290
strength training, 260–61
stress fractures, 237–38
stretches, 109–17
   adductor/groin, 113, *113*
   anterior hip, 111, *111*
   barre, 148, *148*
   calf and shoulder, 117, *117*
   calves, 116, *116*
   external rotators, 114, *114*
   flexor hallucis longus, 115, *115*
   hamstrings, 112, *112*
   quadriceps, 110, *110*
Stroman, Susan, 251
studio etiquette, 11–13, 15
summer intensive programs, 42–45
   clothing and gear for, 44
   evaluations, 44–45
Sunflower Moon (a.k.a. *Lunar Sea*) (Pendleton for Momix), 288, 291
Sunset (Taylor), 289, 291
supported arabesque penché, *30*
Surfer at the River Styx (Tharp), 284–85, 291
sur le cou-de-pied, 94, *94*
Swan Lake, xiii, 51, *118*, *265*
   adagio in, 154
   ballet blanc in, 92
   (Petipa), xiv, 127, 158, 225, 243, 273, 291, 294, 296
   petit allegro in, 158
   turns in, 68, 174

Sweet Charity (musical), 251
swimming, 249, 263
syllabus, in ballet school, 4
Sylphide, La, 96, *118*
   ballet blanc in, 92
   (Bournonville), 82, 158, 291, 294
   as first full-length ballet on pointe, 118
   petit allegro in, 158
   Romanticism in, 41, 50, 51, 243
Sylphides, Les (Fokine), 92, 205, 242, 274, 291, 295
Symphonic Variations (Ashton), 259, 277–78, 291, 297
Symphony in C (Balanchine), 154, 185, 229
Symphony in D (Kylián), 283, 291

T

Taglioni, Filippo, 118
Taglioni, Marie, 82, 118–19, *118*, 126, 294
   ballet slippers of, 119, *119*, 187, 188
   dancing en pointe, *50*, 51, 118
   Le Papillon, 96
   in *Pas de Quatre*, 95, *95*
Taglioni, Paul, *118*
Talking Heads, 289, 290
Tallchief, Maria, 229, 297
Taming of the Shrew, The (Cranko), 280, 291
Tanztheater, 151
tap dancing, 25
Tarantella, 161
Taylor, Paul, 21, 151, 243, 287, 289, 297, 298
   Aureole, 289, 290
   Piazzolla Caldera, 25
   Speaking in Tongues, 289, 291
   Sunset, 289, 291
Tchaikovsky, Pyotr, 127, 184, 185, 273, 279, 290, 291, 294
Tcherkassky, Marianna, 243
tech (technical) rehearsals, 35
technical director, 34
technique shoes, 18–19
tendons, 245
tendu, *see* battement tendu
tennis ball, rises with, 108, *108*
Tharp, Twyla, 151, 243, 251, 265, 284–85
   Known by Heart, 284, 285, 290
   Push Comes to Shove, 284, 291
   Surfer at the River Styx, 284–85, 291

Photography and Illustration

Photography

The photographs demonstrating ballet technique are of Maria Riccetto, American Ballet Theatre, and Benjamin Millepied, New York City Ballet. Unless otherwise noted below, photography is by Eduardo Patino/NYC.

Edwin S. Gaynor, pp. XIII.

Eliza Gaynor Minden personal collection, pp. 41, bottom left; 50; 51, top left; 95, top left; 96; 118, top right.

Victor DeLiso/NY, p. 10.

Francesca DeRenzi, p. 17; fitter, Karen Lacy; student, Mireille Gaynor.

©Paul B. Goode/STEPS on Broadway, p. 24.

Dina Makarova, pp. 33; 225; 265; 271.

©2004 Rosalie O'Connor/Used by permission of Ballet Academy East, New York, NY, www.balletacademyeast.com, p. 7.

©2004 Rosalie O'Connor, p. 35; 272.

©Rosalie O'Connor, p. 281. Choreography © Jerome Robbins, by permission of the Robbins Rights Trust.

Jessica Thelen/the School at Jacob's Pillow; dancer, Meghan French, p. 43.

Richard Merrill. Courtesy Jacob's Pillow Dance Festival Archives, p. 151, top right.

©Costas, pp. 51, bottom right; 92; 224; 228; 264; 276; 278.

©Costas/Used by permission of the American Academy of Ballet, p. 47.

©Costas, pp. 280. Choreography by George Balanchine © the George Balanchine Trust.

©Patricia Barnes/the Image Works, p. 56.

©John Kane/Pilobolus, p. 53.

MIRA, pp. 58; 242, top right.

©Eduardo Patino/NYC/Pointe Magazine, Lifestyle Media, Inc., p. 74.

Georgian State Dance Company, Columbia Artists Management, p. 223.

Herbert Migdoll, courtesy the Joffrey Ballet, p. 277.

Walter Strate, courtesy the José Limón Dance Foundation, p. 288.

Eduardo Patino/NYC/Gaynor Minden Collection, p. 243, bottom right.

©Paul Kolnik, p. 229, top left. Choreography by George Balanchine © the George Balanchine Trust.

©Paul Kolnik/Alvin Ailey American Dance Theater, p. 286.

Arks Smith/Jerome Robbins Dance Division, the New York Public Library for the Performing Arts, Aston, Lenox and Tilden Foundations, p. 83.

©Johan Persson, p. 127.

©Lois Greenfield/the Ballet Tech School, p. 283.

©Rick McCullough 2004, p. 36.

Dance Notation Bureau, p. 67.

©Clive Barda/PAL/Topham/the Image Works, p. 259, top right.

Donald Southern/Evening Standard/Getty Images, p. 258.

Hulton Archive, Getty Images, p. 204, top left.

Jerry Cooke/Time Life Pictures/Getty Images, p. 150

©Martha Swope, p. 229, lower right. Choreography by George Balanchine © the George Balanchine Trust.

©Icare/Ballet de l'Opéra National de Paris, p. 41, top right.

Illustration

Anatomical illustrations on pp. 226, 227, 233, 239 and 240 by Bonnie Hofkin.

Illustrations on pp. 18, 19, 28, 37, 78, 79, 81, 191, 194, and 252 by Monica Rangne.